Margaret R. Miles

and **Believing**

Religion and Values in the Movies

Beacon Press
25 Beacon Street
Boston, Massachusetts 02108-2892

Beacon Press books
are published under the auspices of
the Unitarian Universalist Association of Congregations.

00 99 98 97   8 7 6 5 4 3 2

Text design by Elizabeth Elsas
Composition by Wilsted & Taylor
Printed on acid-free, recycled paper

Library of Congress Cataloging-in-Publication Data can be found on page 256.

For Wendell,
a serious lover of film

Contents

Preface

While I worked on this book I was frequently asked about what I was writing. To my answer, "religion and values in film," the most frequent response was "bet you don't find much religion *or* values in film!" But, of course, I do. In fact, the frequency of slurs about religion in popular film is itself evidence of North Americans' anxiety about religion. We, as a society, seem to seek evidence that will substantiate and reinforce our belief that religious practices are ineffective, and that religious beliefs are wrong, misguided, and dangerous. We apparently need to be reassured that it is quite safe to ignore religion both as personal motivation and as a voice in public discourse. Popular film both reflects a popular consensus that traditional religion is deeply untrustworthy and reinforces our public rejection of religion.[1] Many people find it difficult to imagine that a scholar of religion might find anything useful to say about popular film.

On the other hand, it is frequently difficult to convince friends and fellow religion scholars that studying film in the social and cultural context of American society is anything but a lark, a departure from "serious" academic work, a kinky side-interest of a scholar who should really be doing something else. She should, some friends believe, be studying ancient Greek or Latin theological texts. Or she should support with her scholarship the important efforts of those who seek to remind the religious academy that the study of religion is incomplete and impoverished when we study religious language to the exclusion of religious art. For religious images have informed the religious lives of our historical antecedents far more pervasively and profoundly than our slender attention to them in the academic study of religion would acknowledge.

These tasks—the interpretation of historical religious texts and images—are, I agree, immensely important. Lacking vigorous ongoing critical appropriation, historical texts and images quickly lose their potential to provide perspectives and offer suggestions for living in the present. Scholars of religion, however, can no longer—if we ever could—afford to assume that we can effortlessly engage a broader audience than the six other scholars in one's own field who will undoubtedly read whatever one writes. We will have earned the perennial accusation that we live and work in an "ivory tower" if we do not address more directly and accessibly the anxieties and problems of the present.

I work on popular film because it provides an index of the anxieties and longings of a large audience. I do so out of the conviction that religious scholars ignore this contemporary cultural "text" at the cost of failing to engage the pressing concerns of this historical moment. Moreover, far from being a frivolous side-interest, analysis of popular film requires and exercises my training as a historian. For the ultimate test of a good historical training is to bring it to the analysis of one's own society and its cultural exchanges and to observe the adequacy—or lack thereof—of one's historical method for illuminating features of the present.

One way to describe the project of this book is to say that it is an exploration of the intimate connection between seeing and believing. On the face of it, it seems that as many Americans believe less and less, we want to see more and more. But what if there is some important reality in the old proverb, "Seeing *is* believing"? Does the "voluntary suspension of disbelief" to which we must consent if we are to be entertained affect us in ways we ignore?

I am often alarmed to find that the people most concerned about this issue seem to be political and religious conservatives. While I too would like to see the present violence, poverty, and insanity of American society overcome, I do not imagine, as conservatives often do, that this could result from a backward step into some earlier version of our society. The inequities and the prejudices of earlier times are too evident to encourage me to think that a return to a society unaware of its glaring injustice, its chauvinism and racial intolerance, would be a step in the right direction. Rather, we must go forward to a society of equality and mutuality that we have never known and for which we have no blueprint. Censorship in any of its overt or covert forms is not the answer. I hope in this book, then, to provoke thought, to propose questions, and to suggest a method for exploring a film's "voice" in public discourse about issues that press American society with their urgency.

My own relation to "the movies" is one that may not be shared by many readers. My immigrant fundamentalist parents forbade moviegoing. My childhood was spent visualizing the scriptural stories I read and acted out with my sisters. In an iconoclastic branch of Christianity, one in which "graven images" were feared as idolatrous, the only images I saw were on the Sunday School papers I received weekly. I remember two of these images vividly. One Sunday, a small girl with chubby arms leaned on a windowsill gazing out into the starry night. The text beneath read, "There is no God beside me." Unaware of the secondary meaning of "beside" as "other than," I was puzzled. I had thought that every effort was being made, at home and in Sunday School, to remind me that there *is* a God beside me. That illustration failed to communicate its intended message. Another memorable series of Sunday School papers carried colorful cover pictures each week illustrating the breaking of one of the Ten Commandments. Being ten years old by then, I eagerly anticipated the seventh week. It was a disappointment. It pictured a milkman pouring a pail of water into a large vat of milk. The caption read, "Thou shalt not commit adultery."

My childhood repertoire of images largely failed to stimulate and challenge my psyche. I turned to words and soon learned to scorn any book that had pictures. But I could not walk by the movie marquee without devouring with my eyes the fascinating pictures they carried. From those guilty glances I learned a great deal. I learned that great passion occurs only to young beautiful heterosexual people, though I certainly had neither the word nor the concept until much later. I learned from those marquees that war is noble because the enemy is evil and must be slaughtered. I learned that fat people were laughable, and that people of color were either servants or sidekicks. I learned to yearn to be or at least to resemble those beautiful women on the posters. I learned all of this—and more—in the split second before the parent or grandparent walking with me noticed that I was looking and reprimanded me. "The movies" assumed for me an intense fascination, augmented, no doubt, by the family prohibitions around them.

I saw my first movie, *The Glenn Miller Story*, when I was seventeen, without my parents' knowledge or approval. It was a riveting experience; a new world was opened to me. In the world of the movies people did and said daring things, looking beautiful all the while, and confident, somehow, that everything would come out right in the end. It has taken me forty years to put the movies in perspective. I needed, and could not, until recently, find a way of considering popular films that acknowledged their tremendous quasireligious power but did not overrate the extent of that power or assume its malevolence.

The sparse literature I found that touched on religion and film divided neatly into two approaches. The first approach, consisting largely of articles in the journals of conservative religious groups, deplored "Hollywood" and its influence, finding it the "Whore of Babylon," the quintessential American problem. Movie critics, on the other hand, sometimes found religious themes—alienation, grace, forgiveness, or redemption—in films whose content was not explicitly religious. It seemed to me imperative to extend the discussion of religion and film to include an analysis of the values circulated in films with box office appeal. It seemed important to find a way to assess the influence of those values on the popular audiences that consume films. Yet the crabbiness that characterized the warier approaches seemed solipsistic and not likely to attract thoughtful adherents.

Indeed, the field of "religion and film" has been burdened by several less-than-fruitful approaches. Many reviewers for religious media have assumed that unless a film's primary content was explicitly religious it did not fall within the purview of religion and film.[2] Thus, discussions of religion in film tended to focus nearly exclusively on such films as Bergman's *The Seventh Seal*. Because the examination of values was not considered a religious concern, many or most popular films simply failed to attract the interest of religious reviewers.

Recently, I have found in the emerging interdisciplinary field of cultural studies some useful suggestions for thinking about film. Cultural studies approaches consider a film as one voice in a complex social conversation, occurring in a particular historical moment. Since every film is produced and circulated within a particular climate of public events, conversation, and concerns, it is only in relation to that "moment" that what a film communicates may be adequately examined. Reconstructing the film's contemporary social framework when one thinks about a film helps to minimize impressionistic or idiosyncratic readings. It also limits the unacknowledged perspective of critics who confidently address their readers as "we": "we feel," "we know," "we almost gasp," "we wonder."[3]

A different kind of interpretation is often done by feminists and by representatives of sexual and racial minorities. I am very sympathetic with the longing for more adequate representations of the variety of American lives that underlies this kind of interpretation, the practice of reading "against the grain." In order to enjoy Hollywood films, women and minorities have learned to ignore commonly accepted social meanings of particular dress, language, and actions, and to create their own meanings of characters and plots. That is not, however, what I am about in this book.

The cultural studies approach to film that I will use throughout the book—and will discuss more fully in chapter 1—refocuses attention from the film as a text to the social, political, and cultural matrix in which the film was produced and distributed. I begin by understanding a popular film as demonstrating one, or several, vexing social issues as they affect the lives of particular characters and then proposing a resolution. Most filmgoers, consciously or unconsciously, will see and discuss the film they watch in relation to the common quandaries of the moment.

I hope that this book will demonstrate the importance of thinking about popular films' treatment of religion and values from a cultural studies perspective. This importance needs to be demonstrated because many people, including some of my academic friends, believe that one should not study popular films because one will—at best—become tainted with their triviality, their invidious superficiality; at worst, one will absorb their highly questionable values. Others claim that popular films simply do not merit or repay thoughtful scrutiny. Neither of these responses takes seriously an influential medium that circulates attitudes and values across a broad spectrum of Americans.

A different kind of objection to the serious study of popular film frequently arises: the movies are simply entertainment, "good clean fun," relaxation. The proposal that popular film should become the object of scrutiny seems fussy, overly scrupulous. Art films, films that cannot claim to be "entertainment," much less "box office," because they are difficult and frustrating to watch, may be worthy of scholarly analysis, but surely popular film, commercial film cannot. Besides, the pleasure of an entertaining film is spoiled by serious criticism.

It is, I will argue, precisely these cultural presumptions that need, and will reward, investigation. They operate strongly in the socialized psyches of most Americans. They are present in every casual and classroom discussion I have ever had because they are firmly embedded in my own psyche, as well. This difficulty, this resistance, should itself alert us to an area of cultural blindness. And anyone who has undertaken the never-ending work of knowledge of self and society will feel a surge of excitement at the identification of such a blind spot, recognizing it as a potential site for insight and growth.

I have implied thus far that scrutiny of one's entertainment is an individual task, a task whose fruits are personal self-knowledge and flourishing. This may, indeed, be a rewarding by-product of a greater sophistication and attentiveness in watching films. Providing direction for personal growth is not, however, the purpose of this book. I hope that the book will contribute, in some small way, to a collapse of the dualism of personal and social. One of the most damaging mistakes of a society fascinated with therapies of all sorts is to understand social problems as personal problems. Ultimately, for the individual to flourish requires a just society. And achieving a just society will entail changing the consistent, cumulative verbal and visual representations of people, attitudes, and lifestyles that the media widely circulates.

Change, of course, is inevitable, in ourselves and in society. If we would like to help shape the changes that will occur, we will first need close and accurate analyses of the present state of American popular culture. And the pulse of a society, its interests and longings, its fears and anxieties, can be taken by examining its repetitive self-representations. Accurate and insightful analysis is, of course, only one of the myriad contributions needed for social change; alone, it is not enough. I do not agree with cultural theorists who insist that attention to discourse is the key to positive social change. It is not sufficient, but it is necessary.

Film is an accessible medium in which competing issues of public and private life in a pluralistic society are formulated and represented for consideration and interpretation. Communications scholar James Carey put it well when he remarked that media entertainment should be seen as a site of "imaginative possibility, without which we would be unable to try new models, new roles, new theories, new combinations of behavior."[4] Films articulate a range of values, fleshing out these values in characters, and narrating the conflicts that arise as characters endeavor to live out their commitments. They explore what happens, in particular contexts, when one character's values meet, question, contest, or resist those of another.

Films represent the most intimate and private confrontations of values—such as lovemaking—as well as the most public moments in which values come out into the open, clash, and are violently or peacefully negotiated. They are successful at the box office when they accurately identify and explore a current area of discomfort and anxiety and visualize a possible resolution. In the decade 1983 to 1993, issues related to race, age, ecology, family, education, addiction, abortion, violence, gender, class, United States foreign policy, fundamentalist Christianity, the New Right, "family values," reproductive technologies, AIDS—to give only a partial list—permeated popular films. In short, film supplies the historian of the present with an incomparable resource for describing and prescribing for the problems and struggles of the moment.

I acknowledge with gratitude the Henry Luce III Foundation from whom I received a grant for writing this book. I thank Susan Worst at Beacon Press for her encouragement, advice and thoughtful editing of the manuscript, and Susan Meigs for the final editing. I could not have written this book without the skilled research help of Jess Gugino, Julia Baird Miller, and Adrienne Nock, who, in addition to providing research, also prepared the index. Irene Monroe gave invaluable bibliographical suggestions. Addie, my stepson, bought me the VCR I would probably never have bought myself, and without which this book would not have been possible. My husband, Owen Thomas, read the manuscript, raising interesting and important questions and making suggestions that have helped me to say what I think. And students in my courses contributed the vigorous conversation that stimulated, nourished, and often challenged my thinking about film.

Religion in Popular Film

The importance of the visual to religion has long been recognized. Within historical Christianity, religious images gave a focus to and informed piety.[1] Cinema can be seen as continuous with a long tradition in which images have been used to produce emotion, to strengthen attachment, and to encourage imitation.[2] However, the connection between film and religion has not always been obvious or simple. For example, during the first decades of the twentieth century, when film was becoming increasingly popular, religion was retreating from public to private space. New media for public communication—including film and radio—reached a vastly larger audience than books and newspapers had formerly reached. Because it affected so many more people, the new media began to challenge "the interpretive monopoly of religious and state authorities"[3] in a way that newspapers and books had not.

Where do contemporary Americans receive our values and our images of ourselves and one another, of our social world, and of our relation to the natural world? As a society, we do not primarily get our informing images from the walls of churches as historical Christians did; we get them from the media culture in which we live. Movies, television, magazines, and billboards saturate us with images, images that have cumulative effects. Just as examining historical religious art can reveal a great deal about the society from which it came, exploring media images tells us something about the preoccupations of our society. Media images are one of the most pervasive means by which Americans receive representations of identity and diversity, relationships, and social arrangements and institutions.

Although religion is hardly a preoccupation of contemporary film, images of religion and religious commitment circulate in the public sphere through this popular medium. In Part I, I will examine some images that were, as their box office success indicates, widely distributed. I believe that Hollywood films generate and maintain attitudes toward religion that have far-reaching effects in American social and political life. The constriction of the use of the term "religion" to conservative or fundamentalist forms of religion is one such effect. That the effects

3

of representations of religion in film are difficult or impossible to define with precision makes them no less important to study.

The purpose of this book is (1) to examine popular films that treat three of the most numerically prevalent religions in North America—Christianity, Islam, and Judaism—roughly in the decade 1983 to 1993, and (2) to propose a method for identifying and analyzing the values imaged in films, especially those related to race, gender, and class. Since popular entertainment films are value-laden, it is important to examine the values that are being circulated in this popular medium. Two primary questions focus my exploration: (1) How is the social phenomenon of religion treated in Hollywood film? What forms of religion are "box office"? and (2) What values are circulated?

1

Moving Shadows: Religion and Film as Cultural Products

An ancient image curiously anticipates modern film; Plato's myth of the cave is a strangely approximate description of cinema. Moving shadows are projected onto a wall by passing a series of images across a light placed behind the spectators, who sit in darkness and in isolation from one another. Plato writes:

> Think of men dwelling in an underground cave which is open to the light along its entire width. They have been in this cave since childhood, with their legs and necks fettered, so that they have to remain motionless, looking straight in front of them and prevented by the fetters from turning their heads. There is a light from a fire burning high up and some way behind them; and between the fire and the men in fetters is a raised gangway along the side of which a low screen has been erected, like that behind which a showman conceals himself when he exhibits his puppets. Now imagine men passing along behind this screen carrying all sorts of figures so that they show above the screen, figures of men and animals in wood and stone and all sorts of artificial objects; the carriers as usual sometimes talking and sometimes not.
>
> "What a strange image," said Glaucus, "and what strange fettered prisoners."
> "They are like us," said Socrates.

The difficulty of examining film images is also anticipated in the myth of the cave: the release of the prisoner and his emergence into the light of day happens only when the prisoner is "compelled": "When one of them was unbound and suddenly compelled to stand up, turn his head, walk, and look towards the light, each of these actions would be painful and he would be too dazzled to be able to see the objects of which previously he had seen only the shadows."[4]

Like all analogies, this myth is an imperfect metaphor for the difference between thinking of film as entertainment and critically examining it. Audiences can only metaphorically be described as chained to their seats and unaware that the film they see on the screen is not reality. And even the most insightful critic does not finally "look directly at the sun," as does the prisoner in Plato's myth. Nevertheless, the myth of the cave uncannily anticipates—by approximately twenty-three centuries—cinema's mechanics and effects.

From its beginnings, film has had a strong relationship with religion. Photographic film was invented by an Episcopal priest, Hannibal Goodwin. The first photographic film shown was *The Passion Play of Oberammergau*, on January 31, 1898.[5] It was directly patterned after medieval Passion plays and featured thirteen tableaux of about a minute each from the trial and death of Jesus. Another early film, *The Temptation of St. Anthony* (1902), began with a monk reading an ancient manuscript; suddenly he sees a naked woman, but as he moves toward her, she turns into a skeleton! The first motion picture theater opened on Broadway in 1913; by 1916, there were twenty-one thousand of them in the United States.[6] In 1923, Cecil B. De Mille's *The Ten Commandments* was produced at the then-unheard-of cost of one and a half million dollars.

A viewing public was emerging in America for whom religion and vision were intertwined. The concurrence of religion and spectacle was not new, and it is not accidental that film's first topics were religious. Film, like the religious drama of earlier ages, was understood to have a tremendous capacity for generating and focusing the desires not only of individuals, but of societies.

The history of public "entertainment" also points to a larger purpose.[7] Martha Nussbaum describes audiences' expectations of Greek drama:

To attend a tragic drama was not to go to a distraction or a fantasy, in the course of which one suspended one's anxious practical questions. It was instead to engage in a communal process of inquiry, reflection, and feeling with respect to important civic and personal ends.[8]

Whether this state of mind was common to all members of Greek audiences cannot be known. But that public entertainment *could* be taken this seriously suggests that film could—and can—be as well. For, like classical drama, film represents the particular class, behavior, and loyalties of its characters. It also often provides nuanced explorations of emotion.[9] Moreover, popular film represents characters in situations and quandaries that often bear a marked resemblance to our own, making visible social issues that could not be presented with comparable immediacy and power in any other format.

In ancient Greece, as Nussbaum persuasively describes, theater was understood to identify and explore a central question, namely, the question of "how human beings should live."

To respond to [the performance of a tragedy] was to acknowledge and participate in a way of life—a way of life . . . that prominently included reflection and public debate about ethical and civic matters . . . To respond well to a tragic performance involved both feeling and critical reflection; and these were closely linked with one another.[10]

It is not, I think, a far-fetched claim that popular films can also be seen as implicitly, if not explicitly, addressing the question of how human beings should live. Someone will object that the Greek tragedies, because they depict epic heroic struggle, are far more worthy of thoughtful analysis than are popular films. We have that impression, I believe, primarily because Greek tragedies have been treated with seriousness not only by their society of origin but also by a long line of respected intellectuals, reaching to our own time. But if the narrative content of a Greek tragedy were summarized as if it were a film plot, it might be difficult to see its profundity. *Medea*, for example, is the story of a woman who loses her husband to a younger woman and in vengeance kills her children; in the end, a chariot swoops down out of the sky and carries her away. If our attention were solely on the "action" in Greek tragic drama, the play could be reduced to this description.

On the other hand, if popular films were understood as responses to the question, How should we live?, we might notice that they propose diverse answers—some highly dubious and others rather profound—to that important question. Is not the behavior glamorized by a film (implicitly) proposed as a partial answer? Greek audiences may have recognized more communally and consistently than do late twentieth-century moviegoers that the serious question of how one should live lies beneath the surface of drama. But popular films—from *Witness* to *Alien 3*—can certainly be seen as addressing that question in myriad ways.

Contemporary popular film and Greek drama, then, cannot easily be distinguished according to their content. But Nussbaum's argument was that Greek spectators came to a public drama *expecting* to identify and discuss its proposal about "how we should live." Similarly, for many filmgoers one of the most prominent pleasures of moviegoing is that of thinking and talking about the film they have seen. If theater was not entertainment for ancient Greeks, neither is film "pure"—meaning mindless—entertainment for many Americans.

Nussbaum's description of Greek audiences has helped us to imagine twentieth-century spectators who want to think deeply and talk intensely about a popular film. But spectators who enjoy serious discussions of films are not the only ones who watch movies for suggestions how to live and what to value. They are, instead, among the few who do so consciously, who do not merely *take in*, but also critically *evaluate* a film's depiction of life. One can choose whether to accept, reject, or adopt in part a film's proposed values only when the question of how to live is consciously brought to watching and thinking about a film. Failing that, image is simply heaped upon image, proposal upon proposal, without clarification of the potential choices of "how we should live."

Of course there were also enormous fundamental differences between fifth-century BCE Greek audiences and twentieth-century Americans, two of which are instructive. First, an important aspect of Greek tragedy was its setting. Ancient theater "took place during a solemn civic/religious festival, whose trappings made spectators conscious that the values of the community were being examined and communicated."[11] Nothing signals to modern spectators that questions concerning how to live their lives are to be engaged in the film they attend.

Second, twentieth-century Americans do not think of filmgoing as an especially social or communal activity. Each person is effectively isolated in the darkened theater. We are next to each other but cannot make eye contact, and we are requested not to talk during the show. By contrast, ancient audiences, "sitting in the common daylight, saw across the staged action the faces of fellow citizens on the other side of the orchestra."[12] They simultaneously saw the dramatic action, felt in themselves the emotions elicited by the action, and observed their fellow citizens' reactions.

Clearly, late twentieth-century moviegoers lack the communal religious setting that signalled the fundamental seriousness of drama to Greek audiences. Can we, who love to be entertained but who also insist on thinking about "how we should live," gather material for considering our lives from the movies? I think we can, and already do. Can we consider the question of how to live to be a question about the common good as well as one about individual flourishing? I think we must.

While considering a film one has seen, one's idiosyncratic, subjective perceptions can be transformed by discussion into social criticism. Just as the ancient philosopher Socrates needed interlocutors—friends—in order to explore the dimensions and implications of an idea, so too do filmgoers need friends with whom to discuss, to disagree and argue, with whom to negotiate the multiple meanings of a film. Even before interpretations can be proposed, friends are needed to reconstruct the film, to point out details one has missed, the tone of voice, the camera angle, the arrangement of actors on the screen, the soundtrack, the framing, the facial expressions. Friends are also needed to help reconstruct what public concerns and issues there were at the time the film was produced and distributed and to discern how the film might relate to them.

Discussions about film are valuable for another reason: to compensate for the inevitable blind spots everyone has. Most Americans have watched films with attention and delight all their lives. Each person has a film repertoire of information and associations that no one else exactly shares. This means that, although each person has intensive preparation and a store of knowledge, none "controls," "commands," or has "mastered" this voluminous body of work.

Moreover, at the same time that we have a great deal of personal knowledge of films, we are also well-trained to respond to filmic conventions in predictable ways. The serious discussion of films should unsettle, challenge, even disassemble these socialized reactions. As one learns to question, to investigate, and to make explicit the strategies by which a film produces—or at least directs—our responses, the pleasure of watching a film changes subtly but profoundly from that of passive spectatorship to that of active critical engagement.

A spectator's impressions of a film, then, are simultaneously informed by her education and life experiences and trained by film conventions and viewing habits. This does not mean that the strong feeling a film may elicit should be discarded or overlooked. Rather, the emotion a film evokes should be acknowledged and understood as the starting point for an exploration of the filmic strategies that elicited it. The purpose of paying serious attention to film is twofold. On the one hand, the ability to analyze filmic representations develops an individual's critical subjectivity. On the other hand, films reveal how a society represents itself to itself. I will have more to say in subsequent chapters about the self-knowledge a society can gain by analyzing how its reiterated representations relate to its social and institutional arrangements, its public concerns and interests, and its fears and longings.

What is the role of pleasure if we want to think about a film, not primarily as "entertaining," but as communicating social roles and expectations, values, and constructions of desire and the desirable? In her 1975 essay, "Visual Pleasure and Narrative Cinema," Laura Mulvey made the rather startling statement that in order to challenge the "basic assumptions of mainstream film," one must first "destroy" the pleasure produced by the film.[13] This seems to me a particularly problematic way to understand religion and values in popular film. It reproduces, in secular language, an ancient Christian mistrust of pleasure, calling for a sort of visual asceticism that assumes that one can work and learn only when pleasure is absent.

I would put it differently. Our task is neither to deny nor to destroy visual pleasure in order to do the sober work of analysis, but to trust our pleasure as a primary tool of interpretation. Certainly a film's implicit claim either to entertain or to mirror reality needs to be examined. Yet to assume that visual pleasure serves *only* to seduce viewers into mindlessly accepting the film's values distorts a spectator's experience and eliminates the primary motivation for analyzing a film. Visual pleasure is the place to begin because by producing visual pleasure, a film communicates values. Roland Barthes once remarked that one "gets" the cultural message at the same moment one gets the pleasure.

Spectatorial pleasure, far from being jettisoned, must be noticed and examined. Pleasure can be examined by (1) identifying the filmic strategies or devices that produce it, and (2) by developing a critical method, an ability to articulate the assumptions and values underlying and informing one's reactions to a film. For the film does not contain and determine its own meaning; meaning is negotiated between the spectator and the film.

This does not mean, however, that a film permits an infinite number of interpretations. Films certainly endeavor to make viewers see what the director wants communicated. The primary tool governing the communication of meaning is film conventions, repeated stylized interactions between the actors that viewers have come to expect from watching countless other films of the same genre. I will say more about film conventions in chapter 2. Here, an example will suffice: in romantic narrative film we expect closure, an ending. Trained by Hollywood conventions, we may even expect a "happy ending," by which is usually meant one in which a heterosexual couple finds each other. If such an ending is denied us, we are likely to feel dissatisfied.

Filmmakers outside the mainstream often subvert film conventions in order to make them evident. For example, in Joan Micklin Silver's *Chilly Scenes of Winter*, the couple separates in the end, which caused several reviewers to complain that the film had no ending. It had an ending; it even had—in the circumstances depicted in the film—a happy ending, but because of the expectation that only if the couple were reunited would there be a happy ending, the film felt unfinished. Similarly, in Claudia Weil's *Girlfriends*, a film convention in which marriage constitutes a happy ending is overturned. A woman's marriage is presented as interrupting her work and confining her character development, as well as undermining her relationship with an important woman friend. Spectators' displeasure is often the first signal that a film convention has been disrupted.

To sum up, then, I believe that taking a film seriously does not require that the pleasure of entertainment be replaced by boring analysis. Rather, it involves taking pleasure (and displeasure) seriously enough to be willing to inspect them, detecting the filmic strategies by which they were evoked.

Resistance to examining the values films circulate, and to investigating their depictions of religion and religious motivation in particular, is common, however. Marx's maxim, "The critique of religion is the prerequisite of every critique" has filtered into a widespread skepticism about religion and its effects,[14] which is apparent in Hollywood's bias against religion. Marx's distrust of religion has also been widely and uncritically adopted by otherwise critical theorists.[15] In academic as well as popular literature, religious belief is frequently characterized as slavish and irrational, based on foolish longings for transcendence or immortality.[16] I will examine in more detail in subsequent chapters the subtle and not-so-subtle forms the secular bias takes in Hollywood films.[17]

Moreover, news and information media often fail to differentiate among different religious commitments, considering all forms of religious loyalty as actually or potentially dangerous to the "impartiality" and freedoms of the public sphere.[18] Media attention tends to be focused on fundamentalist religion, probably because these forms—whether Christian, Jewish, or Moslem—seem to inspire in their members the most dramatic public actions. Liberal religion, or religion that seeks to be self-critical, tends to be ignored by the communication media that give many Americans our sense of what is real. Yet different forms of religion have distinct attitudes toward public life and the common good.

The representation of religion in the media often reduces it to flawed institutions, discredited myths, and morally flawed practitioners. But this understanding excludes too much; it precludes exploring the way religious loyalties function in human lives and communities. Religion, as a cultural institution, must perform cultural work; it must organize people's social arrangements and suggest attitudes toward individuals' lives, toward the religious community, and toward others. To examine religion as a cultural product is to ask: How does it work?

Like religion, films describe and define their characters' orientations and attitudes to the world. They invite the question, "How does this character's life *work*?" Are her values, and those of the people with whom she lives, adequate? If one considers the interest in values and relationships common to religion and film, both can be approached as parts of a common cultural matrix. But to make this connection clear, a more adequate understanding of religious orientation and its role in human life will be needed. I will propose a revised understanding of religion later in this chapter.

There is also resistance to investigating serious issues in popular film because of the social and institutional construction of what constitutes serious scholarship. A tradition that has persisted since the West was founded as a cultural and intellectual entity rejects empathic emotion as a method for learning and insight. And the movies both feature and incite emotional engagement. The antitragic tradition in the West, fathered by Plato, has consistently valued rationality, contrasting the use of reason and argument with emotion. This tradition has feared emotion, advocating that emotion be eliminated as much as possible from public and private decision-making. Emotion, especially strong emotion, for adherents of the antitragic tradition, was and is suspect, dangerous, and potentially destructive for both individual and community. The tragic tradition, as exemplified in Greek drama, however, finds it worthwhile and valuable to "nourish the element of pity in us, making it strong."[19]

Since the Enlightenment, the antitragic tradition has sought to establish the ideal of rational impartiality in public discourse, relegating emotion to the private sphere, and empathic emotion to the private arena of entertainment.[20] Furthermore, the public sphere of politics, law, and institutions has been identified with men, while emotion is identified with women. As the ancient tragic tradition knew, the response that drama's powerful images elicited was empathic emotion.

Film, like ancient tragedy, is considered a less than serious focus of study in that it is thought to evoke pity rather than reason as a formal means of participation. Similarly, film reviewers usually rely on a presumed common perspective in discussing their impressions of a film. Thus, a serious study of popular film must establish its relative impartiality, its claim to a method of analysis that maximizes objectivity, and its rejection of impressionistic and subjective readings. While I do not believe that emotion is unqualified to inform decisions and actions, I acknowledge that evaluative interpretations should not appeal to a presumed common feeling, but should endeavor to provide negotiable grounds on which to discuss the judgment at hand.

Finally, there is resistance to examining the treatment of religion and values in film based on the opinion that popular film is simply unworthy of serious scrutiny. The objection is either that popular films cannot reward scrutiny with an enhanced understanding of anything, or that the pleasure of spectatorship will be destroyed by examination. I hope that this book will demonstrate the inaccuracy of both claims.

Yet the idea that analyzing a popular film "spoils the fun," removing the pleasure of spectatorship, is not to be lightly dismissed. It acknowledges a human need for pleasure, a longing to relax and be entertained. I have already described the use of pleasure in serious film criticism, but it must be acknowledged that the pleasure of entertainment is not identical to the learned pleasure of analysis. Anyone who has endeavored to teach film criticism as a disciplined study will attest to the strength of the settled habit of regarding film as entertainment. It is, then, no small thing to ask that a reader tolerate an examination of contemporary popular film as a transmitter of attitudes and values, and to ask that pleasure be scrutinized. There are, on the other hand, some good reasons—like enhanced self-knowledge and understanding of American society—that someone who certainly enjoys entertainment might want, on occasion, to think seriously about what she sees at the movies.

Fundamental to this book is the contention that religion has centrally to do with the articulation of a sense of relatedness—among individuals, within families, communities, and societies, and with the natural world. Religions also provide a picture of the greater whole in which all living beings are related. Understandings of relatedness underlie religious beliefs, narratives, and institutions. Defining religion in this way means that relationships and practices between people in faith communities, as well as attitudes toward those outside the group require scrutiny. Thus, understandings of race, gender, class, and sexual orientation are not accidental or incidental to religious perspectives but, as *a concrete way religious perspectives are articulated*, are central to religious values. Spiritual hunger arises from relationships that lack equality and mutuality and from unjust institutions and social arrangements as surely as it comes from inadequate theology or belief.

If religion is centrally about relationships, about a network of connections, then religion is also centrally and essentially about the values according to which people conduct their relationships. To recognize that religious communities are centrally concerned with the formulation, exploration, and practical application of *values* is also to recover one of religion's public functions, that of critically examining secular values and providing alternatives. Within Christianity, the numerically dominant religion of North America, there are profoundly ambivalent attitudes toward secular society. Conservative Christians often see secular culture as the enemy, while liberal Christians largely assimilate secular society uncritically, even as they temporarily escape its problems in communities of the like-minded. Neither of these stances encourages an engaged, critical, and prognostic relationship with popular public culture.

Religion is hardly prominent in contemporary popular film, reflecting the public sphere's secular self-image. Yet the claim that American society is thoroughly secular is overdrawn. It is also elitist and regional. Although it might be a fairly accurate description of the East or West coast, it ignores a wide middle portion of the United States where there are still traffic jams on Sunday mornings just before eleven o'clock.

In fact, Americans may be ambivalent about, not uninterested in, religion. The number of articles in the popular press purporting to analyze national trends in religious attitudes, beliefs, and practices, indicates that Americans are somewhat preoccupied with their religious profile. Toward the end of the 1980s, *Reader's Digest*, the second-highest circulating magazine in the United States, carried an article titled, "How Religious Are We?" Forty-eight percent of the respondents reported "a rising tide of interest in religion in the United States."[21] This constituted a 300 percent increase over a 1970 poll. Although it is difficult to specify precisely what constitutes "religiosity," the 1994 public debate over legislation that would permit prayer in public schools, places of employment, and government offices indicated renewed popular interest in religion. Moreover, by 1986 there were 1,100 religious radio stations, 200 religious television stations, and 4,100 religious bookstores in the United States. Church membership and attendance figures also support perceptions of "rising interest." True, increased membership in fundamentalist churches (35 percent) and orthodox Jewish congregations (100 percent) is partially offset by declining membership in mainstream Protestant churches and decreasing attendance at mass by Roman Catholics. Still, 76 percent of the Americans polled had attended a religious service during the previous year, and 95 percent professed belief in God or a universal spirit.[22] A resurgence of religion in the United States appears to be occurring, in spite of the decline of mainstream Protestantism.

Hollywood films of the last decade reflect the hypothesis that Americans are not so zealously secular as is often claimed. Although religion is often not treated very respectfully in popular film, it is at least there. The treatment of religion in a 1979 film, *Hardcore* (a box office failure) is typical of films of the 1980s. The protagonist, a Dutch Reformed Church minister, is searching for his adolescent daughter who has disappeared. He fears that she has been abducted by a group that produces pornographic films, so he enlists the help of a teenage prostitute to find her. To pass the time while they are waiting for a bus, the young woman asks him to explain his religious beliefs. He does so, to her amazement, by reciting the Calvinist beliefs condensed in the acronym "tulip": total depravity, unmerited salvation, limited atonement, irresistible grace, and perseverance of the saints. Finding it difficult to comprehend the belief that a person's eternal destiny to salvation or damnation has been established from "before the foundations of the world," the young woman remarks pensively, "And I thought *I* was fucked up!" Religion is sometimes used as a foil to demonstrate the greater seriousness of "real" issues, such as sex, power, and possessions. At other times, film characters may adhere to religious belief passionately and mindlessly, usually causing personal and social mayhem and damage.

The films I will discuss are mostly Hollywood films produced by large studios and widely distributed. They are mostly narrative films whose box office earnings were relatively high.[23] I have chosen to work with films that contain complex and interesting—though frequently problematic—treatments of religion and values. Most of them deal explicitly, if not centrally, with religion; all of them depict values under negotiation. I have chosen not to treat avant-garde, experimental, or "alternative" cinema for the simple reason that none of these has managed either to gather a diverse popular audience or to affect mainstream film production.[24]

Several other considerations have also directed my choice of films. Although moderately successful in terms of box office profits, most of the films I chose to discuss were not the largest box office successes, even in the week of their highest profit. One could argue that, to know with the greatest clarity and precision how issues of common concern are treated in films, one should choose those films with the largest box office. I did not choose them because I wanted to examine films that were presented to the American public as treating issues of common interest rather than as "cheap thrills," featuring sex and violence. The largest social group that determines box office success is male teenagers.[25] While I do not imagine that this audience saw such films as *Hard Target*, *Lethal Weapon 3*, *Hot Shots*, *Wayne's World*, or *Days of Thunder* simply for escapist reasons, I acknowledge that I am less interested in how contemplating such films might inform the issues with which young men must deal in our society. I hope that someone else will write that book.

The films I discuss also illustrate well the fruitfulness of the cultural studies approach I discuss later in this chapter. In Part I, films that focus on religion—Christianity, Judaism, and Islam—are examined. In Part II, I have chosen films that highlight issues of individual and social values, especially as they concern race, gender, sexual orientation, and class.

In short, I address adult readers who want to see and think about what they look at in movie theaters and on video. The large number of movie reviews in newspapers and magazines indicates that many people enjoy thinking and talking about films they have seen. I endeavor to provide such readers with a conceptual framework and methodology for analyzing popular films in the social context of American public life within which they were created and circulated. The book addresses the same diverse audience that made the films I discuss at least moderately "popular."

I consider films that have been produced (roughly) within the last decade so that a more or less accessible historical experience (national and global) can be assumed. Films, like paintings and plays, are not timeless objects; they arise in, and respond to, concrete historical circumstances. Thus, they cannot be adequately analyzed without reference to the social anxieties and aspirations that prompted their production and that had a great deal to do with whether or not they became successful at the box office. While it would be interesting to compare films across several decades, it could not be done responsibly without reconstructing the social interests and concerns within which the film took voice, a task too demanding for this book. The primary context for a film, I believe, is not other films but the public world of events, institutions, and multiple vexed negotiations of values and behavior.

It is notoriously difficult to predict the box office success of any film.[26] Dramatic mistakes have been made—frequently, and on both sides. Small-budget independent films have sometimes been successful beyond all expectations, and films that apparently have everything—big budgets, stars, and all the mandatory titillation—have bombed. My hypothesis is that films that succeed at the box office are those that identify currently pressing social anxieties and examine a possible resolution. My discussion of particular films will seek to demonstrate that the film played a role—provided a voice—in the clamor of public conversation. A director can imagine, and a film can visualize, the resolution of a situation so that cinema audiences can picture more concretely how the issue might be dealt with, what it would look like and feel like if a particular resolution were to be adopted.[27]

If indeed a film's success at the box office is largely determined by its accurate identification of an issue or problem about which people are presently puzzled and concerned, films that were made even a few years ago must rely on viewers' interest in the skill and technical expertise of actors, director, and crew. Even slightly dated films can begin to bore precisely because the issues they explore are no longer the same as those that we are encountering.

Having stated what I hope to accomplish, I must decline several agenda that might at first appear consonant with the method and aims of the book. I do not seek to interpret particular films persuasively, if by "interpret" is meant to argue that a certain underlying theme or problem contains the real meaning of the film. I will not seek to show that contemporary popular films are, in general, invidious, though I will argue that caricatures of religion and the unproblematized representation of certain social and institutional practices are detrimental.

I will not focus on secular reinterpretations of traditional religious themes, like the near-death experience depicted in *Resurrection*, or the moving secular resurrection scene at the end of *Longtime Companion*. Neither am I interested in identifying religious themes—such as forgiveness, grace, or redemption—in Hollywood films. Films may help people to recognize the operation of such realities in contemporary dress and everyday life, but often religious motifs are in the eye of the beholder, requiring a theological perspective and theological language in order to recognize them. They will not announce themselves to most spectators.

A brief overview of popular films of the 1980s and early 1990s reveals some patterns in the treatment of religion in film:

1. No "old-fashioned reverential films" (like the earlier *Greatest Story Ever Told*) were box office successes.[28] There were, however, some films about religion and religious leaders, such as *The Last Temptation of Christ*, which, film critic Tom O'Brien says, "revived the idea that one could make a serious film about religion—a taboo in Hollywood . . . since the 60s."[29] Unlike earlier films, recent films about Christianity are largely iconoclastic: Jesus is pictured as a "real man," troubled by sexual fantasies; or as a media figure (*Jesus Christ Superstar*, originally a successful Broadway play); or as a

contemporary inner-city African American (*Brother from Another Planet*); or as a critic of capitalist consumerism (*Jesus of Montreal*). Moderately successful box office films on religious leaders included *The Chosen*, which presented two forms of Judaism, and *Gandhi*.

2. A few films that critiqued society from a religious perspective had moderate success at the box office (*Romero*, *Chariots of Fire*, and *The Long Walk Home*).

3. Several films (such as *The Day After*, a film made for television, and *Testament*) depicted religion as helpless and ineffectual in the face of human suffering and social chaos. In *Testament*, the priest stutters, "We just don't have all the answers; . . . we are trying to find out." Religious resources for ethical or moral decision-making are equally suspect in Hollywood films. According to popular films, there seems to be little possibility that moral choices involving and affecting a broader public sphere could be religiously motivated. Ethical decisions affecting institutions, national and global politics, and business are seen to require a more complex frame of reference than traditional religious principles offer. In *Coma*, the surgeon says, "Hospitals are the cathedrals . . . [to] a whole nation of sick people turning to us for help." Many films made in the last decade imply that traditional religious authority has been replaced by psychoanalysts and psychotherapists, politicians, lawyers, and business leaders.

4. Religion was frequently represented as a social problem in 1980s Hollywood films (*Jesus of Montreal*, *Everybody Wins*, *The Handmaid's Tale*, *The Day After*, *Jungle Fever*, *The Rapture*). Religious feeling, when it was represented as motivating behavior, was typically fanatical and rash (*Black Robe*, *The Mission*, *The Rapture*).

5. A few movies included religiously motivated characters, but, with one dramatic exception (*Witness*),[30] they were not successful at the box office (*The Trip to Bountiful*, *Babette's Feast*, *Tender Mercies*).[31] Films tended to picture religious motivation as personal and individual, rather than as communal (*Romero*, *Chariots of Fire*, *Black Robe*, *The Mission*). If communal religion was pictured, it was not mainstream religion (*The Long Walk Home*, *The Chosen*). Perhaps largely because American public discourse is filled with the rhetoric of individuality, those of us who are religious usually think

of ourselves as religious *individuals,* not as members of religious communities. Yet, as Fred Inglis said, "The big structures of society play through our being all the time, and our only chance of freeing ourselves from them is to catch them at work."[32]

6. Religious "otherness" was represented from the perspective of a dominantly Christian culture. *Not Without My Daughter,* a film I discuss in greater detail in chapter 4, is a striking example of a popular film's irresponsible treatment of Muslims.

7. Films that urged an explicit message bombed at the box office. "Too-serious" movies—with the notable exceptions of *Schindler's List* and *Philadelphia*—failed to recover their costs, even when well reviewed (*The Last Days of Chez Nous, Lorenzo's Oil, A Dangerous Woman, A Dry White Season, Cry Freedom*).

Despite popular films' largely dismissive treatment of *religion,* films are profoundly interested in *values,* that is, in "the material, relational, social, and political 'goods' that a person or people identify as centrally constitutive of the 'good' life."[33] Values include attitudes, opinions, institutional loyalties, and particular behaviors—sexual and social—that people find indispensable, or at least worth working or struggling for. Values are what people want to be able to take for granted in their society. While others' values can be—often are—questioned, rejected, or resisted, one's own often seem to have an "obvious" or "natural" rightness. Yet experience, and examination of experience—one's own and others' representations of their experience—continually brings received values into question. Values are constantly negotiated, both by individuals and by societies; some values are contested and those deemed no longer adequate are resisted, and different "goods" are proposed.

In short, if we want to understand the values circulating in the public sphere at any time, media culture is a good place to start. Directors have frequently denied that films communicate values. Sam Goldwyn, in an often-quoted aphorism, once said that "anyone looking for messages should go, not to the movies, but to Western Union." Clearly, if they are to be successful, films must entertain. But this study owes a great deal to Roland Barthes's important suggestion, already quoted, that one "gets" the cultural message at the same instant that one gets the pleasure; the cultural message is coated or masked by pleasure, so that the greater the pleasure, the less one notices and examines the cultural message.

A moment's reflection is convincing proof that the problems of American social life are a staple of popular film. Whether or not a film explicitly questions the behavior it shows, if it displays behavior widely practiced but considered problematic, many people will want to see it. To suggest only a few of the many popular films that frontally treat common dilemmas and issues of contemporary life: *Jungle Fever*, which takes on drug use, inner-city poverty, and racism; *Something Wild*, which examines drug use, unsafe sex, and lawlessness; *Star Trek IV: The Voyage Home*, whose plot revolves around an ecological crisis; *White Palace* and *Thelma and Louise*, which depict drunk driving and unsafe sex with a stranger as fun. Racism is central to *The Long Walk Home*, *Jungle Fever*, *Do the Right Thing*, and *Boyz N the Hood*. Sexism is depicted as unproblematic—irritating, but "just the way things are"—in most popular films, including *Thelma and Louise* and *The Piano*.

In this book, however, I will endeavor to avoid a kind of cultural pessimism too often engaged in by critics of contemporary culture and society. Films that depict problematic behavior do not always serve to promote that behavior. Considering particular films in the social context in which they were produced, careful discriminations can be made as to whether the film depicts a damaging or destructive social behavior uncritically, or depicts it in a way that reveals its personal and social costs, in order to critique, or even to present an alternative.[34] And so much depends, as I have argued, on the viewer's use of a film, whether for "entertainment," or for considering how we should live.

It is easy enough to criticize films; so few are perfect. Most treat some issues well, others not so well. People of minority racial, ethnic, religious, and/or sexual orientation groups within American society, whose interests have been consistently misrepresented for decades, often appreciate and support any effort to more accurately and sympathetically represent them.[35] Films that attempt to deal honestly and fairly with issues and images of marginalization and oppression should be acknowledged for their courage as well as criticized for their shortcomings.

"I strain after images," Plato said. We all do. We cannot begin to live a life we cannot first imagine, and images stock the imagination's repertoire. I believe that popular films should help people to imagine richly diverse relationships and a generous society. To the extent that Hollywood film conventions reiterate a narrow range of desires and repetitiously designate what is desirable, they constrain the collective imagination and impoverish the public symbolic repertoire.

The premise of a cultural studies approach is, as J. Hillis Miller put it, that the cultural products of a given time are "deeply embedded in history, in a particular language and class structure, in specific modes of production, distribution, and consumption."[36] Unlike a film critic, a cultural critic is not solely, or even primarily, interested in studying the film as an independent "text"; rather, as a historian of contemporary society, she also studies the particular cultural moment in which the film originated.[37] In contrast to methods of film criticism that think of films solely as texts—psychoanalytic, semiotic, Marxist, feminist, *auteur*, or genre criticism—a cultural studies approach scrutinizes them as products of the culture's social, sexual, religious, political, and institutional configurations.

In his 1987 field-defining article, "What is Cultural Studies Anyway?," Richard Johnson specified a careful and thorough historical method for studying contemporary societies.[38] Cultural studies, he said, examines the "life cycle" of a film, the circuit from production, to distribution, to reception, as well as the film itself. The "cultural context must be studied not in order to melt the work back into it, but as an indispensable analysis undertaken to identify the differentiae that make the work different" from other works.[39]

Culture theorists also think of the spectator differently than do film critics (as I discuss more thoroughly in chapter 2). For now it is enough to say that cultural critics understand film audiences as active interpreters of a film rather than as passive, helpless recipients of the information and values communicated through media. Cultural critics work from the premise that people see differently according to a complex preparation they bring to spectatorship: social location, race, class, sexual orientation, gender, education, age, to name only some of the potential variables. Moreover, spectators are understood primarily as social, rather than as autonomous individuals. That is why the social and historical context of a film's production, circulation, and reception is important. Finally, cultural studies is more concerned with popular culture than with the so-called fine arts, which are seen by comparatively few people.[40]

Cultural studies' approach to media calls for an exploration that goes beyond "impressions" to documented description of the broader social "conversation" within which the film is one voice. Culture theorists do not reject other approaches to film criticism, such as psychoanalytic, Marxist, *auteur*, or feminist; rather, they think of them as insightful but partial pictures of how film works in society. In concrete terms, then, a cultural studies approach requires information about a film's funding and production; its distribution to theaters; the director's intent, as described in interviews; the box office earnings; and the diverse critical perspectives given in reviews. It also analyzes the screenplay, camera-work, narrative, and soundtrack.

Moreover, the "cultural space" taken by any film must include what Barbara Klinger has called "digressions," that is, advertising, interviews, trailers. These designate the film's topic and "consumable identity"; they attempt to make the film appeal to the broadest popular interests, explaining why diverse audiences should want to see the film. Intermedia coverage of films leaves few Americans ignorant of the topics of the best-marketed films. In fact, a film's box office success depends on its supporting digressions.[41] I do not discuss them in this book only because to do so would extend dramatically the book's length.

All cultural messages are timely; they refer to a historical moment and depend on the visual associations and particular perspectives of the viewers whose interest in the film creates its success at the box office. Thus, any identification of a film's cultural messages can only be suggestive, never final or complete. It is, indeed, likely that my positioning of a film within a historical set of public interests and anxieties will not be fully convincing to a thoughtful reader who has noticed different news items or engaged in different conversations than I have. Since a cultural studies approach depends, for its accuracy and insight, on determining which features of society are crucial to a reconstruction of a film's communications, it is always vulnerable to suggestions that a central aspect of common experience has been overlooked. And sometimes information one would like to have is not available. When the necessary context is accurately identified, however, a cultural studies approach to film criticism promises to reveal the functions of popular film in American public life. In the appendix I list the questions I asked in analyzing each film and its treatment of religion and values.

The development of popular film coincided historically and geographically with the emancipation of public life from church control and patronage. "Congregations" became "audiences" as film created a new public sphere in which, under the guise of "entertainment," values are formulated, circulated, resisted, and negotiated. The public sphere is an arena in which various overlapping minorities can converse, contest, and negotiate, forming temporary coalitions.

The point of my study, then, is not to identify films that treat Christianity and/or other religions "positively." Nor is it to praise or deplore the values represented in films. It is, rather, to acknowledge that the representation and examination of values and moral commitments does not presently occur most pointedly in churches, synagogues, or mosques, but before the eyes of "congregations" in movie theaters. North Americans—even those with religious affiliations—now gather about cinema and television screens rather than in churches to ponder the moral quandaries of American life. Religion and film *share* an interest in, and attention to, values. I will endeavor to show that looking at religion and values in "the movies" through the lens of a cultural studies approach can demonstrate the importance of bringing critical religious perspectives to popular public discourse. Finally, the movies help Americans consider the ancient and perennial question of human life: How should we live?

2

"Were You There When
They Crucified My Lord?"

> The Last Temptation of Christ
> Jesus of Montreal

Two films that take the life and work of Jesus as their topic will help to illustrate the complex processes entailed in watching any film; they also foreground some interesting continuities and discontinuities between historical Christians' devotional uses of images and twentieth-century spectatorship. In investigating some of the implicit and explicit claims of narrative realist cinema, I make some—I hope, provocative—suggestions about whether, or in what sense, a film about Jesus can be a "religious" film.

The power of vision to encourage imitation has been recognized since Plato. The power of vision, then, is the topic of this chapter—indeed, of the book as a whole—but it is not easy to say how powerful vision is without either over- or underestimating it. Perhaps the best conceptual model is Michel Foucault's notion of "strong power," that is, the power to attract. While the communication media of a society are able to attract members of the society to the behaviors and skills required for the maintenance of society, there is no need to resort to "weak power." Weak power is coercive power, which may run a continuum from its subtler educational forms to actual physical force.[1] Movies are an important part of the strong power of contemporary American society. Popular films cumulatively—not any one film but the areas of consensus among many films—make the desires and behavior repeatedly depicted on the big screen seem both "natural" and right.

The Last Temptation of Christ (hereafter *Last Temptation*) and *Jesus of Montreal* (hereafter *Jesus*) are realist films; that is, they ask the spectator to believe that the film simply shows things "as they really are." Moviegoers "know" when we watch a film that this is not the case, but the film's entertainment value lies in its ability to make us forget that it is in fact a representation, or construction. In order to be entertained, we need to believe—however temporarily—and we are annoyed if we cannot.

David Freedberg has described the attraction realism held for many historical Christians.[2] The more realistic the religious images they could behold, the more devoted they became. Tableaux illustrating the life and death of Christ were popular as long ago as the fifteenth century and still are, for many Christians, in the twentieth century. Tableaux feature naturalistic figures, often with real hair and clothing. At St. Anne de Beaupré near the city of Quebec, millions of visitors each year enter the huge round cyclorama to view a realistic representation of the day of Jesus' crucifixion. Visitors circumambulate the scene, pausing to pray at "stations" or balconies overlooking the central events of the crucifixion day. In so doing, they imitate, as best they can, fourth-century Christians who undertook arduous journeys in order to be present at the holy places, primarily to see, but also to touch and smell the alleged scenes of scriptural events. Ancient and modern pilgrims testify to the religious value of imaginatively entering a scene from Christ's life or death through gazing on such a scene.

For a Christian, the act of inserting himself, emotionally and, if possible, physically, into a religiously momentous scene was not merely a matter of visiting a *sacri monti*; it was an achievement, the result of long instruction and practice in the devotional use of vision. By contrast, twentieth-century filmgoers are usually unaware of the extent to which our own visual practice is trained. Yet film spectatorship requires visual training at least as complex as that of religious devotion. For example, realist films require spectators' consent to two rather contradictory illusions. Spectators must agree to believe—or at least to suspend disbelief for the duration of the film—that the world of the film and the world of the spectator are separate and unconnected.[3] Spectators must assume that characters in the film are oblivious to the fact that they are being watched. Secondly, realist narrative film implicitly claims to function as a window; the "eye" of the camera reports—without distortion and without selection—"an uncoded reflection" of the "real world."

In short, the spectator agrees to see, in grainy marks on a flat screen, human beings acting and interacting in a three-dimensional world. The "structure of cinematic perception is readily translated into that of natural perception, so much so that we . . . rely on information" we get from films to supplement our knowledge of the real world.[4] "The aim of realism is to obliterate our awareness of the medium and its conventions and to make us take what is represented for a reflection of a natural reality. Realism sees itself as holding a mirror up to life."[5]

Camera strategies contribute to the illusion that the screen is a window, especially the use of long takes, long shots, and the moving camera. "Long takes give the impression of real time; long shots allow us to see complete figures in the context of their milieu; the moving camera knits time and space together in a contiguous whole so that events can appear to be actual."[6] The darkened auditorium helps to create the realist illusions. We are effectively isolated from our accustomed visual and spatial reality, our attention focused on the screen. What we hear on the soundtrack verifies what we see, establishing a strong link between the film and our experience of a real world of conversation and sound. Finally, realist film places its characters and action in a particular social and historical setting. Are you "there"—or not?

Although film implicitly claims to present the world of experience as it is, it actually represents, or replaces, a world that does not exist; that is, a world that is missing, in that the events are not happening as we see them. Painstaking selections among multiple possible visual and audio features create what is essentially "the presence of an absence."[7] Again, the comparison with a devotional image-user is instructive. Christians—past or present—who use images religiously believe that their images represent a reality that is invisible—present, but unseen. For believers, the image reveals a world that is more real than the visible world, a reality that has created, and that still informs and sustains, the visible world. This important difference between the religious use of images and contemporary entertainment is crucial to pondering the question of whether a film about religion can be a religious film, a question I return to later in the chapter.

As film spectators we enjoy the illusion that we are transported into an alternative real world, but we know simultaneously that the image is not life. And so there is a "fissure (or gap) which we sometimes leap, sometimes refuse to leap, and most often straddle."[8] When we refuse the illusion of realism, we experience the screen not as window but as frame, frame into which figures and objects are purposefully placed. It then becomes clear that selections are marked by the perspective of the director and his advisors. The implicit—and frequently explicit—claim to depict a true story cannot explain the many choices that have created the representation. One can never argue, then, that a filmic representation includes the elements it does because it is simply accurate-to-life, or, in the case of *Last Temptation* and *Jesus*, to scripture. The selections for which the director takes responsibility must achieve persuasiveness, not by referring to a real world, but on the film's own terms, in the interrelation and coherence of its many elements.[9]

Although films neither refer to nor present a real world, a film is *itself* a world in two senses. It presents a constructed world—a world that is (more or less) coherent and comprehensive—and it is an intricate set of codes and conventions. Although fiction films do not reveal the real world, they can and do reveal the representational systems of the cinema.

Considering films one at a time, it is easy to overlook the agreement on issues of values in popular films. Consensus among them becomes evident, however, when one looks at their use of Hollywood conventions. "Conventions" are frequently used devices by which visually trained audiences interpret what they are seeing. Is there an American who does not know seconds after the first appearance of a character whether that character is a "good guy" or a "bad guy"? Late twentieth-century audiences do not need black and white hats to convey this; if a character is beautiful, we know s/he will probably be "good," not necessarily in traditional terms, but according to the cultural values of the moment.

Hollywood conventions shorten the distance between seeing and believing. Conventions may be as encompassing as the formula genre film or so subtle that they are not noticed by any but the most perspicacious observer, but they function to make most films as formulaic as a Byzantine icon.[10] For the viewer hoping only for entertainment, most Hollywood conventions bypass conscious recognition.[11] Yet the vast majority of successful Hollywood films are genre films, films which permit spectators familiar with Westerns, or horror, family melodrama, or romance to predict both the narrative and the conclusion of the film.[12] Americans prefer familiar scenarios overlaid with a thin veneer of novelty.

Let us move now to considering the viewer's interaction with a film. Realist cinema invites the spectator to identify with what is seen in two ways. The "primary identification," first named by Christian Metz, is with the "look" of the camera: audiences can see only what the camera sees, and we construct an imaginary wholeness and unity around the figures and objects it shows us. We initially agree to believe that the camera omits nothing essential to the film. If we want, for purposes of analysis, to resist this complicity with the "eye" of the camera, we can do so by examining not only what is there, but also what is not there— what is excluded by the camera's monopolizing gaze.

The "secondary identification" is with a character or actor. We accept, however fleetingly, the perspective of one or more of the film characters, consenting to see what the character sees and to interpret the world of the film as he/she does. However, secondary identifications are very complex. Rather than identifying with a single character who is very like oneself (in gender, race, age, class, or sexual orientation), most spectators make multiple and shifting identifications in the course of viewing a film. (I will have more to say about identification a bit later in this chapter.)

Spectatorship is a learned skill. Two stories about people seeing early films for the first time illustrate the power of the illusion for the untrained spectator that what one sees is real. The first account tells of a man who, not having learned to distance himself emotionally and intellectually from the action of the film, and "overly susceptible to the filmic illusion of the real, flees in terror at the sight of [an] advancing train."[13] Another account describes a woman at one of the earliest demonstrations of cinema who went to the screen and poked her fingers at the image on the screen of a woman's face, convinced that the whole thing was a hoax and that there was a real woman standing behind the screen and projected onto it.[14] Both spectators were enthralled by the screen images; clearly, they had not learned to distinguish between the world of the film and the "real" world.

For spectators to acquire the distance from the screen that we experience and yet remain emotionally engaged by the new medium took approximately a generation. The spectator who could not maintain spectatorial distance was likely to interfere with the picture show by protesting the actions of the villain, dancing with the Parisian dancer in the film, or stopping a filmic fight by tearing down the screen. Indeed, a 1902 film, *Uncle Josh*, shows exactly these incidents in order to "dramatize the unabatable surprise that vision could be dissociated from the body and mechanized in a way that left the body of the spectator untouched, unaffected."[15] The film viewer must learn a new skill; like the medieval viewer, she must train herself in the arts of identification appropriate to film, but she must also learn the complex set of consents I have described above.

These stories illustrating the detachment necessary for viewing realist film are even more vivid when they are compared with the explicit visual training that medieval spectators underwent. Consider the viewer of Fra Angelico's frescoes in the corridors and cells of San Marco, a Dominican monastery in Florence. The subject of these frescoes is the life, death, and resurrection of Christ. The monks who saw these frescoes daily were instructed to identify with the figures in the paintings, with the scriptural human beings who had surrounded the Jesus of history. Yet each painting contains at least one peculiarly unhistorical figure: a Dominican friar, dressed in monastic clothing contemporary with the painting. The function of this figure is to invite the viewer to identify with the devotion of the painted Dominican by imitating the gestures and body postures of piety.[16]

Dominican monks were not the only medieval Christians who were advised to appropriate the postures, gestures, and—through them—the feelings of devotion represented by painted figures: other monastic orders similarly counseled their members, providing religious images to direct their devotional practice. Laypersons were also guided by popular devotional manuals like the fourteenth-century *Meditations on the Life of Christ* to imitate the intense emotions acted out by the figures in religious paintings. Moreover, the imitation required was not thought of as occurring in some timeless, spaceless realm. Christians who engaged in committed religious practice strove to reconstruct mentally the original scene in detail—to imagine the smells, the temperature, tactile sensations—in order to be emotionally present in it. Their religious lives were formed and informed by such identifications. In short, medieval Christians cultivated an altogether different relationship to visual images than late twentieth-century spectators' trained detachment. Historical image-users knew—or at least were repeatedly instructed—to regard religious images as representations of the image's prototype. Some misunderstood, and attached their devotion to the image itself, prompting iconoclastic controversies. In such controversies, the power of images became the basis of arguments both for and against their devotional use.

However, neither the intentional attachment of the Christian to her religious images, nor the detachment of the twentieth-century spectator should be exaggerated. Both combine attachment and detachment in their engagement with images. The stories of early film spectators indicate that what twentieth-century spectators needed to learn was detachment, while Christian devotional literature abounds with instructions for cultivating devotional attachment, not to the religious image itself, but to the spiritual world to which it points. It is easy to see that with the invention of moving pictures, images were all the more powerful, requiring the alien feat of detachment if spectators were not to run screaming from the theater when the image of a train bore down upon them.

Consider, for example, the case of the filmic thrill. As Tom Gunning has pointed out, the thrill promises "an excitation of the body without the accompanying threat of breaching its integrity."[17] Rapid alternation between anxiety and reassurance produces the phenomenon we experience as a "thrill."

Fascination with the moment and circumstances of death is perhaps the most dramatic instance of the spectator's oscillation between engagement and disengagement. Fascination with death combines what is perhaps people's most primitive anxiety with the safety of a comfortable seat, fortified with popcorn, and the knowledge that the body dying on the screen is at the greatest possible distance from one's own.[18]

Sadism and masochism are both components of film audience's well-documented interest in death, especially in violent death.[19]

In one way, the thrill can be seen as a paradigm of cinema. If a spectator experiences no engagement, he gets neither entertainment nor the emotional experience the film seeks to evoke. Yet the spectator's identification with a character in peril is never so great that she believes her body to be endangered. She is engaged enough to identify and she is detached enough to maintain a comfortable distance.

Films purporting to retell the life of the founder of Christianity raise interesting and important considerations about spectatorship and identification. In the post-Christian West, the devotional practices I have described are still evoked when the life of Christ is depicted. The ancient devotional emphasis within Christianity on imitation of Jesus Christ and his immediate followers, raises the question of whether—and who—one might go about imitating in *The Last Temptation of Christ* or *Jesus of Montreal*. Can these films be understood ahistorically as "nothing but" entertainment?

The Last Temptation of Christ (1988)

In interviews, director Martin Scorsese, a Roman Catholic who once studied for the priesthood, spoke of his own faith and his struggle to make the film as a "personal religious testimony." He wanted, he said, to make a film about Jesus that represented "how it felt" to be simultaneously fully God and fully human.[20]

In spite of Scorsese's evident sincerity, the reception of the film was surprisingly varied. Some liberal clergy praised it, calling it a "pioneering attempt to portray . . . the full humanity of Christ." The Episcopal bishop of New York, the Right Reverend Paul Moore, said it was "artistically excellent and theologically sound."[21] Some film critics agreed: Peter Bein called *Last Temptation* "reverential."[22] Terrence Rafferty, film critic for *The New Yorker*, wrote: "It's speculative, but you'd have to be pretty touchy to call it blasphemous."[23] But Stanley Kauffmann, writing in the *New Republic*, called the film "an overheated rendering of a sophomorically daring idea. . . . The idea of Jesus agonizing about whether he would rather be human or divine is interesting enough, but its relevance to our own lives is pretty limited."[24] The Italian director Franco Zeffirelli said it was "truly horrible and totally deranged"; he withdrew one of his films from a festival in which *Last Temptation* was to be shown.[25]

In contrast to the praise from liberal clergy and the mixed reactions of critics, *Last Temptation* caused international outrage among more conservative Christian groups. The United States Catholic Conference of Bishops said it was "morally offensive." Both the Roman Catholic and the Mormon churches condemned the film and urged their members not to see it. In France a theater in which *Last Temptation* was showing was firebombed, and the film was banned in Ireland.[26] The primate of the Greek Orthodox Church, Archbishop Iakovos, called for a boycott of the film.

In addition to questions about blasphemy, *Last Temptation* stirred another controversy. Charges and countercharges of anti-Semitism were exchanged. In spite of the fact that only one Jew, the producer Lew Wasserman, was associated with the film,[27] Christian protesters claimed that it was Jewish anti-Christian propaganda. Some Christian groups demonstrated outside Wasserman's home; another protest featured a man representing Jesus being whipped in the streets of Beverly Hills by another man representing a Jewish producer. And demonstrators outside Universal Studios acted out a tableau in which Lew Wasserman was depicted nailing Jesus to the cross.

Harper's Magazine printed an exchange of correspondence between Abraham H. Foxman, national director of the antidefamation league of B'nai B'rith, and Pat Robertson, chair of the Christian Broadcasting Network.[28] Foxman called on Robertson to speak out against the allegation that *Last Temptation* was a Jewish affront to Christianity. Robertson politely refused, calling on the antidefamation league to condemn the film and in doing so to demonstrate that "*The Last Temptation of Christ* does not have the endorsement of the Jewish leadership in America." Foxman replied, "The 'Jewish leadership' is not the film industry. . . . Why should Jews be put on the defensive because age-old stereotypes unfortunately still exist? We will not be blamed for the crucifixion a second time."[29] The stereotype to which Foxman referred was the Christian accusation that "the Jews" killed Christ, a racial caricature that has incited Christian hatred of Jews and has led to violent recriminations and immense suffering through the centuries of the common era.

But the major protest came from Christian fundamentalists like Pat Robertson. A crowd of 7,500 picketed the studio (ironically, they parked in the studio parking lot, netting the studio $4,500 in parking fees). Pat Robertson called the movie "an offense to a hundred million Christians. It ridicules and blasphemes the faith that we have all committed our lives to." Bill Bright of the Campus Crusade for Christ offered Universal Studios $10 million to allow him to destroy the film.

Clearly, many Christians felt that *Last Temptation* was a direct attack on their faith.[30] They found that Jesus was portrayed in the film as an "anxious neurotic," who could not make up his mind about his mission. Protesters also objected to the film's rewording of gospel accounts of Jesus' statements, so that, for example, the message of the Sermon on the Mount (Matthew 5) is altered. But the most offensive aspect of the film for many fundamentalist Christians was the scene in which Jesus engages in sexual intercourse with his wife, Mary Magdalen. One Protestant minister said of *Last Temptation*, "[It] casts as mentally unbalanced the man who established the teachings that became the guideposts for an entire civilization. It's an outright distortion of history and a devastating assault on the personal values of hosts of people."[31]

Distribution of the film was carefully planned to begin in the cities considered the least likely to protest: New York, Los Angeles, San Francisco, Chicago, Minneapolis, Toronto, Montreal, and Washington, D.C. At least partly because of the enormous publicity produced by protesters, the weekend of its release the film made $400,000, an unusually high amount for such a short period. But the film's expansion into other areas was more problematic as demonstrations in less liberal cities apparently made people reluctant to see it. The studio tried to counter the protests by placing large ads in leading newspapers emphasizing First Amendment rights.

Last Temptation tells—and significantly revises—gospel accounts of the life of Jesus of Nazareth (played by Willem Dafoe). Period dress and Middle Eastern music contribute to the realism of the film. As the film begins, Jesus is building crosses for the use of Roman soldiers. Tortured and conflicted about his identity and vocation, Jesus looks on as a series of men make love with his childhood companion, Mary Magdalen

(Barbara Hershey). He declines when she offers him her body. Instead he goes off and engages in a series of confrontations: with Judas Iscariot; with members of a community of desert ascetics who will become his disciples; and with John the Baptizer. As viewers are informed in the opening credits, the narrative is structured around the struggle of spirit against flesh. All the female characters represent the flesh side of the struggle. In one of the dramatic temptations in the wilderness, the serpent speaks to Jesus with the voice of Mary Magdalen.[32]

The film dramatically departs from the gospels at the point of Jesus' death on the cross. A sweet-faced adolescent girl/angel takes his hand and leads him away from the crucifixion scene and to a waiting Mary Magdalen, who cleans his wounds and makes love with him. When she dies in childbirth nine months later, the angel leads him to Mary and Martha of Bethany, saying, "All women are one, the same woman with a different face." Jesus then lives as an "ordinary" man; married to "Woman" (meaning several women), he fathers children. A model of domesticity, he carries a basket to market and plays with his children, ignoring the religious and political issues and customs of his day. Always counseled by his angel-savior, Jesus grows old. As he lies dying, his disciples gather around him. They express their disdain for the life he has led and the disappointment of their youthful hopes and expectations. The angel vanishes, and, shamed by their rebukes, Jesus returns to the cross and finishes—by dying—the salvific work he undertook so long ago.

Throughout, Jesus is represented as unsure of himself and his message. Is he a romantic hero ("the law is against my heart"), or a political revolutionary? Should he endeavor to heal this world, or is the next world all that matters? Should he save the world or should he make love? *Last Temptation*'s fundamental conservatism becomes evident primarily in the binaries by which it is structured, binaries that reiterate and reinforce popular caricatures of Christianity: spirit/flesh; suffering/pleasure; spirituality/sexuality; man/woman. These traditional dualisms are reiterated rather than revised in *Last Temptation*. Scorsese's Jesus cannot, finally, figure out what he wants, sex and home, or, as he says in one of the last scenes, "I want to be the Messiah." He is a Jesus who "wants it all."

What was the last temptation of Christ? In Kazantzakis's novel, the primary conflict is between the cross and simple domestic contentment, but this conflict is neither dramatic enough for film, nor in accordance with film conventions, in which daily life usually lacks specific focus and value. In the film, the last temptation is sex, reflecting a modernist reduction of all sin to sins of the flesh. Film audiences have no difficulty recognizing sex as a powerful motivation—powerful enough, *Last Temptation* implies—to make even Christ forget and forsake his salvific mission.

Is the Jesus of *Last Temptation* a figure who invites identification? Is Scorsese attempting to give contemporary Christians a "hero" who is accessible, imitatable precisely because of his weaknesses and confusions? In this matter, the director's intentions can only be surmised, but if this is the plan, it does not work. Scorsese's Jesus gives few and ambiguous clues as to how he might be imitated. In addition to his confusion, he has a repertoire of miracles to which no ordinary human can aspire; he also hears voices and bounces self-destructively between extremes of asceticism and hedonism.

Medieval devotional manuals often advised imitating Jesus' nearest followers rather than Jesus himself; perhaps the film proposes that viewers' secondary identification be made with a disciple. Although no historical devotional manual advocated identifying with Judas, I suggest that Judas is the figure in *Last Temptation* with whom a spectator can most readily identify.[33] He is portrayed as an emotional, volatile, and loving character who finally betrays Jesus only at Jesus' insistence. Judas is convinced that nothing but betrayal will initiate the series of events that must lead to Jesus' crucifixion and, thus, to the salvation of the world. Judas is depicted as a "normal" human being. His character steadily develops from a flamboyant revolutionary—a "hothead"— who wants to overthrow the Roman occupation of Jerusalem to one who understands that Jesus must die, that his kingdom is "not of this world."[34]

The character of Judas also seems to be used to comment on the influence being felt at the time the film was produced of the liberation theology movement. I will say more in chapter 3 about the conflict between Latin American liberation theology and the Vatican, a theological and political clash that was prominently reported in the news media, but it is interesting to observe that *Last Temptation* puts liberation theology into the mouth of the young Judas. Judas argues that "pity for men" and the overturning of oppressive government should be central to the mission of Jesus. At the end of the film, however, an older and wiser Judas has realized that Jesus' kingdom is a spiritual kingdom for which Jesus and the disciples must choose persecution and suffering rather than either ordinary family life or political activism for justice.

Finally, possibly to increase the viewer's identification with Judas, *Last Temptation* omits the scriptural scene in which Judas, full of remorse, hangs himself. Although faithfulness to the original script—whether novel or scripture—is not a factor in analyzing a film (since film is not a window or mirror), departures from the original "script" do signal decisions the director and/or scriptwriter have made to accomplish the aims of the film.

The radical iconoclasm many Christians protested in *Last Temptation* can be seen only on the basis of its representation of a Jesus who is "human, all too human" in his sexuality. Theologically, through Judas's rejection of liberation theology, the film represents the self-serving judgment of a wealthy and powerful church: namely, that Jesus' message was spiritual rather than political. Socially, the film is equally conservative. Men and women are stereotypically portrayed: men act and think, while the women lack both subjectivity and intelligence. Instead, they are there to seduce (Mary Magdalen) or to weep (Virgin Mary).[35] The brief moment in which the angel advises Jesus that "all women are one" is not redeemed by the sudden revelation, close to the end of the film, that the angel is, in fact, a devil who has deceived and misled Jesus.

Last Temptation does raise one religious issue, the conflict between sexuality and spirituality; is the issue a lively one for contemporary Christians? It certainly is for many Roman Catholic priests, sworn to celibacy and tortured by sexual cravings and guilt.[36] But they are likely to be a small proportion of the film's audience. Of the other likely audience members, secular people are largely bored with the issue, although many have abandoned religious belief and practice because of childhood experiences of inadequate religious instruction on sexuality. Liberal theologians have recognized the unacceptability of posing sexuality and spirituality as contradictory attractions, so many or most liberal Christians are no longer gripped by guilt over sex because of their religion.

But the issue of sex versus spirituality may still be important for a large number of Americans, specifically the millions of "born again" Christians for whom sex outside of marriage is forbidden. A new emphasis has been placed on sexual chastity recently in reaction to the sexual misbehavior of several televangelists. Christian rock music, "the fastest growing form of popular music" and a billion-dollar-a-year business, repeatedly extolls sexual "purity" until marriage.[37] Some Christian recording companies require musicians and singers to sign "morality clauses" in their contracts. "One Christian record company even produces album covers that include a message from the president of the label: 'You have a right to expect that the singers and songwriters live real Christian lives.'"[38] "Real Christian lives" is a circumlocution for sexless lives—except in marriage. In short, there are many people for whom *Last Temptation*'s primary issue is a pressing concern. But, ironically, these were also the people who boycotted and picketed the film. Apparently the image of a sexual Jesus, even though the image was overturned by the film's conclusion, was intolerable for conservative Christians. The Jesus with whom most evangelical Christians cultivate a "personal relationship" is the divine miracle-worker of gospel accounts.

Reviewers commented most frequently on the film's preoccupation with the related issues of sexuality versus spirituality and spirit versus matter. But a somewhat more subtle dualism also permeated *Last Temptation*: a life of simple pleasures versus a life of suffering and sacrifice. Jesus realizes, at the very end of the film, that without sacrifice and suffering there is no salvation.[39] Is this, perhaps, a contemporary issue?

Clearly, one of the first duties of any religion—and Christianity is no exception—is to make sense of human suffering. The idea that suffering can be productive, rather than that it causes nothing but waste and loss, is one of the most central insights of Christianity. It was also, no doubt, an invaluable idea during long centuries in which there was little or no alleviation for involuntary human suffering.

Yet several twentieth-century theologians, among them Dorothee Soelle, have strongly questioned what they see as the glorification of suffering in Christianity. The high value accorded suffering, they argue, has obscured more productive values. These criticisms, however, come at a historical moment in which, although there is still massive involuntary suffering, there is also more ability to control or contain physical suffering than has ever existed. Antibiotics and anesthetics have changed the way most Americans think about suffering. Few choose to suffer when relief is available.[40] If one consistently volunteers to sacrifice or to suffer with no reward or benefit—spiritual or physical—in mind, it is interpreted as a psychological problem rather than a religious discipline. Neither *Last Temptation*'s exploration of a tension between spirituality and sexuality, nor the suffering versus comfort issue seem to have attracted large audiences.

The fundamentalist Christians who protested the release of the film may have recognized something that liberal and religiously indifferent reviewers failed to notice. Clearly, Christians who protested screenings of *Last Temptation* felt that the film undermined Christianity by slandering its founder's image. For another American population, however, this may have made the film attractive. I suspect that the audiences that made *Last Temptation* a modest box office success were composed at least partly of secular people who were drawn to the film because they expected—from advertising and from news reports of the controversy—to see a caricature of Jesus' life and death, a caricature that would reassure them that Christianity is indeed a dead force. They expected, in other words, to have their belief in unbelief reinforced. Ironically, fundamentalist protests intended to discourage attendance actually boosted ticket sales by alerting people that the film was some kind of a "sendup" or "put-down" of Christianity. Scorsese's repeated insistence that the film represented his respectful interest in Christianity was dramatically at odds with the film's effects. I will return at the end of this chapter to the question of whether *Last Temptation* can be considered, in any sense, a religious film.

Jesus of Montreal (1989)

Jesus of Montreal presents a story about the compromises and struggles of a group of actors in a large city who reenact the story of Christ. One critic called the film "an entertaining satire about show business," saying that it is "as much about actors and media as it is about Christianity."[41] Other reviewers found it to be an attack on the hypocrisy of modern life. In interviews, however, director Denys Arcand emphasized the religious content of the film. Arcand, who was raised a Roman Catholic in the years before Vatican II, said:

> There will always be a yearning for that time in my life when religion provided soothing answers to problems to which there were no answers. To this day I cannot help but be moved when I hear: "Where your treasure is, there your heart is also," or "If you love those who love you, what merit is there in that?" Through the thick haze of the past comes the echo of a deeply disturbing voice.

"Of all the wise men in history," Arcand said, "Jesus is the one talking to me in the most urgent manner, and his voice is irreplaceable."[42]

In *Jesus*, religion provides a critique of contemporary urban values; it is, in a sense, a liberal answer to the question so frequently posed in Sunday School classes: "What would Jesus do?" But the film does not claim to retell the life of Jesus. Rather, it reconstructs the story in modern dress and setting as a conflict of values. The Jesus character, Daniel Coloumbe (Lothaire Bluteau), a not-very-successful actor, accepts a priest's suggestion that he revise and strengthen the Passion play which is given each year on the church's grounds. Becoming engrossed in the project, he gathers a few friends, unsuccessful actors like himself, to act in the play, which is a great success. The play within the film, however, is iconoclastic in its departure from traditional beliefs; the Virgin birth is explained away, and a "social gospel" is given prominence. Outraged by this message, church authorities cancel the Passion play. Daniel is struck on the head by the cross as he is arrested for wrecking a commercial photographer's equipment, and a long denouement follows in which Daniel fanatically proclaims the gospel of his play in a subway just before his death.

In the United States, reviewers were mostly positive: Tom O'Brien, critic for *Commonweal*, commented that *Jesus* succeeds exactly where *Last Temptation* failed—in its treatment of sex.[43] In *Jesus*, sex is not absent, but it is absent from the screen. Intimacy between Daniel and Mereille (the Mary Magdalen character, Catherine Wilkening) is alluded to, not shown. The temptation Jesus faces is deceit and power, greed and celebrity, not sex. Arcand's interpretation also represents Matthew 4 better than does *Last Temptation*. *Jesus* avoids clichés of belief and of disbelief; instead, it represents "a search for something to believe in." But Suzanne Moore in *New Statesman and Society* was more critical. "Saying that capitalism is nasty and that Christ was a closet Marxist seems a little obvious," she wrote.[44]

In *Jesus*, Daniel encounters two characters who challenge his interpretation of God's will. The priest who commissioned the play is having an affair with the actress who plays Mary, the mother of Jesus; despite his own transgressions, however, the priest represents and defends a conservative, institutional, traditional religion against Daniel's revisionist theological agenda. (This depiction of a priest has become fairly typical: in popular films of the last fifteen years priests and religious institutions usually come off badly.[45]) The narrative also includes a devil, a slick lawyer who tempts Daniel to capitalize on his successful Passion play. These two foils for Daniel, different as they may seem, are not unrelated: like the devil, the priest just wants a gripping show, and the devil's name is Richard Cardinal.

The conflicts of the 1980s between traditional religion and the social gospel of liberation theology are as evident in *Jesus* as they are in *Last Temptation*. The commercialism of consumer culture, at its height during the conservative Reagan and Bush administrations, is the film's other primary foil. Although *Jesus* is a Canadian film, commercialism, as many Canadians see it, is a value imported from the United States. In a decade when the largest moneymakers among Hollywood films valorized fame and money rather than work, generosity, or other values, Arcand, in *Jesus*, warned Canadians against a similar addiction to money and success.[46]

The heroes of *Jesus* are the actors who want to minimize, if not eliminate, Christian doctrines in order to highlight Christianity's ethical teachings. The priest's idea of a Christianity that comforts and sustains, that helps people to "just live happily," is in conflict with the ethical imperatives of Christianity as understood by Daniel and his actors.

Curiously, however, there is little conflict in Daniel. There is no wilderness experience, no Garden of Gethsemane, and wealth and fame seem not to genuinely tempt him for a moment. Yet, after he is injured by the cross, he slides from the ultra-"normality" attested to by a psychologist who examines him (declaring that Daniel is "more normal than most of the judges") to the craziness of the penultimate scenes in which he harangues people in the subway. By what inner process did he change so dramatically? Daniel actually becomes the character he plays in the Passion play, but viewers do not know why. One reviewer commented: "Even a Christ-figure needs more of an interior life than Arcand gives Jesus."[47]

The depiction of interior religious life is an interesting cinematic problem, a problem encountered by many films in which protagonists act out of religious commitment (*The Mission, Thérèse, Agnes of God, Black Robe*). In fact, contemporary Hollywood films have not developed conventions to signal religious motivation and commitment. Something as interior and invisible as religious commitment is difficult to communicate, but in a medium in which things must be visible to be real, is it impossible, lacking such conventions, to show religious commitment?

There are film conventions for revealing what is considered centrally important. Perhaps voice-over is the primary convention for representing subjectivity; it could be used to reveal and articulate religious commitment. And there are many conventions for signalling another invisible state—love—in Hollywood films: camera angles and soft focus, as well as acting strategies. It does not, then, seem impossible that conventions might be developed to show religious commitment, if it were an interest and priority of filmmakers.

Issues of race and gender also arise in *Jesus*. The only black woman in the film intervenes in the Passion play (just as the naive spectator did in the early days of film) and must be restrained. She is depicted stereotypically as defined by her emotions, unable to understand the difference between the drama and reality. The treatment of gender is more complex. On the one hand, sexism is presented explicitly as a deplorable feature of consumer culture. Mereille's producer boyfriend tells her, "Your talent is all in your ass"; a woman auditioning for a beer commercial is told, "Bank on your bikini, not your voice"; and the devil has a voluptuous seventeen-year-old on his arm. Yet these explicit messages are undermined by other filmic moments, for example a gratuitous shot of Mereille's breasts in a scene in which she auditions for a beer commercial. An irate Daniel overturns cameras and equipment and leads Mereille away. He rescues her from the beer commercial, but the director does not rescue her from the film's peep-show display. By contrast, a moment in which male nakedness might have been expected—Daniel/Jesus on the cross—is deftly elided. This is not, of course, surprising to any spectator accustomed to a media convention that displays women's bodies and conceals men's, but it does demonstrate the film's adherence to this convention.

Although women are portrayed as adjuncts of Daniel's life and death, considerably more subjectivity is granted to women in *Jesus* than in *Last Temptation.* Mereille's description of how her life had been altered by acting in Daniel's Passion play is a rare filmic moment given to a woman's subjectivity.[48] However, even this moment is ambiguous, subverted—almost annulled—by the guffaws of other characters (and the audience) at the brief suggestive comment by one of the actor/disciples that follows. In another scene, Mary's (Constance Lazure) explanation of why she sleeps with the priest: "It gives him so much pleasure, and me so little pain"—is a classic statement of the sexually passive, eager-to-please woman, not acting on any desires of her own. In short, in *Jesus of Montreal*, the treatment of gender is muddled, muddied, and ambiguous. Text and subtext conflict—reflecting a historical moment in which gender roles have been called into question and are heavily contested, creating social anxiety, but without resolution.

Traditionally, the central moment in Jesus' life was his redemption of the world through death on the cross. *Jesus* subtly redefines the salvific in contemporary terms. In the last scenes of the film, Daniel's body becomes the "source of life" (heart) and vision/sight (eyes) to others through organ transplants. His spirit, however, is not salvific in anything but brief moments, quickly effaced by "reality." Several reviewers saw the conclusion of the film, in which Jesus posthumously "saves" several people through his organs, as a cheap shot: "many a cheap horror film has explored the idea of eternal life or possession through donor transplant with considerably more verve than we get here."[49]

Daniel's last words are an apocalyptic scriptural harangue in the subway addressed to amazingly tolerant bystanders. But are these rantings anything but craziness in relation to the human needs to which the priest is so sensitive, or to Daniel's previously articulated message of social justice? Do they provide an alternative to the preoccupations of the corporate world? Do they suggest possible resolutions for the myriad social and personal exploitations of contemporary urban life? Finally, must religious passion be pictured as craziness in the movies in order to be credible? These questions raise the related question of whether or not *Jesus* and *Last Temptation* can be considered religious films, films that *act* religiously, rather than simply films about religion, an issue to which I now turn.

Were *Last Temptation* and *Jesus* religious films? If we find that neither film effectively supports or augments Christian devotion, is there a sense, nevertheless, in which they are religious? I decided in chapter 1 that the question raised in Greek tragedy, "How should we live?" is essentially a religious one.[50] Although we have seen that movie theaters are not conducive to such a question, the question is not decisively excluded. The viewer who comes prepared to ask the question, and who leaves eager to discuss it with others, can consider these films as proposed answers. And just as the setting does not prohibit engagement with our question, neither do the films themselves, for if they were screened in a church, it would be assumed by all who attended that the point of showing them was to discuss the religious images and values in them. The question would be not only likely, but nearly inevitable. If by "religious" we mean that the films seriously examine the values they propose and the relationships they depict, then both films can be seen as religious.

But consider another perspective. Both Scorsese and Arcand insisted in interviews that they wanted to make a religious film, a film that exposed and examined religious questions. But did they? Is it even possible to make a religious film using Hollywood conventions? Although it is impossible to make a narrative film without engaging film conventions of many different kinds, the more loaded with such conventions a film is, the more difficult it is to see it as anything but "entertainment." Thus, *Last Temptation* presents itself as entertainment more than *Jesus* does. Its historical setting, costuming, and music signals the spectacle, the extravaganza. Moreover, the inevitable association of special effects with entertainment further contributes to *Last Temptation*'s categorization as entertainment. Its conventional treatment of gender and its foregrounding of sex puts it squarely in the realm of entertainment film. *Jesus* is not innocent of Hollywood conventions. It does, however, apparently seek to minimize these elements, although it fails utterly, as I have suggested, at several crucial moments.

But if we mean by "religious" that the films would act to intensify one's devotion, as medieval viewers expected their religious images to do, neither film meets that criterion. Of the two, however, *Jesus* comes closer to posing, in character and event, the religious question of how we should live. It stimulates thought and discussion of the pressing ethical issues of capitalistic urban society, and it is valuable in doing so. It is not, however, a religious film in the same sense that a crucifix or a Madonna and Child is a religious image. It is a secular film that raises religious issues. Neither our imaginary medieval image-user, nor a contemporary pilgrim to St. Anne de Beaupré would find it religiously helpful, primarily because it does not attempt to reveal the invisible world of spiritual reality, evoked for the devout by religious images.

But perhaps we need a more inclusive definition of "religious," a definition that includes the posing of issues that require secular ethical decisions. In chapter 1, I argued that a quality of relationships rather than particular beliefs are constitutive of, and central to, religion. The advantage of this expansive definition of religion is its cross-cultural applicability; all religions seek to inform their members' lives and to order their relationships. This definition also places attention on a feature of religion that is obscured when it is defined strictly in terms of beliefs and institutions. Finally, however, "religion" and "the religious" cannot be spoken of in the abstract. To speak concretely about religion, one must locate the phenomenon one seeks to explain within a complex historical tradition.

To say that a film "raises religious issues," as I have said of *Jesus*, is somewhat different than saying that a film acts religiously. Films that represent the life of Jesus invoke a specific cultural artifact. Christianity itself is a cultural entity in which painted representations of Jesus have a very long and explicit history. To use the word "religious" with substantive content in the context of representations of Jesus' life and death, then, demands that we acknowledge the history of the devotional use of religious images. On these grounds, both films fail to inspire imitation of their protagonist, or even to communicate clearly what such imitation might look like or feel like. In spite of the intentions of both directors to present spectators with important religious dilemmas, the films' effects are likely to be governed more by the theater setting in which the films are shown, by each viewer's training in detachment, and by our expectation of entertainment than by the directors' intentions. This does not, of course, mean that the films could not be read "against the grain" of film conventions in order to allow them to act religiously; it does mean that their ability to do so would have more to do with the spectator than the films.

3

Seeing (as if)
With Our Own Eyes

The Mission
Romero

Popular films have not always lacked conventions for communicating religious commitment. Contemporary films are reacting against the earlier use of some exceedingly obvious and banal conventions for indicating religious feeling and motivation. One need only recall the echo-chamber voice with which Jesus spoke in *The Greatest Story Ever Told* (1965), the heavily vibrating violins in the background, the soft lighting and/or photographing through gauze, and the camera's "eye" looking up at Jesus from below. *The Ten Commandments* (1956), *The Robe* (1953), and *Ben-Hur* (1959) used similar conventions. In films since the 1960s these conventions have been mercifully avoided, but not replaced.

Films of the 1980s found it difficult to picture, or even to acknowledge, religious conviction or commitment. Even the most obvious instances of religious motivation tended to be shrouded in other motivations. And it was not only flamboyant religiosity, such as that depicted in *Black Robe*, that was discounted as motivation for behavior. *Shadowlands* treated the quietly committed life of C. S. Lewis, the author of many popular books on Christianity, as thoroughly secular.

But lack of attention to religious motivation was not the only filmic strategy by which religious commitment was marginalized. In films of the last decade, religious characters were often represented as sinister, devious, or crazy. A priest's collar came to signal questionable morality; a nun's habit was the first visual clue of hypocritical innocence (*Agnes of God*), or of masochistic craziness (*Thérèse*). Protestant ministers fared little better; pastors and evangelists were represented as ineffectual at best (*Testament, The Day After*), and, at worst, as greedy frauds (*Leap of Faith, Poltergeist II*). Or religious commitment is caricatured, as in *Alien 3*, in which a group of incorrigible violent criminals is represented as a monastic community.

The films I consider in this chapter treat religious motivation somewhat differently than the films mentioned above. Both *The Mission* and *Romero* present characters who act as they do explicitly because of their Christian faith. Both films claim, in addition, to present accurate accounts of historical events. Before considering each film, however, I will sketch some features of their social context.

In 1986 four films about religion achieved both box office success and critical attention in the United States, an unprecedented number since the early 1960s: *Thérèse*, the story of a Carmelite nun; *The Name of the Rose*, in which a fourteenth-century Italian monastery is the setting for a murder mystery; *The Sacrifice*, made by a Russian director, Andres Tarkovsky; and *The Mission*. There are some general reasons, I think—and at least one specific reason—why films with religious themes interested popular audiences in the mid-1980s.[1]

Nineteen-eighty-six was a year fraught with political and social upheavals, such as the Iran-Contra scandal. Horrifying accidents occurred: the explosion of the space shuttle Challenger and the Chernobyl reactor fire in the Soviet Union. Over twelve thousand new AIDS cases were diagnosed in the United States. None of these events or conditions would necessarily prompt Americans to suddenly take an interest in religion, of course, but 1986 was nevertheless the high point of a resurgence of religious interest that was documented by a study done by Hartford Seminary. Analysts believed that religious interest was the "result of the baby-boomer generation returning to churches and synagogues as they entered middle age, raised families, and confronted questions about life, death, and meaning that have confronted every generation."[2] These perennial questions would probably, however, not have been sufficient to revitalize interest in religion if a more specific public interest in religion had not also existed.

For when we ask, What makes religion successful at the box office?, we learn that when religion makes newspaper headlines, the cover of *Time*, and the talk shows, it also makes money at the box office. In the second half of the 1980s, the movement within the Roman Catholic Church called "liberation theology" was in the news, at least partly because of its conflict with the world leadership of the Roman Catholic Church. The Roman Vatican was wary of liberation theology's attention to the political situation and material realities of poor people's lives and incensed by the refusal of many liberation theologians to be subject either to "hierarchical control or academic assessment."[3]

The term "liberation theology" originated in Latin America. It was coined by Gustavo Gutiérrez, its father and mentor, who was born in Peru. In Latin America, the struggle for liberation primarily resisted two perceived evils: first, poverty caused by economies based on supplying commodities at low cost to the "developed" nations; and second, political repression generated and supported by dramatic differences in the standards of living of the rich and the poor. Meeting in 1968 at Medellín, Colombia, a group of Latin American bishops proclaimed that the Church should exercise what they called a preferential option for the poor. But liberation theology claims not to be a new theology; it is rather an "attempt to interpret the Bible and Christianity from the perspective of the poor," and "an effort to look at the life and message of Jesus through the eyes of those who have been excluded or ignored."[4]

Reading the gospel from the perspective of the poor brings the realization that even the poor and oppressed can initiate social change. Although no individual can singlehandedly create change, it is possible for a community to confront repressive regimes and to improve the material condition of the poor. Liberation theologians criticize mainstream Christianity's spiritualization of the Christian message of hope. The promise of pie in the sky has been invoked all too often to urge oppressed people to acquiesce to their own oppression. Liberation theology has called attention to Christianity's shameful past in legitimizing structures of injustice.

Liberation theologians also protest the spiritualization of the gospel.

Liberation theology is not focused on an internal spiritual life; it is similarly critical of the idea of the individual as the subject of religious commitment. Instead, the primary organizational tool of liberation theology in South and Central America is the base Christian community, a relatively small group of people who meet to study the Bible together, to worship together, and to participate in social action together with other base communities. It has been estimated that, by the end of the 1980s, there were close to one hundred thousand base communities in Brazil alone.[5] Most of their members live in farming villages or urban slums, and they are crushingly poor. They are led by laypersons and priests who emerge as leaders from within the group without elections or appointments.[6]

In *The Silencing of Leonardo Boff*, theologian Harvey Cox describes the Vatican's increasing criticism of Roman Catholic liberation theologians, beginning in the mid-eighties. Several prominent theologians and church leaders were disciplined for their doctrinal or moral teachings: Edward Schillebeeckx, Hans Kung, Gustavo Gutiérrez, Charles Curran, and the liberal Archbishop Hunthausen of Seattle. The incident that most drew media attention, however, was the silencing of liberation theologian Leonardo Boff in 1985. Cardinal Joseph Ratzinger, prefect of the Sacred Congregation for the Doctrine of the Faith (the Vatican office charged with protecting Roman Catholic doctrine from dissenting interpretations), ordered Boff to cease writing and teaching for a period of ten months.

Each of the films discussed in chapter 2 and in this chapter achieved its modest box office success at a time when the media was widely reporting on liberation theology's growing momentum. Each portrays a powerful institution in conflict with a local and nonconforming interpretation of the central message of Christianity. As I pointed out in chapter 2, *The Last Temptation of Christ* puts liberation theology into the mouth of the young Judas, but by the end of the film, an older and wiser Judas has repudiated it. *Jesus of Montreal* criticizes both a conservative institutional church and a consumer culture, but offers only individual resistance and personal integrity as the alternatives to a cowardly church and a corrupt society. *The Mission* explores divisions within a powerful and worldly institution and depicts the missionary zeal of a small group of committed Jesuits. *Romero* takes liberation theology in El Salvador as its central topic. The specific drama that caught the media's attention and was at the heart of each film is the resistance of an individual or small group of people to an authoritarian institution, an institution accustomed to being obeyed.[7]

The confrontation between individuals and powerful institutions occurred so frequently in films of the 1980s that it became a convention. Sympathy for the individual over an institution or group was, and is, to be taken for granted in media culture. Yet identification with heroic individuals is oddly out of tune with liberation theology's insistence on the primacy of communities. Ironically, in framing the issue as one of individuals against an institution, each film simultaneously capitalized on the public's interest in liberation theology and disregarded one of liberation theology's central tenets, that the community is the basic unit of decision and action. For liberation theology, the conflict is not between an individual's private conviction and an institution's authority, but between different "communities of resistance and solidarity."[8] The difference between heroic leadership and communal solidarity is evident in sociologist Mary Douglas's description of communal solidarity:

> Solidarity involves individuals being ready to suffer on behalf of the larger group and their expecting other individuals to do as much for them. . . . Anyone who has accepted trust and demanded sacrifice or willingly given either knows the power of the social bond. Whether there is commitment to authority or a hatred of tyranny or something between the extremes, the social bond itself is taken to be something above question.[9]

Although heroes may sacrifice themselves for others, they also typically speak and act for others. Given a long Hollywood tradition of attention to individual rather than ensemble performances, it is perhaps impossible to produce a film about a community that would succeed at the box office. The decision-making and activities of a base community, for example, are too complex and dispersed to permit strong secondary identifications without the focusing device of a hero.[10] Nevertheless, liberation theology's central principle is distorted when its protagonists are pictured as individual leaders and heroes.

The Mission (1986)

The Mission announces its intention immediately after the opening credits: to tell the "true events" of the Jesuits' settlements, or "Reductions," in Paraguay and their Christianizing of the Guarani tribes. The film depicts the Jesuit mission of San Carlos, above the Iguazu Falls; the story takes place in the mid-eighteenth century, when Jesuit missionaries had been in South America for one hundred fifty years.[11] The powerful image of a crucified Jesuit falling headfirst into the Iguazu Falls in Paraguay opens the film. There is no historical record of such a martyrdom, "though many Jesuits died violently in the establishment of the missions."[12]

The Mission depicts a conflict over Jesuit power in political states in Europe and in their many and far-flung missions. Historically, Clause 18 of the 1750 Treaty of Rome prohibited Jesuit missionaries from protecting the native population from legalized Portuguese slave traders and from illegal Spanish slave traders. As papal legate Altamirano put it in the film, this rendered the indigenous people "free to be enslaved by the Spanish and the Portuguese," to become the so-called "red gold" of slave commerce.[13]

Because the powerful Jesuit Order had come under suspicion in several European states, Cardinal Altamirano has been dispatched by the Vatican to investigate and determine whether the Jesuit settlements should be maintained or disbanded. The film's action centers on his decision and its disastrous effects. When Cardinal Altamirano decides against maintaining the settlements, an army of mercenaries moves against the Jesuit mission. The mission's leader, Father Gabriel (played by Jeremy Irons), dies celebrating mass with the Guarani people among whom he has worked. Mendoza (Robert DeNiro), a former slave trader who has killed his brother in a quarrel over a woman, is converted and joins the Jesuits, then reverts to violent action in a vain attempt to save the settlement. In the end, as Daniel Berrigan, a radical Jesuit priest who advised and acted in the film put it, *The Mission*'s intended message is quite simple: "How is [a religious person] to die? Either with gun in hand or with sacrament in hand. Both die with the people."[14]

The dilemma may be simple—fight or continue to function until death—but the message of the film is not. As armed mercenaries approach the San Carlos mission, Mendoza straps on his sword and goes to ask for Father Gabriel's blessing. Gabriel refuses, but the two embrace, both profoundly moved. Then Gabriel takes from his own neck the simple cross and gives it to Mendoza. It is the wooden cross he had found in one of the earliest scenes of the film, the cross worn by the original Jesuit missioner when he met his death strapped to a cross and tossed over the falls. A strong gesture, but what does it mean? Does it imply that Mendoza and his sword can represent the spirit of missionizing more adequately than Father Gabriel's passive resistance? The film does not decide. Mendoza, fatally wounded, watches as Gabriel is struck; they die together. One reviewer remarked, "If this is moral history, it's hard to see what the subject is."[15]

It was impossible, in the paragraphs above, to describe the narrative of *The Mission* without mixing fact and fiction. *The Mission*'s claim, in the opening credits, to depict true events is intriguing. On the one hand, it is impossible to know how closely the film adheres to historical events, since historical evidence is not available. Ultimately, however, as I described in chapter 2, accuracy to a text—whether historical event or scriptural or novelistic account—is irrelevant to an analysis of film as film. The filmmaker is not primarily a historian whose job it is to find out what happened—"the facts in the order they occurred."[16] Rather a director is responsible for the film's internal coherence and unity.

By definition, no film can accurately represent "true events." First, all histories, whether filmic or textual, are selections among what happened. This does not mean, however, that since the past is irretrievably lost, all histories, whether imaginatively reconstructed without evidence or competently researched, are nothing but best guesses at what really happened. A thoroughly researched and documented account of a historical event is, of course, better history than a historical novel. Nevertheless, all accounts must organize the extant evidence in order to present a coherent narrative.

Second, all historical accounts are *interpretations* of what happened. A history film must take even greater license than any historian would permit herself with "events as they occurred." For a Hollywood film must aspire to popularity, that is, to box office success. It must meet the audience's expectations for entertainment, and to do so it must employ film conventions. For example, the fact that Mendoza kills his brother over a woman, a crime that leads to Mendoza's conversion, owes more to a film convention than to historical record. The coherence of the film narrative required it. Mendoza's dramatic repentance, his sudden change from slave trader to Jesuit missionary, required an incident on the scale of fratricide to precipitate his change. And to provoke fratricide? What, but a woman, would do?[17] A believable narrative—that is, one that film audiences recognize as explanatory because they have seen it many times in other films—is more important to a film than historical accuracy.

Why, then, do spectators feel that a film has betrayed them if they discover that the director has imagined and interpreted historical events with a free hand? Consciously or unconsciously, a viewing public expects films to perform a public function in defining, or giving a plausible and intuitively accurate account, of the way things were. This expectation might be more-or-less vociferously denied by any individual, but *across* audiences of entertainment films, seeing is believing. The historical narratives we enjoy are those which fortify our present beliefs and attitudes; a film's claim to depict actual events, then, is part of its entertainment value.

The Mission's closing scenes, like the opening scene, are questionable as history. It is likely that the film has improvised at this point to provide a conventional narrative in which heroic individuals resist tyrannical authoritarianism. There is no reliable historical record that any Jesuits were killed when the missions were terminated. Daniel Berrigan writes about the original event as follows: "The armies move on the mission and destroy it; the Jesuits are seized, jailed, shipped back to Europe in chains. Many of them die in prison."[18] A few pages later, however, he writes about the order to dissolve the mission: "Some Jesuits obey, as do a number of the Guarani. Others . . . resist."[19] Again, intriguing as it is, the actual response of Jesuits is incidental to the film *as* film. If the film had been dedicated to representing a historical moment of great spiritual and physical anguish in Jesuit history rather than to box office success, it might not have ended in the mandatory carnage of an adventure film. As Keith Tribe put it, this history is "recognized as Truth by the viewer not by virtue of the 'facts' being correct, but because the image looks right."[20]

Is religious motivation depicted effectively in *The Mission*? Are viewers helped to understand the loyalties, beliefs, and practices that motivated Jesuit missioners? They are not, although the difficulty of conveying religious motivation, as we have already observed, is not unique to *The Mission*.[21] The only devotional practice depicted in the film is the Jesuit missioner Fielding (Liam Neeson) praying briefly during the opening credits. The director, Roland Joffé, himself acknowledged in an interview, "I found I couldn't create religious fervor. I'm rather an awed atheist myself."[22]

The Mission is full of religious symbolism, some of it more subtle than the crucified missionary with which the film begins. Critic Harlan Kennedy points out that the film's topography is itself a rather heavy-handed symbolism: "Most of the white men and the urbanized Indians live below the falls. The primitive Indians and the virtuous Christian whites live above them. It's a geographical Genesis in which 'above the falls' and 'below the falls' mean 'before the fall' and 'after the fall.'"[23] But religious symbolism is not enough to express religious commitment.

Roland Joffé expected viewers to connect the theme of the film, which he defined as individuals resisting institutional authority, with the contemporary religious struggle between the Vatican and South and Central American base communities. He stated in an interview that he intended *The Mission* to be "'modern and relevant' to struggles taking place within the Roman Catholic Church, and throughout the world today" and described the film as mirroring "the contemporary debate between Rome and its radical priests in Central and South America over 'liberation theology.'"[24]

Yet Joffé either misunderstood liberation theology, or he consciously capitulated to film conventions that overrode an accurate depiction of historical events. The film represented, as he put it, "a struggle between individual values and those of political or religious structures." But by assimilating liberation theology to an ideology in which individuals "question authority," *The Mission* conforms to a cultural commonplace that actually functions to absorb and neutralize social protest. David Tetzlaff wrote:

> Individualistic rebellion is constantly validated in our culture; it is an easy staple of popular music, films, and literature. Therefore it offers an easy model for so-

cial and political opposition. Active experience in collective struggle . . . teaches a different lesson: that some sort of unity is the only way to get things done.[25]

Ironically, films that may be intended as radical protest become conformist by representing collective action as individual rebellion. The distortion of presenting individual heroes as leaders of movements that in fact achieved their victories on the basis of group action also occurs in *Romero*, a film that represents liberation theology on location in El Salvador.

I do not wish to belabor an obvious point. *The Mission* was a Hollywood film informed, as every Hollywood film must be, by a profit motive.[26] It appropriates a roughly sketched historical event in order to present some moments of high drama. How might the film conclude if a more truthful presentation of a moment in Jesuit history were its goal? I will make one suggestion based, not on film convention, but on Jesuit training. To do so, I will need to suggest some salient motifs of Jesuit religious life.

Under the leadership of Ignatius Loyola, the Society of Jesus undertook, in 1542, to serve the Roman Catholic Church under the direct jurisdiction of the Pope. Its two primary tasks were to be educating and missionizing, both of which early Jesuits undertook with zeal and success. Jesuits became the schoolmasters of Europe, and their missionary activities covered five continents.[27]

Jesuit missionizing was distinctive among Catholic Orders in adapting to local customs and traditions, but it also often met with resistance and violence, resulting in martyrdom. Above the high altar of the mother church of the Jesuit order in Rome, the Gesú, hangs a painting of the circumcision of Christ, a unique subject for the place of honor in a church building. The circumcision was significant to Jesuits as the event that associated the shedding of Jesus' blood with his name. And, as one early source says, "We Jesuits must be prepared to shed our blood for His name." And they did, in missions all over the world.

Although literal martyrdom was the ultimate commitment of a Jesuit, the daily martyrdom of obedience to superiors was the mechanism by which the order of the Order was guaranteed. Ignatius himself had placed a high value on obedience. Although *The Mission* emphasized Jesuit collegiality, the discipline of obedience is depicted in the scene in which Father Gabriel orders Mendoza to retract the angry outburst in which he calls a nobleman a liar for saying that the Spanish do no slave trading. Despite the accuracy of Mendoza's allegation, he obeys and retracts his statements. This incident, however, only hints at the continual daily asceticism of obedience. Any description of the Jesuit Order must acknowledge its primacy.

As a discipline, obedience is neither easy nor passive. In late medieval Christianity from which the Society of Jesus emerged, authority was thought of as something with which one wrestled in order to shape a religious life. For not only is outward obedience required of Jesuits, but also the more difficult submission of the spirit. The individual will must gradually be ordered, internally rather than externally, to obedience so that when a demanding occasion occurs, obedience will be the Jesuit's natural response.

The Mission focused on one of the Jesuits' priorities, commitment to death, but in doing so it gave an implausible account of the demise of the mission of San Carlos. Mendoza was disobedient in rejecting nonviolence, but his defection is anticipated, even urged and applauded within the film. A Hollywood adventure film must have violence. Moreover, Mendoza's reversion to violence is credible; he was a convert, lacking the settled habit of obedience. But Father Gabriel is also disobedient. He was ordered to leave the Reduction and he refused. This defection is not plausible. It is unlikely that Father Gabriel's apparently deep and long-practiced commitment to Jesuit principles would be overturned without immense interior struggle. A different film, one interested in the intensity and complexity of religious life would, I think, have had the Jesuits leave the Mission San Carlos when they were ordered to do so. A less conventional film might have shown them wrestling with obedience and the unspeakable anguish of contemplating the undoing of their lifework and the inevitable enslavement of the Guarani.[28]

If insubordination were as frequently and easily practiced in the Jesuit Order as *The Mission* depicts, the Order would not have gained the immense power and privilege that made European sovereigns anxious and for which it was suppressed in Latin countries and their colonies between 1759 and 1768. Many Jesuits fled to Russia, where the order maintained itself until it was readmitted to Europe in the nineteenth century.[29] Clearly—and how should one expect otherwise?—*The Mission* is more about Hollywood conventions than it is about a historical moment in the life of a religious order.[30]

Another aspect of *The Mission* illustrates the primacy of film conventions over other considerations. There is a curious contradiction between the film's use of Wanana Indian actors to represent their forebears and its glorification of European civilization at the natives' expense.[31] From the perspective of the Jesuit missioners, the protection and Europeanization of the native population was the point of their labors. Their attitudes may have been chauvinistic and paternalistic, but they understood themselves to be in Latin America for the purpose of benefitting the Indians—as the missioners understood benefit. If the film were about Jesuit history, it would have shown what the Jesuits valued in the Indians that would make them sacrifice lives of ease and comfort in Europe for a daily martyrdom among them.

But the film is unconcerned with examining the Indians' thoughts, their motivations, even their lives, except as they bear on the lives of the white Europeans.[32] The Indians, once threatening and dangerous, become picturesque and lovable when they become like Europeans.[33] At first they crucify a representative of Christianity and civilization; later, under Father Gabriel's beneficent direction, they work on the plantation.[34] Music symbolizes the Indians' Europeanization: in their first encounter with Father Gabriel, they break his flute; later they make European instruments and play European music.[35]

Apparently aware that the Indians were represented as adjuncts to the spiritual quests of Europeans, *The Mission* tried, at one point, to correct this message. In the scene in which the papal legate Cardinal Altamirano visits the oldest of the Jesuit missions, the Mission of San Miguel, a Guarani is its leader. Yet in reality, far from becoming leaders of prosperous missions, "no Guarani were received in the Order for the 150-year span of the mission." The Jesuits decided "shortly after their arrival," Daniel Berrigan writes, "that no Indian was capable of becoming a member of the Order." Berrigan did not try to correct this blatant unhistoricity in the film but defended it as a sort of wishful anachronism: "I tend to look on the episode as the sign of a better future, for it is also a fact that in our century, all sorts and hues of 'indigenous people' have been received in the Order and are presently exercising considerable authority in our midst."[36]

The next film I will consider, *Romero*, raises questions about film's ability to communicate a social message, to raise consciousness. The power of images has been debated in various religious traditions, just as their secular use is presently under critical scrutiny. Indeed, film is only the most recent medium to join a long history of controversy over images, for the reception and interpretation of images cannot be completely predicted and controlled. Images can support or subvert dominant attitudes, values, and behavior, but iconoclasts—political as well as religious—fear them, on two grounds. First, images can incite individuals to imitate the represented behavior, potentially threatening dominant social consensus on issues of morality. Second, vivid images of poverty and pain may prompt calls for reform or revolution. Aware of these dangers, in 1915 the United States Supreme Court explained why it refused cinema the same constitutional freedoms as those permitted printed media: "The exhibition of moving pictures," the Court said, is "vivid, useful, and entertaining, no doubt but [also] capable of evil, having power for it, the greater because of their attractiveness and manner of exhibition."[37]

As I described in chapter 2, David Freedberg has shown that images gain religious power and devotional efficacy when they are naturalistic. The real hair and clothing of the figures in a medieval religious tableau increase viewers' ability to imagine themselves present at a sacred event. Similarly, naturalistic treatments of poverty, violence, and tyranny give social protest photographs and films their power. Raymond Williams has described the close historical associations between socialism and naturalism:

> As a movement and a method, [naturalism] was concerned to show that people are inseparable from their real social and physical environments. As against idealist versions of human experience, in which people act under providence or from innate human nature, or within timeless and immaterial norms, naturalism insisted that actions are always specifically contextual and material. . . . The

leading principle of Naturalism [is] *that all experience must be seen within its real environment*—indeed often, more specifically, that characters and actions are *formed* by environments.[38]

Romero employs the naturalism and on-location style of social protest film to educate North Americans about the atrocities suffered by Latin Americans. Clearly, the intentions of its producers are on the side of the angels. They seek to contribute to ending violence and oppression by inciting people to protest. A bit later I will question whether those intentions were well served by the Hollywood conventions used in the film.

Romero (1989)

The Mission laid claim to an extrafilmic religious authenticity, that of the sincere religious feeling of several individuals engaged in the filmmaking. Daniel Berrigan, the film's Jesuit advisor, took the star, Jeremy Irons, on a Jesuit retreat in preparation for playing the role of the saintly Father Gabriel. Similarly, Raul Julia, the title character in *Romero*, admitted to something like a religious conversion in the process of preparing for his role in the film by listening to the dictated diary of Archbishop Romero, a Salvadoran prelate who was assassinated in March 1980 for supporting struggle for liberation in El Salvador. Julia graduated from a Jesuit high school in Puerto Rico and attended a Catholic university, but he had turned away from religious practice as an adult. After his return to the Roman Catholic faith, he said in an interview of Archbishop Romero:

> I think he was a saint, but I'm not playing him as a saint, because you just can't do it. Romero experienced himself as being responsible for everything. We're not talking about belief; he actually saw himself, Christ, and the Church as one with the people. But I'm playing him as a human being, committed, but with doubts, anger, and fear. You can't play a saint; you can only get into the experience of this person who others happen later to call a saint.[39]

Romero's claim to religious authenticity rests, then, on its content, its producer's intention, and its star's religious experience.

Yet *Romero* has another, and perhaps even stronger, claim to religious authenticity. It was the first feature film made in the United States by a Roman Catholic organization, Paulist Pictures, and the first church-made film to achieve secular acclaim since *Martin Luther* (1953). For this reason, if not for its very modest box office success, it is important to consider *Romero*. Directed by John Duigan, *Romero* was produced by Ellwood E. Kieser, a Paulist priest who celebrated mass for the cast and crew every week during the filming. *Romero* also received an unprecedented kind and amount of publicity by religious organizations: it was advertised by priests in sermons; there were posters in churches, and churches were asked to organize theater parties for viewing the film.

Yet *Romero* was a "frankly commercial venture aimed at a large audience."[40] Kieser had originally planned a television movie, but his proposal was turned down by the three major networks as "too depressing, too controversial, and lacking in love interest"—as if, Kieser said, "Romero's love for God wasn't a love interest."[41] Proposals for the film were also rejected by several major Hollywood studios, so Kieser raised $3.5 million, most of it from Paulist Pictures, a Catholic filmmaking company. The Catholic Bishops of the United States also contributed $238,000. The central authority of the Roman Catholic Church, the Vatican in Rome, was not involved in funding or making the film, but the pope had demonstrated his respect for Archbishop Romero by praying at Romero's tomb on a 1983 visit to El Salvador. Ironically, the film was rated PG13—not G—at its release.

Romero depicts Archbishop Oscar Arnulfo Romero's gradual conversion to liberation theology. A short time before his assassination, Archbishop Romero said to a journalist: "What sustains me in the struggle is my love for God, my desire to be faithful to the gospels, and my love for the Salvadoran people—particularly the poor."[42] Archbishop Romero understood and accepted the principle of group solidarity, and he did not consider himself a leader or—still less—a hero. He became a hero only in death. In life, he was a figurehead for a grassroots movement with multiple "heroes," none of whom thought of him or herself as leading or speaking for the people of the base communities.[43]

The kind of religious commitment represented in *Romero*, then, is—

or should be—different from Daniel Coloumbe's private countercultural religious commitment in *Jesus of Montreal.* Archbishop Romero's
religious commitment was not the resistance of an individual to a
powerful and worldwide organization. Instead Romero's religious conviction was grounded on the informal, communal, practically and ma-
terially focused liberation theology of base communities. Did *Romero*
convey this successfully? I will return to this question.

How did a film its producer called "an act of evangelism . . . the story
of what God can do in a person's life" fare with the critics?[44] *Romero's*
critical reception was mixed: Bruce Williamson said in *Playboy* that
it was "the most meaningful film so far this year." It is, he wrote, an
"earnest, straight-forward reconstruction" of Romero's life.[45] Stanley
Kauffmann, however, saw it as "somewhat wooden and didactic," with
"heavy writing."[46] Vincent Canby agreed, commenting that "the film's
manner is that of a textbook."[47]

Both Kauffmann and Canby spotted in *Romero* its producer's conscious attempt at social protest and consciousness-raising. Its agenda is
that of a social protest film, using vivid and naturalistic images to communicate information, to sensitize viewers, to cause sympathy or outrage, and to advocate social responsibility. Clearly, Paulist Pictures and
the Catholic Bishops of the United States financed the film because they
considered it an effective way to inform a broad popular audience of
conditions and events in El Salvador and to communicate religious values. Did it succeed? First I must digress briefly to describe the origins
and conventions of social protest film.

Realist film, with its broad popular audience and its capacity for elic-
iting the sympathy of spectators, has long been considered a potent
form of social protest. In the course of its twentieth-century history,
realist film has been repeatedly feared by the rich and powerful as capable of inciting social and cultural revolution. Yet, as a commodity, its
firm foundation in capitalistic consumer society undermines this potential. When we examine *Romero's* effectiveness as a social protest
film, it will also become evident that film conventions weakened the
message being communicated.

Romero claims to present contemporary history—the twelve-year-
long civil war in El Salvador in which seventy-five thousand Salvador-
ans were killed—with documentary objectivity, yet like *The Mission,*

it also makes use of adventure film conventions. The genre requires, among other things, a hero whose character develops while the characters surrounding him remain static. They are there only to mark the hero's progress. Danger and violence are also a staple of adventure films, and there must be one or several young women to act as foils for the male protagonist's struggles. In *Romero*, two women represent the different loyalties between which the archbishop must choose. Arista Zelada, wife and daughter of a wealthy family, represents the expectations of a privileged class that Archbishop Romero will support their interests. Lucia, a poor young woman who works tirelessly for liberation, represents Romero's increasing liberation fervor.

The director and producer did not, of course, deliberately tailor the story of the martyrdom of Archbishop Romero to the adventure genre but wanted to communicate a gripping true story to as many people as possible. One must empathize with their predicament. But no one can make a film in a vacuum of cultural referents. In the myriad choices made during filming, the adventure genre came to dominate until *Romero* engaged and satisfied the expectations and anticipated pleasures of an adventure film.

In depicting a historical event, which can be seen from any number of perspectives, the decisions made about how to represent that event are crucial. There is, of course, first of all the issue of which of the surrounding events to represent. The murder of Archbishop Romero occupied a few seconds, but if viewers are to know who he was in enough detail to experience shock and horror, we must, by the time he is murdered, have accumulated impressions of his life and character. If spectators are to recognize Romero's death as the death of a hero, it must be carefully prepared and precisely framed.

Romero's religious subjectivity was the film's primary device for revealing his heroism. Voice-over scenes described his inner struggle, and prayer and the celebration of mass were also shown to be regular and central features of his life. In rendering Romero's religious motivation as plausible and accessible, the film succeeded where others have failed. But *Romero* also incorporated some filmic choices that subverted its effective treatment of religious motivation.

Film's apparent inability to represent group thought and action has to do, at least in part, not only with narrative focus but with another

box office consideration. One of the surest strategies for attracting audiences is stars. Stars are expensive, so most films boast only one or
two. And, of course, the focus on individual stars inevitably undermines the representation of group solidarity in decision and action. Yet,
in real life—as opposed to reel life—social change usually occurs by
group action, rather than by individual resistance. Thus, film narratives
that focus on the story of an individual, and the use of stars (Jeremy
Irons and Robert DeNiro in *The Mission*, and Raul Julia in *Romero*)
to make an enormous difference in the number of people who will buy
tickets, converge to preclude effectively representing groups of people
who think and act together.[48] The unfortunate result is that the group
solidarity that actually can produce social change is not modeled for
the viewing public; heroic individual struggle is presented as the only
model of social protest. But in the real world of politics and institutions,
individual rebellion can easily be ignored, ultimately providing not
much more than a cautionary tale about the futility of protest.

Other film conventions also mitigate against a realistic representation of religious motivation and social protest. Both *Romero* and *Salvador*—a less commercially successful film about El Salvador—contain
a scene that forcefully reiterates and summarizes the cumulative violence of the film. In both, women are brutally raped and killed. In *Salvador*, this scene represents the actual murder of three nuns and a lay
missioner at a roadblock on December 2, 1980. In the scene, the naked
breasts of the youngest and prettiest nun were shown, along with
graphic depictions of the rape of the women. In *Romero*, it is the murder of the young woman, Lucia. Because by the time of her murder Lucia is familiar to spectators, the scene is far more shocking than the
film's scenes of anonymous mass violence. After Lucia is shot and
killed, the camera's eye, and thus the eye of the spectator, lingeringly
retreats from her body with a long tracking shot of her crotch and leg.
This titillating emphasis on women's bodies fits Hollywood conventions, but it is out of place in films that purport to sensitize and inform.

A further question concerns the effectiveness of violence for
consciousness-raising in popular film. Can depictions of violence work
to sensitize a North American population already saturated with violent images? Films such as *Salvador* and *Romero* claim to circulate images of real happenings in the real world.[49] To do so, however, they em-

ploy the same conventions of film violence that are found in fantasy films from *Apocalypse Now* to *Hard Target*. For media-literate Americans, violence is entertainment; a film cannot use violent images to communicate a different message. Neither can such images provoke social action. Violent images will rarely inform, sensitize, or instill social responsibility in people who are accustomed to assuming a spectatorial distance that yields voyeuristic pleasure without requiring, or permitting, active engagement. In short, a film that employs an adventure film's scenes of sex and violence cannot communicate anything but voyeuristic exploitation of suffering people. The pain of the oppressed is ultimately used for the entertainment of comfortable spectators.

Again, I do not question the intentions of the filmmakers, which I am willing to assume were to represent heroic action as powerfully as possible. I do, however, question the use of Hollywood conventions that fetishize women's bodies and display violence and suffering for pleasure.

I asked in chapter 2 whether it is possible to make a religious film using the conventions of Hollywood film, and I decided that, although Hollywood conventions cannot be entirely avoided, they can be minimized. To minimize them is to increase the possibility that religious issues can receive serious treatment. Simply put, some films are better than others at depicting religion with complexity and sensitivity. In *The Mission*, for example, religious conviction is indicated primarily by close-ups of Jeremy Irons' limpid brown eyes; in *Romero* it is more consistently and effectively represented, probably because of its producer's presumed personal interest in, and knowledge of, religious conviction. Yet *Romero* is dramatically flawed by the use of genre conventions. The sex scene and the naked breasts of the natives in *The Mission*, the long crotch shot in *Romero*, and the visual violence of both films position spectators to get the expected pleasure of an adventure film. In both films, we still see, (as if) with our own eyes, scenes to which we are visually habituated, models of filmic conformity.

There is no villain in this story of the transformation of historical report or social protest into adventure film. Each moment of the filmmaking process develops from the earlier moments, lending an aura of inevitability and intuitive rightness to the whole. But the chain of choices and decisions produces a film that supports the *status quo*, despite its radical subject matter. Despite producers' and directors' earnest intentions to raise consciousness or advocate social action, the financial aspirations of Hollywood film cannot sustain explicit advocacy of radical change. The same Hollywood conventions that produce success at the box office simultaneously subvert social protest.

Rather than blaming directors and deploring popular film's apparent inability to break out of longstanding habits of representation, however, the ultimate message of *The Mission* and *Romero* is that viewers must recognize and accept the limitations of films aimed at a large audience. Although we muster the price of a ticket and get ourselves to the theater because a film's publicity claims that it is decisively different, the satisfaction of a popular audience depends largely on a film's fundamental familiarity. The innovativeness of a film is strictly circumscribed by its bottom line.

Thus far, my examination of Hollywood films' ability to represent religion and religious motivation has not been encouraging. We have seen why some kinds of religion generate interest among moviegoers. And we have identified some filmic strategies and moments in which religious motivation becomes, briefly, plausible. But we have also seen that attending a Hollywood film about religion is not likely to be a religious experience for anyone.

4

Not Without My Other: Representing Islam and Judaism in a Dominantly Christian Society

Not Without My Daughter
The Chosen
Chariots of Fire

Identifying and excluding people who differ in race, class, religion, and gender (to name only what cultural critics call the master differences), is an ancient strategy for self-definition. It is regularly used by individuals, communities, and societies. Not all difference can be excluded, however, so difference that cannot be excluded is marginalized. But first it must be identified. Otherness must be imagined before it can be rejected, and popular film is one medium in which pictures of difference are circulated.

Identifying difference is more complex, however, for picturing otherness relies on picturing sameness. Ideas of sameness are usually based on shared subjectivity, on thinking and valuing similarly. Members are thought of as sharing identical interests in all essential matters.[1] Iris Marion Young has analyzed and criticized this notion of community: "The desire to bring things into unity generates a logic of hierarchical opposition. Any move to define an identity, a closed totality, always de-

68

pends on excluding some elements, separating the pure from the impure."[2]

Young argues that even a so-called individual subject is not a "self-identical unity," but could better be characterized as a process, incorporating many disparate and even contradictory elements. Moreover, picturing sameness as uniform is also the implicit basis for imagining otherness as monolithic. Appeals to community, Young says, have often functioned to deny real differences within, between, and among people. People are urged—implicitly or explicitly—to lay aside their individuality and real differences in the interest of cooperation. And the denial of difference results in a failure to recognize that subjects have different historical and social locations and unequal access to economic and social power. The term "community" itself has been understood as the opposing term to "individual," connoting unity, unanimity, and repression or rejection of dissent. Young proposes that appeals to community be replaced by a "politics of difference" in which people learn from, and delight in, differences.

Popular films, I have argued, must be discussed in the context of the historical moment in which they were produced and distributed, for collective interests largely determine whether a film will achieve the popularity that box office success requires. A crucial feature of the historical moment of the 1980s to 1990s was the increasing visibility of religions other than mainstream Christianity in the United States. According to statistics compiled from various sources,[3] the largest religious populations other than Protestants and Roman Catholics in the United States are the following:

Jews	5,981,000
Muslims	1 to 7 million (estimates vary)
Buddhists	1 to 3 million (estimates vary)
Hindus	estimated at 500,000
Christian Scientists	400,000
Hare Krishnas	500,000
Witches and Neo-pagans	40,000

These figures are estimates; no one has yet counted these populations in any systematic way.[4] However, approximate as these figures are, they reveal a rapidly changing religious picture in the United States. Recognizing the reality of religious pluralism is crucial in any attempt to assess the adequacy of representations of non-Christian religion in America, for representations of minority religions do not occur in a cultural vacuum, but in a volatile and, for many, anxiety-provoking religious situation.

The three films I examine in this chapter all deal with cultural and religious otherness. *Not Without My Daughter* looks at Islam from the perspective of an American Free Methodist woman. *Chariots of Fire* places a devout, conservative Christian in contrast with a secular Jew. *The Chosen* presents a conflict of values within Judaism, examining the passionate secular Judaism of Zionism and Hasidism.

I am critical of most of Hollywood's attempts to represent otherness, whether the difference is race, religion, class, sexual orientation, gender, or a combination. So it is perhaps best to acknowledge at the outset that, in my view, there is no adequate way, no matter how sensitive or insightful the outsider, to represent "the other" truthfully. One can best listen and look, carefully and without comment, at the self-representations of those who have been marginalized from public discourse and from the institutions in which this discourse occurs. Beyond that, it is best to acknowledge one's own perspective and to endeavor to denaturalize the way one sees the world and other human beings, and to painstakingly identify one's own socialization. This laborious and time-consuming process offers the best possibility for achieving the generosity of vision that can begin to appreciate otherness, in oneself as well as in others.

Not Without My Daughter (1991)

Not Without My Daughter (hereafter *Daughter*), claims, in the opening credits, to be a "fact-based story," the true experiences of Betty Mahmoody (Sally Fields), an American woman; her Iranian husband, Moody (Alfred Molina); and their daughter, Mahtob (Sheila Rosenthal).[5] The film begins in the United States, but the Mahmoodys emigrate, against Betty's wishes, when they go to Iran for what she thought would merely be a brief visit. The story is set in the mid-1980s, during the Iran-Iraq war. Once in Iran, Betty and Mahtob become increasingly isolated. Betty is battered and intimidated, as if under house arrest, in the home of Mahmoody's fundamentalist extended family, as Moody becomes jealous and violent. Betty plots to escape Iran with Mahtob, but several plans fail, and she becomes increasingly desperate. The film ends with Betty's and Mahtob's harrowing journey to freedom and the West.

Daughter represents the story of one woman's experience. Betty Mahmoody, presently an advisor to the State Department "on the plight of American women and children held against their will in foreign countries," claims that her story is not unusual. In the book she wrote with William Hoffer, Mahmoody says that there are eight cases a week of international abduction of children, but "international abduction is still not a felony in this country."[6] In the absence of other film representations of Iranian family life and society, the film's depiction of other American women in the same plight implies that Betty Mahmoody's experience in Iran is typical.

Few reviewers found *Daughter* worth the time and ink to review it. Those that did review it agreed that it consisted of approximately 80 percent racism and 20 percent melodrama. For example, Caryn James in *The New York Times* said that *Daughter* "exploits the stereotype of the demonic Iranian. . . . it is an utter artistic failure, and its reliance on cultural stereotypes is a major cause."[7] Moody, she writes, seems to be "a pure product of his culture, a mysterious, misogynist Easterner. . . . the film views fanaticism as the Iranian national character."[8] In short, reviewers agreed that the film is "hysterically overdramatized" and "a feminist's nightmare." Yet *Daughter*, with unrelievedly hostile reviews, nevertheless achieved over $14 million in first run theaters, and, in the absence of other film representations of Iranian religion and society, enjoyed a monopoly in circulating its perspective on Islam and Muslims to a broad popular audience.

A review in *The Los Angeles Times* by an Iranian-American woman, Dr. Nayereh Tohidi, a lecturer at the University of California, Los Angeles, protested the film's "unbalanced and distorted representation of Iranians and Iranian culture": "It fails to distinguish between the state and the people. No clear differentiation is made between the policies and attitudes of the extremist Islamic members or supporters of the present ruling subculture and those of other groups of Iranians."

Dr. Tohidi also asks, Why is it the American woman's story?

> By selectively concentrating on Betty's experience as a white middle-class American woman trapped and victimized by Iranians and not depicting any Iranian women similarly victimized, the filmmakers reinforce the narrow view of "civilized Americans" vs. "savage Middle Easterners."[9]

Dan Nimmo and James Combs discuss the "group-mediated realities" of film and television, saying that media representations of "reality" can often be fantasies. A fantasy, they write, "is a credible picture of the world created when one interprets mediated experiences as the way things are and takes for granted the authenticity of the mediated experience without checking against alternative, perhaps contradictory realities so long as the fantasy itself offers dramatic proof of one's expectations."[10]

By this definition, *Daughter* is much more a fantasy than the "true story" it claims to be. We need not question Betty Mahmoody's experience in order to argue that her experience, as represented by the film, becomes a fantasy, or even a falsehood when it is presented as characteristic of a culture.

If *Daughter* is a fantasy, it was a very timely one. *Daughter* is an easy film to consider as a cultural product, for shortly before the film entered production, the Iran Contra crisis and the Iranian hostage crisis had aroused Americans' curiosity and anxiety about Islamic religion and culture. While *Daughter* was being filmed in the summer of 1990, tensions in the Middle East were building, and in August Saddam Hussein invaded Kuwait. Moreover, *Daughter* was released in January 1991; it reached its highest box office ranking (number 7) the week of January 17, the week the war in the Persian Gulf started. In February of the same year, the Gulf War ended and *Daughter* stopped showing in first-run theaters in the United States.[11]

American involvement in the Gulf War seems an obvious enough context in which to consider *Daughter*. But another fact of American public life also contributed importantly to its cultural context. The film was made and the war occurred at a moment when Islam was rapidly overtaking Judaism as the second most common religion in the United

States. Muslims could no longer be thought of as people at a great distance, but had become—literally—the neighbor, the fellow American, albeit with different, and, for most Americans, unknown, religious loyalties and practices. Americans were at least curious, and many were anxious, about Islamic culture when a Muslim nation became a military adversary; Americans were also nervous about what it would mean to live with Muslims on their own blocks.

Media rhetoric during the Gulf War reflected and addressed these anxieties. Nancy Armstrong, in an article ominously entitled "Fatal Abstraction: The Death and Sinister Afterlife of the American Family," explores an interconnected rhetoric in the American news media that played on notions of family and fear of pollution. Repeatedly, Iraq was characterized as a "cultural rather than a military threat," she writes, and Hussein was featured as a "monster capable of global pollution."[12] His family life was targeted as evidence of his immorality: Hussein's first wife was described in the Minneapolis *Star Tribune* as "a clothes horse, a bottle-blond, head-mistress of a girls' school, a jealous wife, the wife of a killer, and [perhaps most damning of all] her husband's first cousin." Ignoring the fact that the royal family of Iraq has practiced polygamy for generations, American media described Hussein's first wife as having been replaced by his second wife. And George Bush described the war as targeted at a "sick" Hussein.[13] One can readily see how such media rhetoric aroused and cultivated public interest and anxiety about Iranian family life, culture, and religion—all of which are explored in *Daughter*. Armstrong calls this rhetoric "semiotic warfare."

Similarly, newspapers, news journals, and television reporters used sanitation metaphors to describe American involvement in the war: United Nations forces conducted "surgical bombing," using "smart bombs," to "take out" specified military objectives. "Our military aggression," Armstrong writes, "was repeatedly described as an act of purification." This rhetoric served to reassure the American public that the Gulf War was necessary if the United States was to be protected from pollution by an alien culture and to maintain the family values that figure so largely in public discourse.

A religious rhetoric was also part of the selling of the war to the American people. In an address to the National Religious Broadcasters Convention, President Bush said that, although the Gulf War had "nothing to do with religion per se," it had "everything to do with what religion embodies—good versus evil, right versus wrong, human dignity and freedom versus tyranny and oppression." Predictably, Bush aligned the United States with good and right, claiming that America is "armed with a trust in God and in the principles that make men free."[14]

In my discussion of *The Mission* in chapter 3, a film that allegedly represented the historical situation, I argued that a film must work— or, perhaps, does not work—primarily as a film, not as a representation of history. Nevertheless, in a film that claims to represent individual or group history, departures from historical events can alert one to the operation of powerful film conventions that override historical evidence. *Daughter* is a personal story which allegedly bases its authenticity on a concrete historical situation rather than on the perspective of its protagonist. But does it? We must question the selection of events and characters represented, asking, what is there? But we must also ask: What is *not* there? What is subordinated or excluded? Most importantly, we must ask: Is it possible that the more-or-less accurate representation of one person's experience might become a gratuitous falsehood when it is taken to represent a largely unknown—and feared— culture?

Indeed, *Daughter*'s claim to present real experiences prompts questions that are irrelevant to the film as film, but that cannot be ignored when we examine the context and potential effects of the film. Because the script for *Daughter* was based on a book, *Daughter* is a representation of a representation. Although it is ultimately impossible, in either novel or film, to distinguish fact from representation, the novel can be compared with the film to identify divergences that signal decisions made in order to produce a popular film. In *Daughter*, perhaps the most dramatic of many divergences from the novel is the omission of the book's description of Moody's disintegration from happy and relatively successful young husband and father to domestic tyrant. In the film, Moody's personality changes abruptly when he arrives in Iran. The cumulative effect of this and other alterations of the book is to flatten what should be seen as a dramatization of one American woman's experience with one Iranian, a man that even his family—in the book—

came to think was crazy. In the film, one woman's experience becomes the stereotype of a culture.

Ultimately, differences between the book and the film have less to do with the particulars of Betty Mahmoody's story than with the conventions of film narrative. Noel Carroll writes:

> The action in movies, . . . unlike most of the action we encounter outside our cinemas, is imbued with heightened sense, direction, intelligibility . . . movies are not only larger than life but more legible too.[15] [Moreover] narrative film constructs scenes that pose (implicit, unconscious) questions in viewers' minds, and scenes that answer those questions. Audiences expect answers to the questions that earlier events in the film have raised. Some form of narrative is not optional but mandatory in films.[16] A successful narrative tells you, literally, everything you want to know about the action being depicted.[17]

If a character gets lost, dropped between the cracks of a narrative structure, it is because that character has not been sufficiently fleshed out to require that the spectator find out what became of her or him.

These familiar narrative conventions create expectations of films that may even contradict our life experience. For example, although most people's lives exhibit at best a rough-and-ready *post hoc* kind of intelligibility, fictional characters' lives must make sense.

Daughter's representation of Islamic culture and family life as alien and threatening implicitly indicts the religion itself. Islam is represented as largely to blame for the "primitiveness" of Muslims. Lest the viewer fail to draw the conclusion that Iranian culture is monolithic and primitive, Betty repeats throughout the film: "It just seems so primitive sometimes," "This is a primitive country," "It's all so primitive!"[18] The only moment of appreciation for Islam that the book or film can offer is Betty Mahmoody's cavalier description of Islam as admirable in that it is like Christianity:

> I was impressed that [Islam] shared many basic philosophies with the Judeo-Christian [sic] tradition. The Moslem Allah is the same supreme being whom I, and the other members of my Free Methodist Church, worship as God. Moslems believe that Moses was a prophet sent from God and that the Torah was God's law as presented to the Jews. They believe that Jesus was also God's prophet and

that the New Testament is a holy book. Mohammed, they believe, was the last and greatest prophet chosen directly by God. His Koran, being the most recent holy book, takes precedence over the Old and New Testaments.[19]

Within the film, there *are* several suggestions that the narrative it presents may be atypical of Iranian society. For example, because religion is to blame for the fanaticism of Moody's family, one is invited to imagine Moslems who are not so religious and therefore more tolerant. Moody says that his family are "very religious . . . basically uneducated country people," equating religion with ignorance. Also, when Betty complains of the "primitiveness" of Islam, Moody responds rather profoundly, "All religious beliefs seem primitive when they're not your own."

These suggestions that Betty Mahmoody's experience in Iran might not be characteristic of the culture as a whole, however, are maintained at the cost of understanding Islam as the primary primitivizing feature of Iranian culture. Islamic ritual prayer is shown from a distance that blends the gestures and mumblings of one into those of the group. But Betty and her daughter pray to their Christian God from the heart, their tear-streaked, anguished faces shot close-up. An Iranian man screams at Betty, "You must not be careless. Every single hair that is not covered is like a dagger you aim at the heart of our mothers." This scene is shot close-up on faces contorted by rage. The only moment when the possibility of a gentler Islam is suggested—when Betty's rescuer shows her his garden and talks about the ancient beauty of Islam ("The word 'paradise' is a Persian word")—cannot balance the cumulative representation of Islam as unrelievedly oppressive.

The only likable Iranians in the film were so because they had been to the West, or had been influenced by the West. Fortunately, *Daughter* was such a starkly prejudiced account of Islamic religion, family life, and society that many who saw it recognized it for what it was. Across a large popular audience, however, there must have been many who didn't, and whose support for the Gulf War and antipathy toward Moslem neighbors in the United States was strengthened by the caricature it presented. *Daughter*'s effects cannot be measured with precision, but it clearly spoke on the side of fear and hatred of the otherness it represented. Next I consider a film that treats otherness much more subtly.

Chariots of Fire (1981)

Chariots of Fire (hereafter *Chariots*) is a British film that had broad circulation and box office success in the United States.[20] Although it was not made in Hollywood, its popularity in the United States, together with its sympathetic representation of a committed Christian, make it an interesting film to consider. Like several of the other films I have discussed, *Chariots* claims, in the opening credits, to be a true story. In fact, the producer, David Puttnam, created the film from a newspaper clipping, a children's story about the two runners, and the 1924 Olympics record book. He insisted on not using stars because he thought that the absence of famous faces would make the film more believable.

Chariots tells the story of Eric Liddell (Ian Charleson, who died of AIDS in 1990), who won the 400-meter race, and Harold Abrahams (Ben Cross, in his film debut), who won the 100-meter dash in the 1924 Olympics. In the film, Liddell and Abrahams barely know one another, and they race each other only once. The title, *Chariots of Fire*, is unexplained within the film; apparently it alludes to the preface of Blake's poem, "Milton," in which he calls "Young Men of the New Age" to be "just and true to our own imaginations."

> Bring me my Bow of burning gold;
> Bring me my Arrows of desire;
> Bring me my spear: O Clouds unfold!
> Bring me my chariots of fire.[21]

Chariots is about male competition; it is also about conflicts and loyalties between actual and/or symbolic fathers and sons. This theme is established by the opening words: "Let us now praise famous men and our fathers that begat us," while a father and son watch runners on a beach. In the film, Eric Liddell, a Scottish Presbyterian, must choose between symbolic fathers: God and country. Committed, along with his sister Jenny, to becoming a missionary in China, Liddell takes time out to run in the Olympics. Once there, however, Liddell refuses to break the Sabbath by running on Sunday, unfortunately the very day his major race is scheduled.

Harold Abrahams' father was an immigrant Jewish Lithuanian who raised his son to be an English gentleman; Abrahams "runs to become visible in a Christian Anglo-Saxon society that—at best—pretends not to notice [his] Jewishness," and at worst actively disparages it.[22] In the end, Abrahams opts for his trainer, Sam Massabini (part Italian, part Arab), as father figure because Abrahams cannot fully adopt what he sees as his own father's uncritical worship of his country of adoption.

Two filmic devices are used repeatedly in *Chariots*. Slow motion scenes, used especially for running scenes, signal a poetic content. The second device—voice-over—is used to inform and comment; the film is narrated by one of the English runners, Aubrey Montague, whose letters to his mother provide the voice-over comment. Just as the spectator in a darkened movie theater sees without being seen, so the moviegoer overhears without being addressed directly. The narrator's voice speaks from a vantage point over the narrative and is invisible and omniscient. It has "unqualified authority" because the audience is dependent on it for its own point of view.[23]

Critics were polarized in their impressions of *Chariots*. Vincent Canby called it "unashamedly rousing and invigorating, but [a] very clear-eyed evocation of values of the old fashioned sort that are today more easily satirized than celebrated. . . . The director knows the difference between sentiment and sentimentality."[24] Stanley Kauffmann also praised *Chariots*, calling it "gripping, intelligent, rewarding" and commenting puzzlingly that the film is "inspiriting without being remotely 'inspirational'."[25] But Pauline Kael said: "The film is gimmicky, with too many tricks and lots of dead spots, and the two heroes have no real connection—they barely meet. Abrahams is lucky [she adds], he doesn't have to listen to Liddell's right-from-the-heart sermons. We do." Kael called *Chariots* "retrograde movie-making, presented with fake bravura," and with a "mildewed high moral tone."[26] Michael Seitz agreed with Kael: " 'Chariots of Fire' is the most reactionary film I've seen in a long time . . . an exercise in escapist nostalgia. I suspect there is more than a little conservative calculation in the promotion of such a hero for contemporary audiences."[27] Indeed, in a year—1981—in which Jerry Falwell and the Moral Majority were on the rise in the United States, this comment revealed liberal anxieties about the increasing *political* significance of religious fundamentalism.

Steve Neale said of *Chariots* that "representations of masculinity and the male body are the central core, the determining focus around which race, religion, class, and nationality are articulated." Female figures, he says, are incidental: Jenny Liddell is "largely an image of religious rectitude;" Sybil, the actress Abrahams loves, functions as the object of his sexual desire, but his real passion is running.[28] An interview with the actual Jenny Liddell revealed the extent to which the film took liberties with the "true story." Although her opposition to her brother's running was a major motif of the film, Jenny Liddell says that she never opposed it.

Chariots is an unusual film in that it makes Liddell's Christianity central to his character. The uncommonly wide divergence in reviewers' evaluations of the film may have been caused by their differing attitudes toward religion. Discussing Liddell's religious conviction, the producer, David Puttnam said: "This is an expedient world; for people to behave in an unexpedient manner is extraordinary." He was repeatedly told, he said, that "a contemporary audience would not be able to believe that an Olympic athlete would train for the Olympic games, get there, and refuse to run. The guy's a jerk. The audience would laugh." But he persisted.[29]

Interestingly, no reviewers I found questioned Liddell's religious commitment. Whether one appreciated it or not, it was apparently fully believable. How did *Chariots* achieve this authenticity? First, it presents Christian commitment as rooted in religious community rather than in religious individualism. A lengthy part of the film establishes Liddell's answerability to his family and community in Scotland. He is not shown socializing with other runners at the Olympics; his relationships with them are friendly but distant. Second, voice-over and interior dialogue are used at crucial points throughout the film to reveal the commitments, not only to religious ideas but also to people, that inform Liddell's convictions. By contrast, Abrahams' Jewishness, even though it is explicitly pictured as essential—even the key—to his character and motivation, is not articulated. Abrahams is not shown as having family, community, or religious practices. In the scene in which he describes to Ashley Montague what Jewishness means to him, Abrahams shows Montague a picture of his father. But the camera, and therefore the viewer, does not see it. Abrahams talks about his father, but the father never becomes visible to the viewer. The filmic isolation of a character signals his otherness in relation to the perspective assumed by the film, usually that of its protagonist.

Eric Liddell "runs to honor God." What form of Christianity does the film represent? Not one, I suggest, that can be counted on to be immediately sympathetic to a popular audience in the United States or in Great Britain. Liddell's Church of Scotland espouses a Calvinistic doctrine that believes in the total depravity of humankind; salvation cannot be earned but is granted to the few who have been predestined to receive it. Scripture is believed to be the literal Word of God and the absolute rule for faith. And, according to Scottish Presbyterians, God has stipulated how God is to be worshipped:

> He hath appointed one day in seven for a sabbath, to be kept holy unto him . . . in which [men] observe a holy rest all the day from their own works, words, and thoughts, [and their] worldly employments and recreations. (Westminster Confession xxi)

It is this tenet of 1920s Scottish Presbyterianism that provides *Chariot*'s central narrative conflict. I will discuss it shortly.

Scottish Presbyterianism in the early twentieth-century developed what was called a muscular Christianity. Vigorous missionizing was one of the evidences of muscular Christianity. Both in life and in the film, Eric Liddell gave up a career in running to become a missionary to China. Presbyterian missions in China were in their heyday in the 1920s, a time between the Boxer Rebellion of 1900 in which thousands of Chinese Christians and many missionaries were killed, and the revolution of 1949 when the Communists came to power and denounced foreign missionaries as agents of Western imperialism.

The dogmatism and aggressive missionizing of Scottish Presbyterianism is glossed over by its setting as a period piece. It is also masked by filmic devices—especially the hymns sung by Scottish Christians and by Anglicans—that imply its fundamental identity with Anglican liberalism. Moreover, Calvinism's belief in the total depravity of all human beings is never alluded to in the film, helping to make Eric Liddell's religion sympathetic to popular audiences.

Harold Abrahams's running is, as he tells Aubrey Montague, "a weapon against being Jewish." Abrahams, wealthy, but different in ethnicity, religion, and class from his classmates, speaks of his experience of otherness and his resentment of it: "it's an ache, a helplessness, and an anger." Yet, ironically, the film itself politely ignores Abrahams' Jewishness, even while his Jewishness is featured. Before examining *Chariots*' marginalization of Abraham's Jewishness, we need to consider some of the rather subtle ways that ideology can operate in films.

Perhaps the only way to identify an ideology that one happens to share is by observing closely how a film is composed. Ideology, as unstated assumptions and perspectives, is at work in the myriad choices made in the process of production, choices of subject and narrative, scriptwriting, casting, shooting, and editing. Every feature of a film is consciously selected to produce a film that says, as precisely as possible, what its producer and director want it to say. As we have already seen, however, there may be considerable dissonance between a director's intent and the messages viewers with diverse perspectives and interests receive. While a producer and director are focused on telling one story, other stories can often appear in the interstices.

Moreover, films are aimed at particular audiences. They do not represent some "pre-existent reality which [the film] merely conveys. . . . The text is determined not only by the situation to be represented but by its audience as well."[30] *Chariots* provides a good example of this discrepancy between intentions and effects. In addition to an explicitly sympathetic treatment of Christian conviction, a Christian ideology can be spotted by noticing some contrasts between the representation of the two runners' stories.

Chariots explicitly exposes the anti-Semitism of Abrahams' elite Cambridge college and sympathetically represents the pain it causes, but the film nevertheless subverts its own critique in several ways. First, it represents Liddell's and Abrahams's personalities as stereotypes: Liddell is friendly, has a sense of humor, is outgoing and usually takes himself lightly; Abrahams is moody, intense, and lacks humor. Liddell is presented as self-assured and likable, Abrahams as difficult, defensive, and monomaniacal. Liddell runs to "give God pleasure," while Abrahams runs to show a dominantly Christian culture that he can "run them off their feet." A dominantly Christian audience in Great Britain and North America could be expected to find Liddell's motivation more heroic, especially when viewers learn, at the end, of his death as a Christian martyr.

Furthermore, spectators are much more likely to identify with film characters whose subjectivity we have access to than with those we merely see acting in certain ways. Abrahams' self-talk is heard only after he loses an important race, when obsessive images of losing the race occupy his mind. Viewers are encouraged to identify with Liddell, however; at several crucial points we hear the interior voices that explain his motivation or agonize over the conflict he feels.

The operation of a Christian ideology is also apparent in a scene from the end of the film. As Harold and Sybil walk toward one another at the train station on his return to England, a Christian hymn, "Jerusalem," for the scene to follow begins. As they meet, and kiss, the music swells insistently, a segue into the cathedral scene that begins and ends the film. Abrahams' Jewishness is merged into the elite Christian ethos to which he has aspired.

Any one of these examples may seem insignificant, but the accumulation of instances, at myriad tiny points throughout the film, adds up to support racism. It is important to remember that films have always exhibited an extraordinary sensitivity to social attitudes. Films support prevalent attitudes; indeed, they must do so if they are to succeed at the box office. In turn, prevailing social attitudes can be deduced from movies. The massive and ubiquitous racism of the 1915 Hollywood film, *The Birth of a Nation*, for example, would not be tolerated by film audiences today. But more subtle public expressions of racism, matching the present more subtle social practices of racism, still flourish, in films and in society.

In fact, social attitudes are the most recalcitrant and tenacious feature of public life, often proving less flexible and more resistant to change than institutions and laws. According to government records, anti-Semitism is on the increase in the United States. It is, then, important to seek the sources of a broad-based support for such hatred. Perhaps some of that support comes, not from explicitly anti-Jewish rhetoric or activity, but from the circulation of media images that show Christian culture as more attractive than that of other religions. Indeed, if one asks why the protagonist's antagonist should be a Jew, it becomes evident that the Jew is needed as foil for the triumphs of the Christian.

Class is also on *Chariots'* agenda. As the film begins, Abrahams is arriving at Caius College of Cambridge University. Elitism is "just the way things are" at Caius, and who can signal elitism better than Sir John Gielgud, who plays one of the masters? As the musical comedy song in which Abrahams enthusiastically joins, goes, "If everybody's somebody, then nobody's anybody." The upper class is depicted from a middle-class perspective as snobbish, hypocritical, and unfeeling. Abrahams' aspirations to it, based on his new money, are yet another indicator of the shallowness of his character. Clearly, Liddell's staunch middle-classness is the right social position, according to *Chariots*. It could also be expected to further endear him to predominantly middle-class audiences.

In *Chariots*, Christian commitment is depicted in the best possible light. The particularity of Liddell's form of Christianity is elided, making it acceptable to large audiences in North America and Great Britain. The appeal of Liddell's Christianity is also enhanced by its setting in family and community loyalties, by Liddell's attractive personality, and by the happy solution that is found to the conflict of God and country. Moreover, Liddell's Christianity is incrementally strengthened by positioning Abrahams' Jewishness as foil, a device that the film explicitly questions even while it implicitly employs it.[31] The filmic strategies by which a Jew is "othered" in *Chariots* will recur in my discussion of racism against African Americans in a later chapter. Let us turn now to a film that focuses directly on different loyalties within Jewish communities in the United States.

The Chosen (1982)

The stage must be set for my discussion of *The Chosen* by a review of Jews' situation in America in the film era. With the twentieth-century exception of Israel, nowhere and at no time in the last two thousand years have Jews been a majority in any country. In the United States, Jews constitute the only minority defined more aptly by religion than by country of origin. In the twentieth century, the central fact of Jewish life was the Holocaust of six million Jews in Nazi Germany during World War II. Although anti-Semitism in the United States has never been officially sanctioned, it has existed and continues to exist.[32] A virulent wave of anti-Jewish activity following the Great Depression of 1929 prompted Jews to redouble their efforts, throughout the 1930s and 1940s, to assimilate to American culture. "To succeed in America," Patricia Erens writes, "meant assimilation; the overriding problem was to find the proper balance between traditionalism and assimilation." In working out this issue, American Jews largely achieved what Erens calls "acculturation," that is, absorption into the dominant culture without the loss of their ethnic specificity.[33]

Jewish immigrants arrived in America in waves, largely prompted by persecution in Europe. Between 1880 and 1924, about a third of all Eastern European Jews emigrated to the United States. In the 1940s, Nazi persecution of European Jews brought three hundred thousand German Jews to the United States, including "many of Europe's most prominent scientists, scholars, writers, and musicians." More recently, between 1971 and 1980, eighteen thousand Jews immigrated from Soviet Russia. Following the Second World War, and because of Americans' knowledge of the Holocaust, discrimination in the United States eased, and Jews gained widespread access to the professions. A 1964 study of adult males in New York City "showed that Jews accounted for the largest numbers enrolled in college, graduate and post-doctoral work."[34] Twice as many Jews as other ethnic groups were professionals in large cities, and almost no Jews remained in the unskilled labor force."[35] Jews were successful in America.

Cinema was one of the many arenas of this success. Hollywood producers and writers were and are still predominantly Jewish. From the first, Jews also held executive positions in major studios and directed films. Jews have been "the backbone of film production in America; it is their stories, almost without exception that are chronicled in films of the first three decades—tales of pogroms, of immigration, of ghetto living, and of upward mobility."[36] The earliest American films depicted "the contradictions of an immigrant, ethnically and racially segregated society." Unlike other minorities or marginalized groups like African Americans and women, Jews had access to the means of film production and thus have mostly enjoyed a "protected image [in films] despite their minority status in society." Yet, after the first decades of the century, Jewish life has seldom been the focus of narrative film. Perhaps reflecting Jewish success in acculturation, as well as the disinterest of a dominantly Christian society in Jewish stories, Jews in films have usually been presented simply as Americans without attention to their ethnicity or religious lives.

In her book on American silent film, Miriam Hansen describes an early widespread conception of film as "a new universal language" capable of "integrating empirically diverse audiences."[37] Film was considered capable of accurately revealing different ethnic groups to one another in the interests of greater mutual understanding. The desired and anticipated result of such understanding was that ethnic, religious, and class differences would be dissolved in the great American melting pot. In contemporary American public life, however, the dissolution of difference is no longer widely accepted as a desirable goal. Rather, a pluralistic society needs images of irreducible—and respected—difference. I selected *The Chosen* for discussion in this chapter even though, like *Chariots of Fire*, it appeared slightly before the decade (1983–1993) on which I focus, because of its attention to differences between Jewish communities of commitment.

The Chosen was adapted from a Chaim Potok novel about the last years of World War II.[38] At the time the film was produced, *The Chosen* was unique: it is "entirely bounded by the Jewish world"[39]; it respectfully portrays a Hasidic family and community; and it "recognizes the philosophic and religious differences that divide Jews, rather than assuming a unified group."[40] Its story represents two of the possible options for passionate belief and community cohesion among Brooklyn Jews in the 1940s—Hasidism and Zionism. Historian Arthur Goren has written that in the last years of the Second World War, "Support of Israel served as a secular ethnic replacement for, or reinforcement of, religion."[41]

The Chosen's director, Jeremy Kagan, was committed to making the film as visually accurate as possible. He secured the advice and help of the Lubavitcher community, a Hasidic group led by Rabbi Menachem M. Schneerson, on costuming, set design, and the choice of a neighborhood for the filming. Brooklyn school yearbooks from the 1940s were canvassed to get the "looks" of the boys. Forty of the mink and sable hats worn by Hasidic men on special occasions were needed; they would have cost $700 each, so a cheaper version had to be made out of dyed raccoon tails. Not only house numbers, but the facades of buildings had to be changed because typefaces have changed.[42]

The Chosen is a tale of male friendship: that of Reuven Malter (Barry Miller) and Danny Saunders (Robby Benson). Danny, son of a rabbi, is expected to attend a university where he can study the Talmud, but he yearns to study in a secular university. Reuven, son of a secular Jew, expects to attend a secular university but changes his academic interests and career goals in the course of his friendship with Danny.

Although male friendship is represented as providing new understanding and new possibilities, the sons' relationships with their fathers—Danny and his father, the *tzaddik* (Rod Steiger), and Reuven and his Zionist father (Maxmilian Schell)—take precedence over their friendship with each other. A talmudic story at the end of the film sums up the conflicts between fathers and sons; it tells of an estranged son who found it impossible to return to his father: "Return as far as you can," the father says, "and I will come the rest of the way."

The Chosen represents intelligent, passionate, and committed Jews who opt for different goals. Both Professor Malter and Rabbi Saunders are deeply informed by a strong and poignant sense of the suffering of the Jewish people. "How the world delights in killing us," Reb Saunders says, but "we are the leaders; it's up to us to keep our people alive." For Reb Saunders, there must be "no Jewish state without the Messiah." Professor Malter, Reuven's father, has a different solution; he writes and speaks to the point of exhaustion in support of the founding of the state of Israel. Contrasts between Reuven's father's worldly focus and Danny's father's spiritual focus are irresistible. Yet *The Chosen* resists displaying the greater beauty and profundity of either at the expense of the other. It does not polarize political and religious approaches to Jewish existence, nor does it adopt a secular bias, posing Professor Malter as secular and humane, for example, and Rabbi Saunders as a fanatical rabbi. This is an unusual and considerable filmic achievement.

How is this balanced account of two Jewish commitments achieved? Two film conventions are used extensively in *The Chosen*—as in countless other films—to represent the relationship of two characters: point-of-view editing and shot/countershot camerawork.[43] The classic device for representing relationship and, as film critics put it, "stitching" the spectator into that relationship, is shot/countershot: "a character will be shown looking and a responding shot will show what the character sees."[44] Another way to put this is that shot/countershot is a point-of-view pattern that shifts between characters and indicates a 'dialogic' relationship. Thus, if two characters are given roughly equal time looking and being looked at, and if the camera adopts the perspective of both characters for a similar amount of time, moviegoers recognize subliminally that we are expected to believe in the equality and mutuality of their relationship. In *The Chosen*, point-of-view editing and the shot/countershot device signal the mutuality of Danny and Reuven's relationship.

Despite the differences between Reuven and Danny, and between the boys and their fathers, an area of strong agreement, both in the film and in Jewish life in the United States, is on the value of education. Reb Saunders and Professor Malter represent and advocate different kinds of learning, but both urge their sons to cultivate their minds. The value of education is often referred to in films about Jewish life (such as *Yentl* and *Radio Days*), and it is noticeably missing in most other films. Learning, a passion for knowledge, primarily of the sacred Torah, but also, as in Danny's case, for secular learning, is a staple of Jewish film.

Moreover, in *The Chosen*, learning is depicted not only as important, but also as exciting, in contrast to many other films of the 1980s. There are a few films that canonize skillful teachers—such as *Stand and Deliver*, *Lean On Me*, and *Dead Poets Society*. However, many others, especially of the high school and college genres, vilify everything about school, including teachers: *Fame*, *The Breakfast Club*, *Fast Times at Ridgemont High*, *Porky's*, *Summer School*, *E. T.*, and *Wargames* are some examples. In these movies, education is boring, unproductive, and confining. By contrast *The Chosen* depicts learning as valuable and interesting.

Barbara Streisand's *Yentl*, based on a short story by Isaac Bashevis Singer, has a similar theme. Yentl is a young Jewish woman in 1904 "when the world of study belonged only to men." The bookseller in the marketplace cried, hawking his wares: "Story books for women; sacred books for men; picture books for women, sacred books for men." Yentl longed intensely for knowledge; she studied Torah behind closed curtains with her sympathetic father until his death. Then she cut her hair, dressed as a boy, and set off to seek—and to find—further education.

Yentl is, however, a fairy tale, and *The Chosen* is a "realistic" film about the 1940s. Thus, Yentl was somewhat more fortunate in her pursuit of learning than was Danny's sister who, when she tried to read a book, was first interrupted and teased by Reuven, and then ordered to the kitchen to cut vegetables by her mother. After Reuven learns that she is not a possible wife for him, Danny's sister is never seen again in the film. The mother guards her daughter for an arranged marriage, yet she intervenes to release her son from his father's dictates for his education and vocation, giving him a briefcase "to keep your books in," and telling him that he will be permitted to go to a secular college.

As *The Chosen* emphasizes, part of the attraction of learning is precisely that it is a male preserve, an area of male bonding, friend to friend and father to son, to which no woman had access in the 1940s. In common with most communities, gender difference is neither accidental nor incidental to the Hasidic community; it simultaneously articulates and integrates community. By contrast, Reuven and his father stand alone, without mother and wife, without family or visible community. Women in *The Chosen* are either dead (Reuven's mother) or docile (Danny's mother and sister). This story of two forms of Jewish commitment is told without exploring any woman's subjectivity.

Critical responses to *The Chosen* varied considerably. Many reviewers commented on the film's visual accuracy to a 1940s Lubavitcher community. The Crown Heights Lubavitcher community at the time of the filming, under the leadership of Rabbi Menachem Schneerson, remained silent, though Director Jeremy Kagan was eager to know what they thought:

> You would hear Hasidim say that they didn't go to the movies . . . but Rabbi Schneerson felt that, if it existed in this world, then HaShem, the Lord, meant it to be used for holiness. I was anxious to get a reaction to the film from them. I figured that somebody must have seen it. But I haven't had any approval or disapproval. I guess you could say I got the non-disapproval.[45]

One reviewer who reflected on the issues raised in *The Chosen*, Robert Hatch, referred to the "gaiety and security of Hasidic life" but doubted that Reb Saunders would so abruptly change his "autocratic" behavior to allow Danny to go to a secular college and, eventually, to become a psychologist. Moreover, he doubted that Danny's "splendid" personality would be the result of the silent treatment he got from his father all the time he was growing up: "men are not made splendid by cruelty, nor are they free one day and subservient the next. Stories that assume the opposite are fairy tales, not insights into life."[46] Yet one of the issues effectively raised by the film is the possibility that popular wisdom about how to live and how to bring up children may be severely flawed. The film presents the Lubavitcher community as an alternative to a way of life—the nuclear family, romantic love, and materialistic goals—that has not worked well for many Americans.

Consider *The Chosen*'s representation of Hasidic religion. It is not easy to comment on the filmic treatment of a religious community to which one does not belong, and I do so with hesitancy. I am also suspicious of critics who inevitably find their own religion less than ably represented, while they find that others' religions are well represented, simply because the representation fits the critic's preconceptions. Having said that, however, I did find *The Chosen*'s representation of Hasidism remarkably accurate. Contrast, for example, *Not Without My Daughter*'s representation of daily life in a Muslim family with *The Chosen*'s depiction of daily life in a Hasidic family. Though the latter was depicted as containing discomfort and tension, it was also loving, playful, and secure. Also, Hasidic practice and values were implicit, even where they were not explicit, in *The Chosen*, revealing restriction and permission as intimately interconnected. A brief description of the tenets of Hasidism will demonstrate the film's depiction of the interweaving of religion and daily life in Reb Saunders' household.

Hasidism is a movement that originated in a European Jewish community founded by Israel be Eliezer, the Baal-Shem Tov (Master of the Good Name), who lived from 1700 to 1760. "Hasid" means pious man. The term *"tzaddik"* means righteous, proven, completed: when Danny reconciles with his father, Reb Saunders says that Danny will become a *tzaddik* even if he enters the secular world, as long as he does so as a Jew and keeps the Jewish law. Martin Buber, the author who spent more than fifty years describing Hasidic thought to the English-speaking public, wrote in *Hasidism and Modern Man* that Hasidic teachings "can be summed up in a single sentence: God can be seen in each thing and reached through each pure deed."[47] Overcoming a separation between "sacred" and "secular" is the most important duty of a Hasid.

> By no means can it be our true task in the world into which we have been set, to turn away from the things and beings that attract our hearts; our task is precisely to get in touch, by hallowing our relationship with them, with what manifests itself in them as beauty, pleasure, enjoyment. Hasidism teaches that rejoicing in the world, if we hallow it with our whole being, leads to rejoicing in God.[48]

In order to cultivate the ability to act with one's whole being, one must "begin with oneself, but not end with oneself; to start from oneself, but not to aim at oneself; to comprehend oneself, but not to be preoccupied with oneself."[49]

Hasidism has an antiascetic character: "no mortification is needed, for all natural life can be hallowed" if one lives it with holy intention.[50] Moreover, "everyone should carefully observe what way his heart draws him to, and then choose this way with all his strength"—a prominent theme in *The Chosen*.[51]

Ecstasy, the inflaming, is highly valued in Hasidism. The inflaming is an immediate mystical apprehension of life and death, the world and paradise. In the film, the reb's solo dance at a wedding might illustrate a Hasidic saying: "If one has fulfilled the whole of the teaching and all the commandments but has not had the rapture and the inflaming, when he dies and passes beyond, paradise is opened to him but, because he has not felt rapture in the world, he also does not feel it in paradise."[52] *The Chosen* manages to communicate that a religion with strict rules for behavior can be joyful and fulfilling. Because this is an unfamiliar concept for many late twentieth-century Americans, the film's provision of an image of this aspect of religion is valuable.

Let us return to the depiction of difference between Jewish communities of commitment in *The Chosen*. The film begins with Reuven saying to Danny, "You are *weird*," because Danny has never been to a movie and doesn't know who Erroll Flynn or Benny Goodman is. Yet the film ends with an exchange of the boys' "destinies": Reuven decides to become a rabbi ("not like Reb Saunders, but a rabbi for the modern world"), and Danny becomes a psychologist (but one who adheres to Jewish laws). Differences between the two are minimized in this exchange of vocations in a nation of almost infinite possibility. Difference between Jews is overcome or transcended in *The Chosen*. Difference disappears in the last scene: Danny Saunders arrives at Reuven's door, his hair cut, and dressed in a 1940s suit and hat. The Hollywood melting pot psychology I have described is evident in *The Chosen*'s conclusion.

A resolution in which the main protagonists absorb each other's intellectual fascinations, lifestyles, careers, and even clothing may be tremendously satisfying as a narrative closure in a film. I question, however, the film's reassurance that friendship dissolves difference. In the context of a society which, in 1982, was beginning to recognize, and seek ways to accommodate, its incontrovertible diversity, does *The Chosen*'s conclusion offer an adequate model? I do not think that it does. Had the profound difference between Danny and Reuven's values and commitments been maintained and even strengthened by a conclusion in which each learns from the other, yet without changing his own values, however, moviegoers, anticipating the satisfaction of a conflict resolved, a difference transcended, would have been disappointed. The image of a strong friendship in which the friends' different loyalties are not overcome, but continue to delight and intrigue the other, would have provided a valuable model for 1980s struggles with diversity.

The many decisions made in creating a film can all be seen as occasions for expressing complex, ambivalent, or even contradictory responses to questions concerning race, religion, class, or other forms of difference. The net effect, however is often to permit audiences to "lend sympathy for an hour without having to change attitudes or beliefs."[53] The viewer's privileged position is surreptitiously reconstructed as "reality," as just the way things are. We saw, for example, that Abrahams' ultimate triumph was to fit into British Christian society. His Jewishness gave him energy and motivation for a difficult feat; then it became obsolete. There is a gap between the film's intention of depicting racism as painful and the effect of showing Abrahams' assimilation.

Although most textbooks in world religions define the religions of the world by their beliefs, common beliefs alone do not define religious communities; the way in which members and those outside the community are regarded and treated also defines communities. The films discussed in this chapter demonstrated the centrality of relationships within and across religious communities. Did these films, then, adequately represent difference and otherness? *Chariots of Fire* and *Not Without My Daughter* explicitly forefronted issues of race, gender, and religion. But they also subverted, in various ways, their own representation of the pain of racism and sexism.

The cohesiveness of religious communities in the West has been defined by exclusionary practices. On the one hand, defining what is other, what is not "us," is an effective way to define who "we" are. Yet, as we have seen, even in films that specifically address issues of cohesion and exclusion, camerawork, lighting, the musical score, and other filmic elements may clash with the intended message.

Is it possible to represent religious and cultural difference in ways that do not, blatantly or subtly, either subvert or eliminate difference? Are Hollywood film conventions adequate for representing difference as irreducible and delightful? I raise these questions not in order to answer them at this point, but to call attention to the importance of considering them in relation to films that represent religious commitment.

If movies were merely entertaining, caricatures of otherness like *Not Without My Daughter* might not be a problem. But film conventions not only condition our expectations of movies, but they also seep into, and merge with, what we expect from life. In a society in which religious difference is rapidly becoming more visible than it has been in the past, popular film might encourage, rather than inhibit, appreciation for the many forms of religious commitment and community presently existing in American public life. As the reader may have noticed, the movies I have discussed in this chapter are, in their sequence, increasingly skillful treatments of religious and cultural difference. *Not Without My Daughter* caricatured a Muslim society at a critical cultural moment when interest in, and anxiety over, Muslims was strong. Although subtle racism may be as invidious and damaging as overt racism, *Chariots of Fire*'s positioning of a religion, race, and class other than mainstream Christianity as foil for revealing the greater integrity of Christian commitment avoided explicit racism. *The Chosen* managed best to explore the different commitments of two protagonists. That it ended by eliding difference was, in an otherwise commendable film, an unfortunate gesture towards a conventional happy ending. Although I have criticized *The Chosen*'s conclusion, however, the film's evenhanded, sympathetic depiction of both Zionist and Lubavitcher commitments should not be overlooked. It is a rare filmic achievement.

5

There Is a Bomb in Gilead:
Christian Fundamentalism in Film

> The Handmaid's Tale
> The Rapture

What kind of religion is featured at the movies? We have gathered several suggestions in the previous chapters about the forms of religion most likely to draw large audiences. Discussing *Jesus of Montreal* and *The Last Temptation of Christ*, I suggested that the only credible religious motivation contemporary film audiences recognize is fanaticism, psychological imbalance, or derangement. Considering *Romero* and *The Mission*, we saw that current religious conflicts inspired the production of films on similar issues, just as *Not Without My Daughter* was a glaring example of interest in, and/or fear of, religious "otherness" being generated by current events.

Christian fundamentalism has been featured in popular films of the 1980s and 1990s more than mainstream Protestantism or traditional Roman Catholicism, but without much nuance. Films, exhibiting a secular bias common to liberal media, tend to depict fundamentalism as monolithic, fanatical, and threatening to a nation committed to the separation of Church and state. Fundamentalist religion often appears in the news because of the religious right's often vehement political advocacy. Fundamentalism borders on fanaticism in the minds of many; for mainstream liberals, it represents religious otherness at close range.

By "fundamentalists," I mean Christians who believe that the Bible in its most literal sense provides a clear, full, and sufficient guide for living. By the term "religious right," I mean groups that may differ in religious beliefs and membership but who are united in their positions on some controversial issues in American public life, such as gender roles, reproductive technologies, the nuclear family, abortion, sexuality, and sexual orientation. The religious right includes fundamentalists, conservatives, and evangelicals. "Conservatives," by my definition, are Christians who, without subscribing to a party line, tend to make choices that seek to return the United States to the values of former times—times remembered as more stable and God-fearing. "Evangelicals" are Christians for whom the Christian message of salvation and hope is more important than political agenda. Clearly, liberals and secularists fear the religious right for its political advocacy rather than for its religious beliefs.

In chapter 1 we saw that Americans are becoming more religious, but in different configurations than before. In chapter 4 I charted estimates for the largest religious groups in the United States. Within Christianity, there has also been rapid change; the *Yearbook of American and Canadian Churches* details trends within Christianity, modestly designating itself a "snapshot of religious activity," since religious organizations are "in constant flux."[1] There is a "continuing loss in adherents for most mainline denominations: Episcopal, Evangelical Lutheran Church in America, Presbyterian Church USA, United Church of Christ, and United Methodist Church."[2] According to a survey in *Time*, mainline Protestants comprise about 18 percent of Americans. Even though attendance at mass has declined, the Roman Catholic Church remains strong, with an estimated 23.4 percent of Americans as members. Considerable increases are occurring, however, within Evangelical Protestantism. Churches within the Southern Baptist Convention, the Latter Day Saints, and the Assemblies of God and other fundamentalist and charismatic groups are growing steadily. Evangelical Christians presently comprise 25.9 percent of the American population.[3] Surprisingly, the Pentecostal Church has become the fifth largest denomination in the United States. Seeking patterns in church affiliation, the *Yearbook* differentiates denominations according to whether they are governed by a "top-down" or "bottom-up" organization, finding "bottom-up" organizations to be increasing and "top-down" churches decreasing. Moreover, many "bottom-up" members participate simultaneously in more than one church organization.

Christianity in the United States is becoming less white. Two largely African American denominations are in the top seven—the National Baptist Convention and the Church of God in Christ—and six are in the top fourteen. A startling result was reached by adding membership figures in predominantly African American denominations, estimates of African American members in predominantly white denominations, and the one million plus African American Muslims: "When these numbers were added together they came up to almost a hundred percent of the total African American population in the United States."⁴ Not only is religion in America changing color, but African Americans' high rate of participation in religious organizations continues to provide African Americans with a political base from which to advocate social change.

Is this rapidly changing religious picture reflected in popular film? I think that it is, but with some severe limitations. The "bottom-up" Christianity of liberation theology directly inspired *Romero* and *The Mission*. And African American religion is integral to many popular films, several of which will be discussed in the following chapters: *The Long Walk Home, Daughters of the Dust,* and *Jungle Fever. The Last Temptation of Christ* enraged fundamentalists because its representation of Jesus conflicted with evangelical Christians' picture of a Jesus with whom they endeavor to have a personal relationship.

In this chapter I will discuss two films that explore Christian fundamentalism. Since American religious life is changing, and all change is anxiety-provoking, as Alvin Toffler argued in *Future Shock*, one might hope that popular films would display and consider possible ramifications of actual religious changes. Both *The Rapture* and *The Handmaid's Tale*, however, contribute to secular liberals' fear of fundamentalist Christianity without suggesting viable or attractive religious alternatives.

The Handmaid's Tale (1990)

The Handmaid's Tale (henceforth *Handmaid*) was based on Margaret Atwood's 1985 novel by the same name.⁵ *Handmaid* is presented as fairy tale or science fiction—"Once upon a time . . ." it begins. But rather than imagining a future in which the arena of human life has expanded into intergalactic space, as another movie that began with those words, *Star Wars*, did, it pictures a severely constricted human future on earth, one barely worthy of the name "human."[6] Yet the film's stars, Natasha Richardson and Robert Duvall, called it a "love story" and a "romance."[7] Director Volker Schlöndorff said that the film portrays "a war of the sexes much more than any religious-political war." *Handmaid* also shows a racial war; the deportation of blacks and other minorities is a leitmotif woven through the narrative. "Our big mistake was teaching them to read," the Colonel says; "we won't do that again."[8]

As *Handmaid* begins, a civil war erupts; the husband of the heroine, Kate, is killed, and Kate and her daughter are kidnapped and separated as they attempt to cross the border. Kate becomes a Handmaid—essentially a "breeder"—for a high-ranking colonel in the Republic of Gilead. After undergoing grim training in docile behavior and submission in every detail of life, she goes to live with the Colonel and his wife. On ritual occasions, Kate lies in the lap of Serena Joy, the Colonel's wife, while having intercourse with the Colonel. If Kate does not become pregnant within a reasonable length of time, she will lose her job as Handmaid and be relegated to cleaning up nuclear waste in the wilds of Gilead. But the Colonel likes Kate; he initiates forbidden private evenings, bribing her with magazines and hand lotion to play cards and have conversations with him. He even takes her to a secret nightclub, where the illicit vices of the former bourgeois society flourish. But Kate does not become pregnant. Serena Joy, who longs for the child Kate will hand over to her at birth, arranges a tryst for Kate with Nick, the chauffeur, so that she can become pregnant. In brief, Kate and Nick fall in love, Nick reveals himself to be a member of the underground fighting to overthrow the Republic, and Kate soon becomes pregnant. Eventually, Kate kills the Colonel, and Nick manages her escape from Gilead. As the film ends, Kate waits alone for the birth of her child and for news from Nick, who remains in Gilead to continue his subversive work.

Handmaid's reviewers fell rather neatly into two camps. Some, like Ed Doerr, felt that as a shocking reminder of a real possibility, the film deserved "the highest praise and the largest audiences."[9] Others, like

Michael Calleri, dismissed the film, finding it "simpleminded," "unengaging," and obvious in its villainy.[10]

Both novel and film appeared when concerns relating to all the themes of book and film were prominent in American public life. The book was published in 1986, "during the heyday of militant right-wing Christian fundamentalism," before media scandals had temporarily damaged the credibility of such groups.[11] During the production of the film, the rise of the Moral Majority and the presidential candidacy of Pat Robertson contributed to religiously and politically liberal Americans' anxiety about the future of the United States. Militia groups were increasing in membership and activity. Race and gender issues were also prominent during the film's production and first-run circulation. On October 22, 1990, the year *Handmaid* was released, President Bush vetoed a civil rights bill that sought to reverse a recent Supreme Court ruling that weakened antidiscrimination laws on hiring and promoting minority people. The strains of a democracy that was not working well for many of its constituents also were apparent in 1990 in a jobless rate that was at a three-year high.

In *Handmaid*'s Republic of Gilead, a theocracy established by armed religious fundamentalists, order and control have replaced freedom of action and self-expression. As Aunt Lydia, the tyrant charged with socializing the Handmaids, says, "In the days of anarchy it was freedom *to*. Now you are being given freedom *from*." The low-level anarchy of everyday life in the old democracy has disappeared; everyone has a place and stays in it. In the Republic of Gilead, sex is not for pleasure and values are simple and clear: obedience and docility for 99 percent of the population; for the remaining 1 percent, intransigent commitment to eliminating "without mercy" any internal or external enemies. Abortion is punishable by death, as is "gender treachery," that is, homosexuality.

Atwood said in interviews that her book is not "an attack on Christianity," but it is, she acknowledges, a comment on Christianity's historical persecution of dissidents. Atwood said, "I didn't include anything that had not already happened, was not under way somewhere, or that we don't have the technology to do." She collected thoughts and clippings for four years before writing the novel.[12] Her points of reference included the Berlin Wall, slave-breeding practices, the effect of chemical pollutants on human reproduction, the outlawing of birth control and abortion in Romania, Nazi genocide, Iranian public executions and compulsory chador-wearing for women, censorship and book-burning, apartheid in South Africa, surrogate mother controversies, codes of puritanical religious behavior from seventeenth-century New England, and nineteenth-century Canadian executions. Needless to say, the list of past and present atrocities could easily be longer.

Curiously, although *Handmaid* focuses explicitly on gender relations in Gilead, social arrangements and relationships between men and women are so stabilized by coercion that any and all questioning or subversion of gender roles is punishable by disfigurement or death. This leaves little space for the constant and often rather pleasurable gender negotiations North Americans expect in movies, as gender socialization and expectations are tested, questioned, and their limits pressed.

Handmaid imagines a society in which gender socialization is managed through what Michel Foucault described as "weak power," that is, coercive force, as opposed to "strong power," the power to attract people to the attitudes and behavior that a society needs in order to perpetuate itself. For most North Americans, gender socialization is primarily a function of "strong power." Women and men are not forced to adopt the "gender practices" of masculinity or femininity; rather most of us are—more or less, but enough—attracted to the models of masculinity and femininity we are exposed to, as children in families of origin, in media culture, and in social institutions. Furthermore, these models of masculinity and femininity are, to some extent, negotiable; they can be resisted, subverted, if not without some economic and social punishment, usually without risking death.

Gender arrangements in *Handmaid*, then, are less interesting than either those of the social world of North Americans or those of film conventions. They articulate a society's "weak power," power to coerce. Only those at the top of the power pyramid can afford the luxury of negotiation, and even they are unsatisfied. The Colonel finds Gileadian sex impersonal; he wants to "get to know" Kate. He even grants her, on occasion, the option of resisting his sexual advances in order to make her more interesting for himself by enticing her to a personal relationship. Yet, inevitably, her lack of freedom to choose whether to be or not to be his sexual partner makes a personal relationship impossible—at best a farce; at worst it could result in her death. Everyone loses.

Despite *Handmaid*'s specific focus on gender arrangements, however, the character of Kate has been significantly changed in the transition from book to movie. Atwood has said she is happy with the movie version of her novel, calling it "a fairly faithful adaptation."[13] Yet Kate's complexity, strength, and survival skills are weakened in the film; she is presented as a woman who reacts rather than acts and who submits numbly to her oppression. The "strong and cunning Kate" of the novel has disappeared.[14] Moreover, instead of the novel's ambiguous ending, in which the reader never learns what happens to Kate as she undertakes to escape with Nick, the film delivers an ending that places her safely outside the reach of Gilead. Her escape is, however, engineered by Nick; Kate merely consents to it. All of these changes undermine the film's condemnation of repressive gender arrangements. It is difficult to understand Atwood's approval of *Handmaid*.

The novel *The Handmaid's Tale* was written by a feminist author interested in exploring the complex character of her protagonist. In the film, however, the development of Kate's character is ancillary to the creation of a film that will achieve box office success. The issue is finally, however, not whether a film presents a female protagonist who is as strong and self-reliant as the character in the book but how it addresses a female viewer. Is *Handmaid* a "women's film" in the sense that it enhances women's symbolic repertoire for imagining their own lives? Is it possible to read "against the grain" of the film, to offer a resistant or deconstructive reading? To explore this question, I will need to sketch briefly the development of feminist theory on the issue of women's spectatorship.

Early feminist theories of spectatorship theorized the female spectator as "other" in relation to the gaze of the normative male subject, as "repressed," "colonized," "alienated," or "masochistic."[15] More recent feminist film critics, like Christine Gledhill, have argued that films have no absolute power to force spectators to accept certain predetermined meanings. "Meanings are not fixed entities to be deployed at the will of a communicator."[16] Gledhill points to what she calls the "culinary fallacy" in the idea of the viewer as a "consumer" who swallows whole whatever meaning the filmmaker communicates. Rather, the production of meaning is a complex interaction "shaped by a range of economic, aesthetic, and ideological factors that often operate unconsciously and are unpredictable and difficult to control."[17] Spectators use the film's representations to negotiate (multiple) meanings, meanings that reflect and "allow space to the subjectivities, identities, and pleasures of (diverse) audiences." Gledhill proposes a model of spectatorship by which "meaning is neither imposed nor passively imbibed, but arises out of a struggle or negotiation between competing frames of reference, motivation, and experience."[18]

According to this model, meaning is negotiable, perspectival, informed by the spectator's social location, education, interests, and the myriad other influences that determine one's perspective. But the movie "text" a spectator considers must also provide the possibility of alternative readings. It must contain the clues that can ultimately demonstrate that such a reading is not purely imaginary rather than imaginative.

Consider *Handmaid*'s representation of relationships between women. In the Republic of Gilead female friendship is depicted as subversive, nourishing, and crucial to the sanity of the Handmaids. Yet women are also socialized to accept their oppression by other women— the Aunts, led by Aunt Lydia. And Handmaids are utterly dependent on the goodwill of the Wives: Wives and Handmaids can collaborate, as Serena Joy and Kate did, or a Wife can bring about the deportation or even death of a Handmaid. Female relationships, then, can also be dangerous, ultimately punishable by death.[19]

To interpret *Handmaid* as an examination of women's relationships would be to perform what Gledhill calls a resistant analysis, one that can be supported and documented by several scenes in the film, but one that ignores or denies some central aspects of the narrative. For female friendship in *Handmaid* never transcends the bounds of companionship in misery. It does not rescue Kate. Rather it is Nick, the romantic hero, who saves Kate, first from her childlessness and ultimately from the horrors of Gilead, though in the dystopia of the Republic of Gilead, there is no redemption. Survival itself takes the place of redemption, and survival, according to *Handmaid*, requires the *deus ex machina* of a romantic hero.

Women and minority moviegoers have often become expert in "reading against the grain." Lacking varied and complex images of themselves in media representations, they learn to find pleasure in isolated filmic "moments," often ignoring film conventions that submerge those brief moments in the same old representations. But educated idiosyncratic reinterpretations do not indicate how a film will be interpreted by a diverse popular audience. The "raw" reading—the unsystematic, impressionistic way that anyone sees a film for the first time—is by far the most important indication of the range of impressions and interpretations that a popular audience is likely to carry away from the film.[20] It is highly unlikely that a raw reading of *Handmaid* would propose that relationships among women was a central theme of the film.

Handmaid was produced and circulated at a time in North American society when political correctness was becoming a buzzword among those who sought to trivialize concern about the inequities of American society. A film like *Handmaid*, in which men have guns and women are either docile or dead, might potentially have helped people to consider a possible trajectory of racism and sexism. To do so, however, it would need to present a less passive protagonist; it would need to reject a happy ending in which a romantic hero—the "one good one" in a film in which men are flattened to gun-wielding oppressors—rescues the lovely damsel. It would need to represent gender neither as a "war of the sexes," as *Handmaid*'s director characterized the film, nor as a romance, as its stars described it. Even more fundamentally, sex would need to be represented with more complexity and nuance than *Handmaid*'s conventional conflict between conceptualizing sex as either reinforcing marriage and the nuclear family or, as the countercultural movement of the 1960s pictured it, as subversive and liberating. It would need, in short, to avoid the suggestion that the conventional gender relations of Hollywood popular film in which the romantic hero saves the "little woman" are an adequate answer to the gender horrors of Gilead.

Religion in *Handmaid* represents repression. Yet biblical fundamentalism does not genuinely seem to attract any of the characters, even those who, like the Colonel, stand to benefit most from it. Like gender arrangements, religion in Gilead does not possess "strong power" but has become the contentless tool of a political regime. Biblical imagery and language, actual hymn tunes with similar but different words, and pseudoreligious ritual are simply a framework for the state's agenda. Christian fundamentalism in *Handmaid* has few saving features: it is repressive, nightmare religion, full of hypocrisy. *Handmaid* envisions theocracy as inevitably and necessarily coercive, feeding North Americans' fears of a fundamentalist takeover of American public life. Although Kate and Nick long to escape from Gilead, it is not so clear what they want to escape to. "Freedom to" is apparently assumed to be self-explanatory to North American film audiences. The film I discuss next, *The Rapture*, focuses, not on a theocratic society, but on an individual's search for religious meaning.

The Rapture (1991)

Michael Tolkin, director of *The Rapture*, was a religion major at Middlebury College. He first conceived the film when he saw a bumper sticker that read: "Warning: in case of the rapture, this car will be unmanned."[21] Subsequently, he read of a woman killing her three children to send them to heaven. He made *The Rapture*, he said, to investigate the emotional state that might lead someone to such an act. Here, finally, is a film that presents religious belief and commitment as its explanatory thesis. Unfortunately, according to Tolkin, what religious commitment motivates is pathological compulsiveness and murder.

Tolkin wanted to make a film about religion motivating behavior, he said, because religion as motivation is usually ignored. In southern California, he said in an interview, anytime you turn on the television you can see three or four twenty-four-hour Christian television channels. "Within that world there are a lot of different views; there's not a monolithic evangelical movement." He continued:

> In the early eighties I was disturbed by how I saw Christians being portrayed in the media, on television, and in the movies and at the same time I also felt that the anguish of the fifty million people that call themselves "saved" and believe that "the rapture" is likely in their lifetime is nothing to be laughed at. The impulse to want some immediate relief without doing the hard work of organizing some mass political movement is . . . a powerful impulse that I think everybody has.[22]

Although the link between belief in the rapture and the woman who killed her children was entirely Tolkin's invention, he spoke in interviews repeatedly about the actual existence of fundamentalists. In doing so he ignored the fact that, as the *Christian Century* reviewer put it, of the alleged "forty million fundamentalists in the country who believe in the rapture, hardly any of them shoot their children."[23] Despite his expressed empathy with fundamentalists, Tolkin's implicit equation of fundamentalism with murderous insanity supports—and reinforces—a liberal fear.

Tolkin claimed that he sought to understand how a woman might be brought to murder her children by belief in the rapture. He expressed sympathy with "the anguish of the fifty million people in this country that call themselves 'saved' and believe that the rapture is likely in their lifetime." Yet the film's effect was to caricature fundamentalism. Only the reviewer quoted above questioned the unexamined connection between fundamentalism and child murder.

The Rapture begins as the protagonist, the as-yet-unconverted Sharon (Mimi Rogers), and her lover, Vic, pick up couples for group sex. Graphic sex scenes are apparently meant to show that sex-for-fun is meaningless; these scenes also reveal the film's primary commitment to box office success. Two members of an undisclosed fundamentalist religious group try to convince Sharon that belief in God is the answer to her unsatisfying life, but she does not convert until she "hits bottom" and attempts suicide. Surrounded by a light that reveals a shining pearl, Sharon believes.[24]

She marries one of her lovers and they, with their daughter, become a happy and very religious family. Instead of going to church, they attend meetings in a private home in which a young Black boy tells his congregation what God discloses to him. After her husband is murdered by an alcoholic he has fired, Sharon becomes convinced that she has been called to the Southwest desert to await reunion with him in the coming rapture. She departs with her young daughter, who also longs for reunion with "Deddy." They camp in the desert, stealing food once her money is spent, and only the kindly attention of a state patrolman keeps them from freezing and starving. When the child begs again and again to go to heaven now, Sharon shoots her, determined to shoot herself immediately after. But she cannot. She is arrested for the murder of her child. While she is in jail, the rapture occurs, complete with the crumbling of prison bars and the four horsemen of the apocalypse. As Sharon and the kindly highway patrolman escape on his motorcycle, they encounter the wraith of her daughter, who begs Sharon to believe in a loving God and accept admission to heaven. By now, however, Sharon can no longer believe in a God who failed her so utterly, a God for whom she murdered her daughter. She declines, and the film ends, leaving Sharon apparently alone "for all eternity."

The film was timely. As Tolkin wrote *The Rapture*, the popularity of the television evangelist Jerry Falwell was high. Falwell described the rapture—as if elaborating the bumper sticker that prompted the film: "You'll be riding along in an automobile . . . When the trumpet sounds you and the other born-again believers in that automobile will be instantly caught away—you will disappear, leaving behind only your clothes." Falwell's associate Tim LeHaye elaborated: "There will be airplane, bus, and train wrecks throughout the world. Who can imagine the chaos on the freeways when automobile drivers are snatched out of their cars?"[25]

The film's star, Mimi Rogers, who is a member of the Church of Scientology, said in an interview: "On a religious level I never really took the script literally. [But] it spoke very strongly to some idea of spiritual nature as being very important to quality existence." If so, the film never managed to represent spirituality effectively. The use of lighting, especially backlighting Sharon's "big hair," was the film's primary device for signalling this spirituality. A cynic might also observe that the most noticeable immediate result of Sharon's conversion is that her skirts drop about a foot and a half, from mini to midi. Sharon's working definition of "real" appears toward the beginning of the film when she sneers to someone who describes the dream of the pearl: "If everybody's getting this dream, how come it isn't on the news?" By the end, and to signal that it really *is* real, Sharon sees the rapture on television from her jail cell.

The religious problem posed by *The Rapture* is "meaninglessness." At the beginning of the film, as a directory assistance telephone operator, Sharon does not have meaningful work, and kinky sex has not proved redemptive.[26] Sharon talks in clichés of meaninglessness: "Everything just seems so empty. I need a new direction in my life." Her lover's response is also stereotypical: "You're depressed . . . see a therapist." Although meaninglessness has been continuously cited as a root problem of modern life at least since it was named by the existentialist philosophers of the mid-twentieth century, the particular configurations of the problem change with historical social circumstances, and *The Rapture* reflects a particular form of ennui.

In 1991, the year the film was released, an article in *Time*, "Why Is America in a Blue Funk?," explored the "Is this all there is?" syndrome. The author, Charles Krauthammer, cited "low consumer confidence" as evidence of a collective depression indicative of a "loss of faith, a statistical measure of national anxiety." Krauthammer argued that pessimism flourished despite the notable triumphs of 1991: victory in the Persian Gulf and the demise of the Soviet Empire. He offers no explanation for the phenomenon except a very mild recession and a national sense of being "a minute past our finest hour."[27]

In *The Rapture*, meaninglessness is construed as an individual problem, to be addressed by an individual solution. Images of isolation are featured throughout the film, from the first scene in which the heads of telephone operators appear above the partitions of the cubbyholes in which they supply information to other disembodied voices, to the final scene in which Sharon remains alone in a bleak landscape. Sharon's conversion is individual, mediated not by other people, as most religious conversions are, but by a light surrounding her, which turns from red to gold. Later, her religious community declines to accompany her to the desert: "We weren't invited." Sharon is a religious loner.

What kind of Christianity does *The Rapture* endeavor to represent? That is never clear in the film. In the decade prior to 1991, new religious movements frequently drew public attention. It was a decade that remembered Jonestown, a decade that would culminate in Waco and the Branch Davidians. As mentioned earlier in this chapter, it was also a time when membership was on the decline in mainstream Protestant churches. Like churches with "bottom-up" organizations, many new religious movements showed dramatic growth.

Was the group to which Sharon was converted a New Age group? Clearly it was a fundamentalist group, but with unscriptural innovations, like the converting dream of "the pearl." It was also a group with eschatological and apocalyptic beliefs. Sharon's group is difficult to

classify, at least partly, I suspect, because Tolkin invented it on the basis
of his partial knowledge of various southern California groups who believe in the rapture. In any case, while it is not important to identify or
classify Sharon's religious organization, it is important to place *The
Rapture* in the context of a popular interest in apocalyptic religious
groups.

The amount of journalism on the topic of new religious movements
is evidence of interest, both from those who consider joining or have
already joined such a group, and from outsiders who are fascinated by
their different beliefs and lifestyles. Most articles on the subject in religious periodicals are aimed at mainstream Christians who either are
attracted to or fear the new religions.

The label "New Age" refers to a very diverse spiritual movement
whose adherents believe that every human being and the cosmos itself
has a spiritual essence; that there are psychic phenomena that reveal the
spiritual essence; that the spiritual essence is submerged in most people
by their immersion in the material and social world, but that by awakening, becoming aware of, and cultivating, one's spiritual essence, it
can be strengthened and made the center of one's daily life. They believe
that the purpose of existence, and the ultimate goal of the human race,
is to become integrated into the spiritual world. In short, New Age religions teach that "things don't have to be the way they are."[28]

New Age groups also protest and seek to change the dehumanizing
effects of scientific reductionism; the wasting effect of secularism and
materialism; the rape of the earth and its resources; the search for status, fame, and wealth; and the arrogant isolationism of North America
from hunger, disease, and war.[29]

Most countercultural religious groups offer the assurance of salvation
and the attraction of a simple doctrine that is not overlaid by centuries
of dispute. They claim to possess superior knowledge, and they seldom
have a constricting institutional structure. Not least, most of the new
religious movements require a degree of fervor and discipline not characteristic of mainstream churches. Membership cannot be simply
added to one's life, but must become the governing principle of life and
action. While the demand for greater rigor might not immediately seem
to be an attraction, there is every evidence that it does attract members.

In a very different cultural context, the history of early Christianity is compelling evidence that a demanding, secret, persecuted religion can flourish.

Reviewers differed widely in their responses to *The Rapture*. Most reviewers had difficulty assessing the film's use of religion. Lisa Kennedy wrote, "*The Rapture* is an interesting film because the protagonist is a woman. Historically, unless you go way back, women are not the ones battling with God." She adds, "I think some people have a difficult time with the film because it deals with faith and belief, and those are often treated as very lowbrow desires."[30] A *Variety* reviewer wrote: "An utterly undistinguished personality, Sharon experiences crises of conscience and moral struggles worthy of the most hallowed biblical figures."[31] J. Hoberman apparently saw the same thing, but put it differently; Sharon, he writes, "shape-shifts from smile-button Magdalen, to female Abraham, to existential Job-ette."[32]

But most reviewers were dismissive or trivializing. Stating that "the film's budget does not begin to approach what would have been needed for a Hollywood-worthy climax," Janet Maslin sneered at the halo effects around Mimi Rogers in the latter part of the film. Caryn James wrote, "What does a saved woman wear to the Apocalypse? The final message of *The Rapture* [is that] come the Apocalypse, there will be a lot of backlighting and all the women will wear Laura Ashley knockoffs." *The Rapture* is "the story of a woman who trades in sex for God. [The film] gets to have its sex and condemn it too." It "purports to be deep but is as cynical and shallow as movies get."[33]

Directly contradicting the director's stated intention, a few reviewers called *The Rapture* a misrepresentation of fundamentalism by a director with an ax to grind. Marilynne Mason observed that Tolkin relies on a Marxist caricature of religion as an opiate and goes on to demonstrate its disastrous effects. "Tolkin seems to want to reject religion but keep a mean-spirited deity around to despise."[34] Sharon never doubts the unreconstructed God of her religious teachings—only his goodness.

Other reviewers found *The Rapture* merely theologically incoherent. Robert Denerstein said that it is "an extremely confused film, with a very immature reading of theological issues."[35] A *Rolling Stone* reviewer agreed: "Tolkin is trying to be the new Ingmar Bergman and question the existence of God, but his special effects and visions of the apocalypse are tacky and muddled. The great Swedish director knows the difference between a movie and a sermon; Tolkin does not."[36] "In statements and interviews, Tolkin has cited his own religious befuddlement—as though it weren't perfectly evident on the screen."[37]

However, not all reviewers agreed on the inadequacy of *The Rapture*'s representation of religion. Janet Maslin said that it is "a fierce frightening exploration of religious faith pushed to the breaking point, [with] a tough, thoughtful ending that will not soon be forgotten." Despite her criticisms, Maslin assessed *The Rapture* as "a stark, daringly original film that viscerally demonstrates the courage of its convictions."[38]

Maslin referred to "the brazenness of [Tolkin's] having made a mainstream film about religious faith."[39] A *Newsweek* reviewer also commented on a film taboo on religious topics:

> If movies were all we had to judge from, one might never suspect the enormous resurgence of religious faith in this country. The one thing that moviegoers rarely encounter on screen is much talk of God, discussion of religious identity, any whiff of theology. This—certainly not sex—may be the last cinema taboo. . . . *The Rapture* is neither an exploitation movie, an exposé, a horror film nor a psychological portrait of a delusional woman. It is a genre unto itself—call it theological film noir.

"Love this movie or hate it," he concluded, "you haven't seen anything like it."[40] However, when most film reviewers got over the embarrassment of being forced to talk about religion, they often judged it simply a poor film.

However, to my knowledge, no one protested the film, even though it represents religious belief as deluded and dangerous. This may be because the film did not focus on a sacred figure, as did *The Last Temptation of Christ*, or it may be that New Age groups do not have an umbrella organization that could have planned protests.

I have focused in this chapter on what Hollywood thinks of the religious right. What do conservative Christians presently like to see at the movies? In 1994 the Christian Film and Television Commission announced its awards for the best films in the categories of "family picture" and "mature audiences." The best family picture was Walt Disney's *Homeward Bound: The Incredible Journey*, "a movie starring two dogs and a cat." The best film for mature audiences was *The Remains of the Day*. *The Age of Innocence* and *Much Ado About Nothing* were runners-up. The Commission denounced *Mrs. Doubtfire*; it was unacceptable because it "flouts the admonition in Deuteronomy 22.5 that men not wear women's clothes."[41]

If the Christian Film and Television Commission accurately represents the Christian right, its approval and disapproval reveal a lack of recognition of the role of popular film in American public life. The Commission awarded films that avoided offense—"nice" movies—rather than films that represent and explore the pressing problems of society. In other words, the Commission subscribes to the film industry's characterization of its product as "entertainment," ignoring popular films' ability to represent conflicts of values for consideration and negotiation.

In turn, the recent treatments of religious fundamentalism—Christian, Muslim (*Not Without My Daughter*), and Jewish (*The Chosen*)—vary in their examinations of committed countercultural religious belief. *The Chosen* gives the most nuanced account, while the other films misrepresent more than they describe. The sensationalist films I have discussed in this chapter cater to, and perhaps augment, a liberal alarm about the political and social power of large conservative religious groups that can—and do—speak and act together in the public sphere. As long as thoughtful fundamentalists and evangelical Christians consider only the most superficial features of box office films, they will not be able to use popular films to focus the issues and problems of American public life. As long as popular films continue to give a distorted picture of fundamentalism, featuring its lunatic fringe because to do so is good box office, secular and liberal fears of fundamentalism will be strengthened at the expense of public discussion and negotiation of values. Unless they have some knowledge or experience of conservative Christians, movie audiences are not likely to recognize that representing religious commitment solely as madness and motivation for murder is a massive misrepresentation of the function of conservative religious belief in the lives of forty to fifty million Americans.

Liberal Christians are often more critical of fundamentalist Christianity than are secular people, who typically lump all forms of Christianity together as one of the problems, if not the major problem, of American society. I find that, in their eagerness to dissociate themselves from their fundamentalist co-religionists, liberal Christians are often more concerned with ingratiating themselves with their secular colleagues and friends than with constructing an alternative Christian position on matters of public concern. When that occurs, liberal religious people cede the territory and the label of "Christian" to rightists, who make loud use of it to recruit broad popular support.

It is, in fact, exceedingly difficult for Christians who believe in the literal meaning of the King James Version of the Bible to talk with Christians who do not accept prooftexts, and who consider the Bible to be always in need of careful and contextual interpretation. But in relinquishing "Christian" as a description of their concerns and loyalties, liberal Christians permit the category to become monolithic in public usage. Popular film reflects—and supports—the constriction of "Christian" to mean conservative, countercultural Christianity.

Liberal Christians who find the religious right dangerously united on some crucial issues must define thoughtful positions on the same issues and thus demonstrate that various approaches are consonant with Christian belief and practice. In my view, it is important to press on the public agenda a Christianity that holds as its core a gospel of commitment to social and institutional change on behalf of those who are impoverished, marginalized, and oppressed. This gospel stands in dramatic contrast to a gospel of the "straight and narrow way" that insists on adherence to particular social and sexual arrangements and behaviors. To date, conservative Christians have had a higher profile in pressing their concerns in the name of their religious commitment than have liberal Christians. It would, of course, be nice to see the complexity of religious commitments modeled on the big screen. But would it be box office?

Race, Gender, Sexuality,
and Class in Popular Film

No one would contest the statement that gender roles and expectations have been a major public and private preoccupation of the past decade. Focused in public debate by the 1991 Clarence Thomas Supreme Court confirmation hearings, struggles over gender occupied most Americans in the home as well as in the media, at their place of work, and in their religious organizations. But gender arrangements are always thoroughly and intimately intertwined with race and class. As bell hooks, Elizabeth Spelman, and others have recently shown, examinations of gender that omit race and class are fatally distorted. This understanding emerged only after some pioneering women of color, such as the late Audre Lorde, pointed out that excluding race from gender analysis effectively assumed that educated and privileged white women's perspectives are universally normative.

It is impossible to speak of everything at once, but it is always erroneous to think separately about race, gender, and class. In the face of this dilemma, I will organize my discussion around several films that vividly represent the interconnection. In Part I, I discussed issues of race, gender, and class as they arose in films' treatments of religion; in Part II, I will focus on films that highlight issues of race, class, and gender, but my attention will also be on the ways in which religion is either explicitly present, or conspicuously omitted—excluded from the frame—in these films.

6

"Older, Wiser, Stronger":
Representation and
Self-Representation

The Long Walk Home
Daughters of the Dust

The Long Walk Home and *Daughters of the Dust*, two films that represent aspects of the history of African American experience in the United States, cannot be adequately appreciated without first surveying the long and painful history of African Americans' (mis)representation in mainstream Hollywood films. Michael Winston has demonstrated that "media images of Black people were continually reconstructed from previous media representations: first print, then radio, film and television." From the 1920s forward there was also a "thriving, if limited (in distribution) Black film industry, which produced films about, by, and for blacks. But . . . general audiences never saw these films."[2] According to Jacqueline Bobo, "by 1942 there were 430 Black movie theaters (ninety percent White-owned or managed) in thirty-one states, and about two hundred more White theaters with Black sections. By 1943, Blacks were spending about $150 million annually on movies."[3] Nevertheless, Hollywood films ignored Black audiences, many of whom learned to interpret popular films according to their own interests.[4]

Marlon Riggs's 1987 documentary film *Ethnic Notions: Black People in White Minds* discusses the consistent stereotyping of Black people as "loyal toms, carefree Sambos, faithful Mammies, grinning coons, savage brutes, or pickaninnies."[5] These images of African Americans, repetitiously placed before our eyes in the popular medium of film, are implanted deep in the psyches of most Americans, of all colors and ethnic groups. They have contributed substantially, Riggs's film argues, to the oppressive social and psychological conditions against which African Americans continue to struggle. *Ethnic Notions* concludes, "There is nothing wrong with dancing, singing, using your whole body as an instrument. It's lack of serious dramatic presentations and exclusive stereotypes that's the problem."[6]

Indeed, as James Monaco has observed, "In nations in which film is dominant, the cinema helps to define what is permissible culturally; it is the shared experience of a society." Its repetitiously reinforced role models are so psychologically powerful that "it is difficult for people even to conceive, much less act out, roles for which no models are provided."[7] Bell hooks states, "Producing images of blacks in a racist context is [always] politically charged."[8]

According to Miriam Hansen, the racism of some of the earliest American films, such as *Birth of a Nation* (1915), illustrates a major dynamic of American public culture in the twentieth century. Pejorative images of the racial other encouraged immigrant white ethnic groups to identify with white "melting-pot" culture. The "comic display of class, ethnic, and racial stereotypes" provided a "negative foil for a new, ostensibly middle-class identity."[9]

Racial stereotypes of African Americans have continued to play a role in American culture. Extraordinarily sensitive to, and reflective of, popular attitudes, films have mirrored racism in society with what Tom O'Brien has called "a sad rhythm."[10] In the late 1940s, in the liberal mood following the end of the Second World War, a spate of films dealt with racial tensions more or less openly, but in the McCarthy era of the 1950s, to be a real American was to be a White racist. As depicted in *The Long Walk Home*, civil rights workers were often thought of as communists, and communists as evil. It was not until the late 1960s that African Americans began to play nonstereotypical roles, and the

1970s finally saw some serious and important films about African American history and life, like the made-for-television films, *The Autobiography of Miss Jane Pittman* (1974) and *Roots* (1975).

In the early 1980s, African American issues in films were largely on the back burner.[11] Although other racial and ethnic groups were receiving attention in film, only *Places in the Heart* (1984) dealt specifically and centrally with White racism. In the late 1980s, however, the number of films that were serious treatments of racial issues increased, as did the on-screen representation of African Americans. Director Spike Lee's first films came out, and Black actors such as James Earl Jones, Danny Glover, Morgan Freeman, and Denzel Washington played a variety of serious dramatic roles in mainstream cinema. *Do the Right Thing* (1989) and *Mississippi Burning* (1988) were perhaps the most important examples of films that forefronted issues of race and justice in America.[12]

The two films I discuss in this chapter illustrate vividly the difference between having radical subject matter and being a radical film. The 1960s civil rights movement was a radical moment in American public life, but *The Long Walk Home*, in the 1990 context of racial and gender backlash, represented that radical movement in a way, I will argue, that maintained the status quo of 1990s social conservativism.[13] By contrast, *Daughters of the Dust*, which does not treat a radical topic, is nevertheless a radical film.

These two films were released in 1990 and 1992, respectively, and it is within the social discourse of those years that they must be considered. In 1990, President Bush vetoed a proposed civil rights bill which sought to reverse a recent Supreme Court ruling weakening antidiscrimination laws on hiring and promoting. The jobless rate continued to rise.[14] And in 1991, gender and race were publicly debated when African American Anita Hill, a University of Oklahoma law professor at the time, accused African American Justice Clarence Thomas of sexual harassment in his nationally televised Supreme Court confirmation battle. Racial incidents on city streets, in schools and college campuses were common. The years from 1990 to 1992 are a period in which public anxiety about issues of race, gender, and class can be documented easily.

The Long Walk Home (1990)

The Long Walk Home (hereafter *Long Walk*), directed by Richard Pearce, was a very modest box office and critical success. Its topic is historical—the 1955 bus boycott in Montgomery, Alabama, that was a decisive event in the civil rights movement. It focuses on the relationship of two women, Odessa Cotter (Whoopi Goldberg), a Black maid, and Miriam Thompson (Sissy Spacek), her White employer. Miriam is gradually drawn into sympathy with civil rights activists through Odessa's struggle to maintain both her job and her integrity. Miriam eventually defies her husband to participate in the car pool which drove Blacks who boycotted city buses to and from work.[15]

Critical reception of the film was mixed. Janet Maslin wrote that *Long Walk* "avoids shrillness and keeps its potential for preachiness more or less at bay." But Louis Menand wrote, "It's hard to give dramatic resonance to a conflict in which history, justice, and high moral style are all on one side, and the other side has nothing going for it but bigotry and ignorance." He called the film "a predictable and unambitious movie," held together only by Goldberg's performance. He blames the director for what he perceives as a reverse stereotype at work in the film: "the whites run the danger of seeming too dense; the blacks run the danger of seeming too dignified."[16]

My discussion of *Long Walk* will explore—and question—the film's representation of a personal story within the context of a larger social story. Attention to several aspects of the actual 1950s civil rights movement, the situation of Black women domestic workers, and the form of Christianity that took shape in the civil rights movement, will reveal film conventions at work in *Long Walk*. I will argue that film conventions, not history or memory, directed choices made in the screening of the personal story and the social story. As I stated in an earlier chapter, realist films need not reflect historical reality, but when they do not do so, we can often spot film conventions at work.

The bus boycott in Montgomery, Alabama, began with the December 1, 1955, arrest of Rosa Parks, a Black woman who was charged with violating the Alabama bus segregation laws. The boycott ended on December 20, 1956, but, as *Long Walk* notes, the incident was only the beginning of the struggle for civil rights. Although Martin Luther King, Jr. continued to insist that demonstrations by Blacks and civil rights workers should be nonviolent, shootings and bombings of Black churches and Black leaders' homes by White Citizens' Councils continued and increased in Montgomery and other parts of the South.[17]

The boycott, organized by the Montgomery Improvement Association, was crucial to the nascent civil rights movement. The Association demanded the elimination of reserved seating for Whites, and the hiring of Black bus drivers. "Whites Only" signs had been removed from buses twenty years before in Montgomery, but Alabama law still stipulated that a "Whites Only" section be reserved in the front of the bus. The boycott demanded that seating for Whites begin from the front; for Blacks, seating would begin from the back; and that the reserved section, which required Blacks to stand if the Black section was full, even if the White section had empty seats, be eliminated.

The boycott was 98 percent effective. During the year of the boycott, between thirty and forty-thousand fares were denied to the bus company every day. By the first week of 1956, bus companies faced imminent bankruptcy; emergency fare increases of 50 percent failed to solve the problem, and the Montgomery City Lines still lost about $3,200 a day. Since the Montgomery police commissioner threatened to arrest any taxi driver who charged less than the minimum fare, the car pool initiated by Martin Luther King was crucial to maintain the boycott. By the beginning of 1956, there were over three hundred and fifty cars participating daily in the pool. It is this historical situation on which *Long Walk* is based.

Elizabeth Clark-Lewis describes another aspect of the historical situation represented in *Long Walk*. Domestic labor, Clark-Lewis writes, was a site of oppression for Black women since they lacked other opportunities. Moreover, a direct correlation existed between White women's increased employment outside the home and Black women's domestic labor. As White women left their homes for salaried work, they increasingly needed to hire domestic labor. Clark-Lewis found that as job opportunities for white women expanded during the first three decades of the twentieth century, the proportion of black women in household service increased by 43 percent.[18] Her study demonstrates, however, that Black women's domestic labor was not only oppressive; Black women also struggled together to exercise a measure of creativity and dignity. She describes the transformation of domestic service in 1940s Washington, D.C., from live-in to commuting day work. "Black women resisted the personal constraints of live-in service and participated in 'penny-savers' clubs in order to accumulate the necessary money for maintaining their own households." They also rejected the maid's uniforms—symbolic of servant status—their employers supplied. They brought their own work clothes, which they carried to work in "freedom bags—badges of self-respect among Black women domestics."[19] They also took pride in their ability to work efficiently without being monitored.

Although *Long Walk* presents some moments in which Odessa exhibits initiative, pride, and wisdom in the course of her domestic labor, she is largely passive in Miriam's home. The film emphasizes Odessa's oppression in order to make Miriam's transformation plausible. The film minimizes Odessa's struggle to maintain her job and her integrity.[20] She finds the bus boycott little more than a nuisance until Miriam takes an interest in her situation. Empowered by her White employer's help, she understands the importance of the communal action.

In *Long Walk*, Sissy Spacek is billed above Whoopi Goldberg. Narrated by Miriam's seven-year-old daughter, Mary Catherine, *Long Walk* is the White woman's story. The opening scene establishes the focus of the film to be Miriam's change of heart about the civil rights movement: Mary Catherine says, "There's always something extraordinary about someone who changes and then changes those around her." Miriam's consciousness-raising is initiated by Odessa's eviction from the local park while she is taking care of Miriam's children. "It's not like she was paradin' her *own* children around the park, for heaven's sake!" she declares indignantly. By the end of the film, musing over Odessa's tender care for Miriam's sick daughter, Miriam has developed the ability to wonder aloud, "Would I have done that for your daughter?"

But why is it the White woman's story? When African Americans have been so consistently misrepresented in mainstream Hollywood film, should not the opportunity be taken to show *their* perspectives, their subjective experience, and their struggles during the civil rights movement? Even if it is easier for White Americans to identify with the

White protagonist's increasing self-knowledge and recognition of the demands of justice, why—in 1990—yet another film for White Americans? Whoopi Goldberg and director Richard Pearce clashed over precisely this issue when Goldberg suggested that a film about the civil rights movement should be a story about Blacks.[21]

Long Walk is not alone among feature films about important episodes in African and African American history that somehow, on screen, become White people's stories.[22] A similar question—whose film *is* it?—could be asked, for example, about *A Dry White Season* (1989). The director, Euzhan Palcy, was the first Black woman to direct a film for a major Hollywood studio.[23] Her film treats the oppression and persecution of black people in South Africa under apartheid in the 1970s. Palcy said in an interview: "I knew that Hollywood would not do a film about black people unless the main character was a white man."[24] Moreover, in *A Dry White Season*, the White family is repeatedly shown relating to one another intensely, while Black people confer only in the presence of the White man.

The choice of whose film it is—whose story is told—seems to have had more to do with Hollywood conventions and box office aspirations than with either Black history or the director's politics. Hollywood producers assume that to succeed financially, movies must be addressed to White middle-class Americans.

Long Walk is the story of a White woman's political transformation, but it is also about friendship between women of different races and classes. Odessa and Miriam share some common conditions as women. Their work, influence, and authority are confined to the home; the threat or actuality of physical force can be used to control them; and both are constrained economically, though in different ways. When Miriam claims that running the home is her work, her husband Norman replies, "Aren't you forgetting who pays the bills around here?" Miriam works for Norman as Odessa works for Miriam.

Despite their common dependent status as women, however, there are some enormous differences between Odessa's and Miriam's situations—differences of race, class, and economic security. Miriam and her friends are simultaneously disadvantaged in relation to White men and oppressors in relation to Black women.

Despite Odessa's dignity, strength, and courage, her character never departs from a stereotypical representation of African Americans, the Mammy. This is established at the beginning of the film as the narrator, Mary Catherine, says of Odessa, "She was the first woman to rock me to sleep." Appreciation and even affection for African Americans are not incompatible with stereotyping them. *Long Walk* continues, rather than reverses, a long filmic tradition. Bell hooks comments in another context, "Even when representations of Black women were present in film, our bodies and being were there to serve—to enhance and maintain White womanhood as object of the phallocentric gaze."[25]

Long Walk demonstrates in detail the operation of White privilege and Black oppression, from asymmetrical first-naming to the effects of money, power, and a range of choices—or the lack thereof. The film also reveals, if largely implicitly, Odessa's particular oppression as an African American *and* as a woman. She serves in Miriam Thompson's home not only because she is Black, but also because she is a woman. But, largely because of Whoopi Goldberg's performance, Odessa is not solely a victim. Her courage and dignity are evident throughout.

Long Walk minimizes Miriam's role as Odessa's oppressor partly by representing Miriam as more constrained *in her home* than Odessa is in hers. Early in the film, Miriam identifies herself as "Mrs. Norman Thompson." Berating her for driving Odessa to work, Miriam's husband states the previously unspoken rule of the household: "I know you don't keep up on things. . . . Ask me; I know what's best." In Odessa's home, however, her work is appreciated, her wishes consulted, and her physical comfort sought. Miriam's exclusion from the public meetings in which White men debated about civil rights, and her oppression within the home combine to heighten her heroism in eventually taking a public stand with African Americans. Odessa's oppression is obvious and straightforward; Miriam's must be more subtly demonstrated.

Hollywood films are not unique in overlooking Black women as heroes of their own stories.[26] The work of White feminists has, until recently, also largely ignored racial differences among women. Feminist film theory has usually privileged sexual difference, actively suppressing recognition of race, and "reenacting and mirroring the erasure of Black womanhood that occurs in films."[27] Indeed, scholarship has generally neglected women of color. Evelyn Brooks Higginbotham identifies what she calls "the sound of silence" as the failure of historical scholarship "to recognize Black women's history not only as a field . . . but as an integral part of Afro-American, American, and women's history."[28] In fact, she writes, a double silencing of African American women has occurred: "Afro-American history has failed to address gender issues adequately, while women's history has similarly failed to address questions of race."[29] By focusing on the White woman, *Long Walk* does little to redress the lack of public attention to Black women.

The director's intention seems to have been to show that in the intimacy of Miriam's home, two women of vastly different social and economic circumstances could come to understand and identify with one another, overcoming all social and institutional injustice by simple friendship. By contrast, the White men—Miriam's husband and his brother—speak racist cliches and attend hate-filled meetings of the White Citizens' Committee. Focusing attention on differences in the quality of the women's relationships and the men's relationships, however, means that inequalities of race, ethnicity, and economic means between Odessa and Miriam are ignored. Although the film convention that places the White woman on screen as a foil for the White hero is subverted, the suggestion that other differences can be easily swept away by friendship between women is oversimplified and misleading. Institutional racism and economic inequity do not dissolve when individuals get to know one another.

Let us consider *Long Walk*'s representation of religion. By showing church meetings in which civil rights strategies were communicated, the film underscores religion's role in the struggle for civil rights, a frequently overlooked aspect of the early civil rights movement. For those who participated in the movement, civil rights was often a *religious* issue. As Martin Luther King, Jr., a Baptist minister, said in a sermon:

> My friends, I want it to be known that we are going to work with grim and bold determination to gain justice on the buses in this city. And we are not wrong. We are not wrong in what we are doing. If we are wrong, the Supreme Court of this nation is wrong. If we are wrong, almighty God is wrong.[30]

A new kind of theology emerged from the civil rights movement of the 1950s and the Black power movement of the 1960s. Even before it was named Black theology, many Black ministers and congregations understood social justice to lie at the center of the Christian gospel.

Black theology originated in reflection on the Black struggle for justice and liberation in American society. Black theology disputed White Christians' frequent claim that religion and politics do not mix; it also repudiated most White Christians' failure to speak out for racial integration, or their advocacy of very gradual integration. James Cone, author of the first book on black theology, *Black Theology and Black Power*, wrote: "Christian theology is a theology of liberation. It is a . . . study of the being of God in the world in the light of the existential situation of an oppressed community, relating the forces of liberation to the essence of the gospel, which is Jesus Christ."[31]

In addition to showing the civil rights movement as an essentially religious struggle, *Long Walk* depicts the daily support of the church community for civil rights activism. Taylor Branch describes the rhythm of religion and activism that characterized the bus boycott:

> As for the boycotters themselves, the religious fervor they went to bed with at night always congealed by the next morning into cold practicality as they faced rainstorms, mechanical breakdowns, stranded relatives, and complicated relays in getting from home to job without being late or getting fired, or getting into an argument with the employer, then getting home again, perhaps having to find a way to and from the grocery store, and cooking and eating supper, dealing with children and housework, then going back out into the night for a mass meeting [at the church], and finally home again, recharged by . . . the inspiration of King, and then at last some weary but contented sleep before the aching chill of dawn started the cycle all over again.[32]

Two kinds of Christianity that were numerically significant at the time in Montgomery, Alabama, however, are not represented in *Long Walk*. First, White people in the film show no trace of religious conviction or motivation, continuing a recent Hollywood trend of associating communal religion primarily with minority women and men. White people's religion neither supported nor challenged their racism, according to *Long Walk*. When Miriam changed her views, she did not do so for religious reasons. The film's unhistorical exclusion of White Christianity conceals the opposing stands White churches actually took on civil rights. Some White churches actively supported racism: Pat Robertson and Jerry Falwell were members of the openly racist

White Citizens' Council. Others encouraged their members to support, to work for, and even, in some cases, to die for racial justice.[33]

Secondly, there were Black preachers in Montgomery who were alarmed by King's call to political action, choosing to emphasize instead Whites' and Blacks' common religious values and commitments. *Long Walk* simplifies and condenses Black Christianity, representing unanimity rather than any division or conflict among the Black church leaders. Although narrative film often must simplify historical complexity for a film's coherence and power, the assumptions that govern its simplifications should be noticed.

Long Walk's representation of an important historical moment in the United States is flawed by its treatment of gender, race, and religion. I turn now to a film about an African American community that was written and directed by a Black woman.

Daughters of the Dust (1992)

Daughters of the Dust (henceforth *Daughters*) was produced, written, and directed by an African American woman, Julie Dash.[34] *Daughters*, like *Romero* and *Paris Is Burning*, which will be discussed in chapter 8, are anomalous among the films discussed in this book in that they were not financed by a Hollywood studio. I examine *Daughters* because it provides an instructive contrast with Hollywood films. By deliberately overturning some Hollywood film conventions, *Daughters* also helps make those conventions apparent in other films.

Yet Dash paid a price for her unconventional content and treatment. It took Dash about a decade to raise funds for the film, and even after it was made she had difficulty finding a distributor. She began with nothing but a small grant from the National Endowment for the Arts. Later, when she was already on location in Georgia, she got small grants from other foundations. Although she received no Hollywood studio funding for *Daughters*, Dash is optimistic about Hollywood's increasing interest in Black filmmakers: "We need films financed by Hollywood. We deserve them, and it's long overdue. Filmmaking is a business venture. We have stories to be told, and studios have money to be made."[35]

Daughters, which takes place at the turn of the twentieth century, is part of a four-film series. An earlier short film, *Illusions* (1982, Best Film of the Decade from the Black Filmmakers Foundation), is set in the 1940s; and Dash plans to make two more films, one that takes place in the 1960s and one set in the near future, in the year 2000.

While Dash was studying film at UCLA, she was a member of a radical group of Black filmmakers who thought of film as a means of political struggle, continuing and extending the racial struggles of the 1960s. They wrote a declaration of independence (from Hollywood), proposed an alternative curriculum for the UCLA film school, and held off-campus study groups to discuss film politics and techniques. Protesting the preoccupations and politics of Hollywood, their declaration of independence included the following tenets:

1. Accountability to the community takes precedence over training for an industry that maligns and exploits, trivializes and invisibilizes Black people.
2. It is the destiny of our people that concerns us, not self-indulgent assignments about neurotic preoccupations.
3. Our task is to reconstruct cultural memory, not slavishly to imitate White models.
4. Students should have access to world film culture—African, Asian, Latin American cinema—in addition to Hitchcock, Ford, and Renoir.[36]

Dash's *Daughters* evolved in conversation with other Black filmmakers in the movement. Its themes are those that the group identified and used repeatedly to produce films that support the Black community. The values of Black community and family are affirmed and women are presented as strong leaders and initiators. In addition, spirituality and religion are depicted as central to everyday life, and Black history is interpreted by Black people.

Daughters explores the complex relationship of history and myth, showing their inevitable interweaving in stories about the past. Although *Daughters* includes history as well as myth, it does not employ a convention I have pointed out in several other films, the assertion in the opening credits that the film presents a true story. Rather, *Daugh-*

ters is based on collective memory, in which facts and myths combine to establish the identity of a people. "To remember is [also] to empower," bell hooks has written.[37] The purpose of *Daughters* is not to entertain but to strengthen African-Americans' identity and to empower them.

Daughters also reflects Dash's evident awareness that two common assumptions about history are presently being examined and revised. The first myth is that history is narrative, in the sense that it "naturally" unfolds as a story, with a beginning, a middle, and an end. The second is that history is—or should be—about great individuals whose military or intellectual power changes the lives of untold passive masses. *Daughters* does not have a plot, and it is not about individuals—great or ordinary—but about a family.

Daughters is set in 1902 on the islands off the coast of the Carolinas and Georgia, known as the Gullah or Geechee Islands. On these islands, slaves were quarantined and fattened after the grueling Middle Passage and before being sent to the ports of Charleston.[38] The story of the Ibo Landing is repeated in two different versions: "[The myth is that] African captives of the Ibo tribe refused to live in slavery, and upon their arrival to these shores walked on top of the water all the way back to Africa. The reality is that African men, women, and children in shackles walked into the water until they drowned."[39] Both versions of the story have profoundly influenced the Peazant family, inspiring in them courage, anger, and pride.

As the film begins, the Peazant family matriarch, Nana Peazant (Cora Lee Day), has called the family together for a meal before a large part of the family departs for the mainland to make a new life. The family has problems and resentments: Eula (Alva Rogers) has been raped, and her husband Eli (Adisa Anderson) cannot believe that the child she carries is his; Yellow Mary (Barbara-O) has a "past," and comes to the family meeting with a stranger, a woman companion with whom she has a spontaneous intimacy Yellow Mary does not have with her family. Nana Peazant deplores the departure; it will mean that the "old ones," the ancestors—in the soil and in the psyche—are left behind. Haagar (Kaycee Moore) wants nothing to do with "Nana's old stories," root potions, and "that Hoodoo she talks about," while Viola (Cheryl Lynn Bruce) has returned for a visit from the mainland, where she "fell

straight into the arms of Jesus." The family is divided, and Nana Peazant seeks to heal those divisions by creating a ritual. Family members
participate with differing degrees of enthusiasm. The film's tension is
augmented by the fact that viewers know that the mainland to which
the Peazant family members traveled was "no land of milk and honey."
Some of the family "remained behind, growing older, wiser, stronger."

To understand fully the distinctiveness of *Daughters*, we must recall
the stereotyping of Black women and men in film. There are no "Toms,
Coons, Mammies, Aunt Jemimas, bucks, as well as the white folks
around whom all these caricatures gravitate" in *Daughters*.[40] Furthermore, in the world of Hollywood conventions, we have seldom seen
wisdom spoken by an African American woman and attended to respectfully by a community. Yet in *Daughters* there is not just one wise
woman; Nana, Eula, Haagar, Viola, and Yellow Mary each voice their
particular insights with authority and passion.

One of *Daughters'* central themes is memory, the "need to remember
the richness of the past in order to move forward into the future."[41]
"The first voice we hear on the soundtrack is chanting in Ibo; the one
discernible word is 'remember.'"[42] The opening captions say that the
Gullah people actively "recalled, remembered, and recollected" their
African heritage. The role of common memory in constituting a people
is emphasized. Nana Peazant hoards and treasures family memorabilia.
Collective memory informs resistance on myriad levels, from the daily
practical resistances—Eula's unwillingness to identify her rapist, so
that Eli can kill him and, inevitably, be killed himself—to Nana's faithfulness to African religion. As in *The Chosen*, the filmmaker's concern
with accuracy of detail demonstrates her esteem for the people she depicts. "The film's respectful attention to language, codes of conduct,
food preparation, crafts, chair caning, hair sculptures, quilt-making,
and mural painting constitutes a praise-song to the will and imagination of a diasporized and besieged people."[43]

Like the resistances it pictures, the film itself constitutes a series of
resistances. Perhaps the most obvious of Dash's resistances to Hollywood conventions was to foreground Black women and the different
kinds of beauty among them. Dash said in an interview: "I wanted these
women to look like nothing you've ever seen before." She used Agfa-
Geveart film instead of Kodak because she found that Black people look

better on Agfa. Dash's camera lingers on the faces of Black women, recording their thoughts and their emotions. *Daughters* fills the screen with strong, multidimensional Black women.

Each of the decisions made by Dash and her crew was governed by Afrocentrism, by actions and values derived from West African culture rather than European. For example, Dash subverted Western individualism as well as Hollywood films' preference for heroes and stars, by choosing to tell a *people's* story. Several other aspects of *Daughters* also resisted film conventions.

Consider first the camerawork. *Daughters* favors wide-angled and deep focus shots in which, as Toni Cade Bambara put it, "No one is background scenery for foregrounded egos. The camera work stresses the communal; space is shared."[44] By contrast, "conventional cinema space is dominated by a hero, and shifts in picture plane are most often occasioned by a blur," so that the spectator's eye is directed to the central action rather than to characters other than the hero.[45] Unfortunately, some of the spatial effect of *Daughters* is lost in video, because each scene is framed around its central action, cutting off the periphery in order to fit the television screen. In *Daughters*, the periphery is not really the space of marginalization, but the full spaciousness that frames the people of Ibo Landing.

Second, *Daughters'* cinematographer Arthur Jafa varied the standard frame rate of twenty-four frames per second in order to signal different kinds of time.[46] In one scene, a deep focus shot shows the men discussing the decision about "crossing over." The right decision must be made, they say, "for the sake of the children." As they talk, the camera moves, approaching children playing on the beach. But the frame rate is slowed when the children are shown, giving a subtle impression of a timeless place where children are crucial, "eternally valid" as a primary value. Then the camera backtracks to the grown-ups, switching back to "real" time—twenty-four frames per second.[47]

Third, language in *Daughters* is an example of both Dash's resistance and her concern with authenticity. The primary language throughout the film is Gullah or Geechee, "a language created by Africans of several tribes to facilitate intercontinental trade long before the African holocaust."[48] It is a kind of pidgin English, difficult for most spectators to understand. The use of the Gullah language contributes to the film's authenticity, but the effect of straining to understand the language—as almost all spectators must do—also reveals to White Americans how it feels to be excluded from a dominant language—or at least, to have to struggle to figure it out.[49]

In her practical choices, as well as in her filmic choices, Dash demonstrated her loyalty to the UCLA Black filmmakers' Afrocentrism. She cast *Daughters* from actors who had previously been in films made by her UCLA colleagues. For spectators familiar with independent African American filmmaking, these were actresses and actors whose faces would instantly reference, or make connections with, these other films.[50]

> The whole thing was to hire actors and actresses who you know are good and who have also supported Black filmmakers in the past. These people worked months on films for little or no pay at all; so, now that I was finally able to pay them for their work, why look somewhere else?[51]

Although many young filmmakers may select actors from their own artistic community, Dash did so as a matter of principle. Clearly, she construed her answerability to Black filmmakers to extend to the people who supported Black film, as well as to Black film's principles.

Finally, Dash's Afrocentrism is evident in her treatment of religion as central to the concerns of everyday life. Several religions appear in *Daughters*: West African worship rituals, Santería, Islam, Catholicism, and Baptist Protestantism.[52]

Nana's African religion is Nommo, which centers on belief in a "harmonizing, integrating energy that connects body, mind, spirit, self, and community with the universe."[53] It is an inclusive, syncretistic religion, with none of Christianity's exclusive claims (represented in the film by Viola). In the ritual Nana creates, she struggles to bind together—literally and figuratively—the old and the new ways, the ancestors and the future. "Crossing over" is a rich symbol throughout, simultaneously indicating both the binding and the separation that makes necessary renewed connection. While Viola urges the family to cross over to the mainland, "an engraved invitation to culture, education, and wealth," Nana insists that the family must maintain the ancestors' protective custody: "We the bridge where they cross over."

Religion is the ground on which the Peazant family negotiates their different values and longings. Unlike most White cultural critics, many minority critics recognize the centrality of religion to African American culture and society. Bell hooks writes:

> Ironically, despite all its flaws, religion was one of those places that expanded our existence. . . . So this turning away from religion (in black culture from traditional black religion) has also meant a turning away from a realm of the sacred—a realm of mystery—that has been deeply helpful to us as a people.[54]

In *Daughters*, there are two kinds of resistance to Nana's religion, Haagar's and Viola's. Haagar resists all religion in the name of "progress": "Those old people; they pray to the sun; they pray to the moon, and sometimes they see a big star. They ain't got religion in them. No. This is a new world we moving into and I want my daughters to be decent somebodies. I don't even want my girls to even hear about all that mess." Viola resists instead the syncretism of the ancestral religion, the ease with which it assimilates her Christianity to the religion of the ancestors. She prefers a religion of precepts and ultimatums from "the Lord." But only Haagar, the belligerent secularist, ultimately refuses to participate in Nana's farewell ritual. The depiction of several religions coexisting in *Daughters* strongly distinguishes it from Hollywood films, which depict religious commitment either as nonexistent or as fanatical. In *Daughters*, religion does not make people tyrannical, monomaniacal, or violent; it does not separate people or make communication impossible. Rather, characters appeal to each other's religious sensibilities as the basis of a mutual bond.

By rejecting Hollywood film conventions in favor of Afrocentrism, however, Dash became vulnerable to some harsh criticism. A *Variety* reviewer wrote:

> Nobly intended as an investigation into a little known African-American culture, *Daughters* plays like a two-hour Laura Ashley commercial. Wildly indulgent and undisciplined as filmmaking, Julie Dash's feature does possess a unique look and feel that, in addition to its ethnographic interest, will appeal to some people.[55]

This reviewer made the naive assumption that he was faced, not with a different set of values than that of Hollywood films, but simply with a poor rendition of a Hollywood film. Other mainstream reviewers were similarly critical. Some alleged that the film's many subplots were confusing. In response, Dash said of the film's complexity, "This is the way my grandmother told me stories, the way an African storyteller tells stories. It's the way African Americans visualize things. Think of the density and complexity of rap music. We're used to decoding layers of images."[56] A film that disrupts spectators' expectations by creating a fundamentally different visual experience cannot be expected to be unanimously praised by reviewers. But it should be reasonable to expect that reviewers recognize that different values governed the filmmaker's choices.

In this chapter we have considered two films, released within two years of each other, whose topic is Black women and African American community. Using *The Long Walk Home* and *Daughters of the Dust*, we can compare a Hollywood film about an intensely contested moment in Black history made by a White producer and director, with a film about an African American family made by an African American independent filmmaker.

Why would a major film studio decide to release a film about the civil rights movement in 1990? Since films are not made as public service offerings, there must have been reason to think that the issues in the film were timely enough to make it successful at the box office. In the atmosphere of aroused feelings and backlash on issues of race and gender, *Long Walk*—a conservative film about a radical topic—would find a large interested audience and could expect box office success.

Daughters was also a commercial venture, of course, but the filmmaker had other agenda as well. The budget was only $800,000, in a year when the average cost of making a Hollywood film was $27 million. Because of its low budget, *Daughters* had to be shot in a twenty-eight-day period. At every stage, Dash struggled for funds to continue. She described the difficulty of making a film without sufficient funding:

> In independent film, we are never able to pay top salaries. None of us are adequately compensated for the work we do, not the writers, the producers, the directors, the crew, the actors, not one. We do it to create the work. We do it to sharpen our skills. We work with the hope that if the film is good, someone will offer us a bigger budget the next time and then we'll be able to hire and compensate adequately those who sacrificed on the low-budget projects.[57]

The cost of Hollywood conventions is high, literally—in money—and figuratively—in the social stereotypes that are perpetuated. The problems to which the *Variety* reviewer referred may have had more to do with the low budget than with lack of skill.[58] Nevertheless, Dash made a film that supports and empowers Black women and men in their continuing struggle in American society. She did so by revealing their beauty, a beauty evident, not in a single heroic moment, but in their everyday interaction.

Curiously, despite its topic of liberation, *Long Walk* is not a radical film. It appropriates a singular historical moment in African American experience and recasts its importance as belonging to a White woman. Under the guise of recovering a racial memory, it erodes that memory. As critic Keith Tribe remarked, in films "history is recognized as Truth . . . because the image looks right."[59] But to whom does the image look right? At a time in which racial struggle is again prominent in American society, *Long Walk* does little to empower African Americans or to refresh our memories of a heroic moment in an ongoing struggle. It features Black people's oppression and suffering rather than their heroism and creativity—an old story for former slaves. The real glory of the civil rights movement, *Long Walk* implies, was the slow individual change it effected in White people's attitudes. Moreover, by depicting the "olden days," a time when African Americans *really* suffered, *Long Walk* trivializes the present suffering of a people *still* oppressed—and still resisting that oppression—in American society.

Hollywood films, whose overriding purpose is to earn money, have rarely supported or advocated change in American society. As we have seen, even films that seem to do so often subvert the potential for changing attitudes that their explicit content promises. A film may take a radical topic and yet remain well within the old cinematic conventions that make for a conservative message. On the other hand, a filmmaker who identifies strongly with the people she represents is more likely to interrogate and resist Hollywood conventions on their behalf, to show something new.[60] But even self-representation does not always guarantee powerful and honest images. In chapter 8 I will continue to examine the representation of people of color in two films, one by a White woman, Jennie Livingston, and one by a Black man, Spike Lee.

7

Good Clean Fun:
Love in Popular Film

> Thelma and Louise
> The Piano

In the long history of the representation of women in the dominantly Christian West virtually all of the texts and images that represented women were made by men rather than by women themselves.[1] Historical representations of women cluster around two images; women are either romanticized and glamorized—like the Virgin Mary and countless film stars—or they are pictured as daughters of Eve, cause of the evils of sex, sin, and death.[2] Jewish and Christian scriptures support the latter interpretation; Ecclesiasticus 25.24 reads: "From a woman sin had its beginning, and because of her we all die." Many medieval paintings and sculptures represented original sin as a naked, corpulent woman with pendulous breasts.

Although naked women were depicted as dangerous, sinful, and death-dealing, the naked male body often represented spiritual strength and heroic struggle against temptation. There are a few exceptions, but there is no iconographical tradition in the Christian West that identified spiritual struggle or the cultivation of a religious self with the unclothed female body.

As early as the third century of the Common Era, self-shaping desire and intentional agency were recognized as a male prerogative. Late

Roman women who resisted traditional roles in order to create and cultivate a religious self, whether in Christianity, in Judaism, or in one of the philosophical schools, were spoken of as "becoming male." Nevertheless, countercultural religious and philosophical communities of the late Roman world had a religious context for understanding and honoring women who sought to cultivate a religious self.

In societies that have lacked even the notion that women can become male, women who have dared to desire, and who have acted out their desires as unmarried women, or simply as women of accomplishment, have usually encountered scorn, misunderstanding, and, often, violence. Throughout Western secular literature, folk tales, and films, tales of the flamboyant lives of fictional or actual women such as Joan of Arc, Isadora Duncan, Camille Claudel, or Madame Bovary have concluded with their alcoholism, insanity, or painful and ignominious death in early middle age. *Jules et Jim* is the classic film statement of this theme. Indeed, as my examples show, these stories can often claim the status of biography, thereby reinforcing their effectiveness as cautionary tales.

Since feminist theory in general and feminist film criticism in particular have addressed the history of representation of women, I want to give a brief history of feminist film criticism before discussing two contemporary representations of women in popular film.

Feminist film criticism is a rather recent phenomenon; its most important developments occurred in the last two decades. The first issue feminist critics examined was how sexual difference—difference between men and women—is treated in cinema. Early feminist work focused on women as objects of the male gaze. It was largely assumed that women spectators had no option but to identify with the female figures they encountered in Hollywood film. In other words, early critics argued for a clear and simple dichotomy in the activity of looking: men look, and women are to be looked at. Moreover, as Constance Penley put it:

A similar active/passive division of labor controls the narrative structure: it is the man who makes the story happen at every textual level. Through identification with the male character, the spectator is privileged as both the viewer of the woman exhibited as spectacle, and as controller of those events on the screen which unfailingly lead to the male's possession of the female.[3]

In this classic scenario, early feminist critics thought that the female viewer could enjoy the film only masochistically, by identifying with the male hero. She can desire only to be desired. Woman's body is the "site of sight," not the site of subjectivity. Paula Rabinowitz wrote: "the woman's body is everywhere one looks on the screen; yet it is nowhere to be found among the spectators, whose gaze has been relentlessly constructed as that of the masculine voyeur."[4]

Since those early days of feminist film criticism, feminist authors have expanded their early positions on the "gendered eye." Critics like Jackie Stacey still notice that women usually occupy stereotypical roles in most popular Hollywood films, but they now posit the possibility of partial, multiple, diverse, and perverse identifications with film figures.[5] Moreover, as I suggested in discussing *The Handmaid's Tale*, it is possible to enjoy more complex pleasures than simple identification, for example, the pleasures of analysis and "reading against the grain,"—active rather than passive pleasures.

Recently, Judith Butler has argued that spectatorial identification is a foundational human activity. It is not simply "an imitative activity by which a conscious being models itself after another; . . . identification is the assimilating passion by which an ego first emerges."[6] Not only is identification profound, but it is also more complex than early theories of cinematic identification indicate. Butler argues that identification with an object is not incompatible with desire for the same object.[7] This theory includes the lesbian eye, so frequently excluded from analyses of spectatorship. Moreover, many or most women, not only lesbians, Butler claims, enjoy female film characters. Posed as desirable within a male aesthetic, women spectators as well as men respond to female characters' desirability with desire.

Hollywood films are changing as society changes. In some films, the heterosexist presumption of most Hollywood films is questioned or problematized, at least briefly. In films such as *Personal Best, Desperately Seeking Susan, Thelma and Louise*, and *Fried Green Tomatoes*, deep social and erotic bonding among women provides a lesbian subtext. Furthermore, it is viewers and not films who produce meaning, and by reading against the grain, moviegoers can imagine alternatives to both dominant cinema and dominant interpretations.

Yet, as I have argued throughout the book, if what one wants to examine is the role of a particular film in a complex social discourse on pressing social issues, reading against the grain is of limited significance. It has little bearing on how large audiences will understand a film. That can only be reconstructed by examining the convergence of film conventions with social interests and anxieties at the historical moment of a film's production and circulation. Feminist critique must be included in a broader and more concrete study of contemporaneous culture and society if it is to achieve its greatest potential for understanding filmic communications in North American society.

Within the last two decades, the focus of feminist criticism has also changed substantially. Early work tended to identify inequalities between women and men; feminists pointed out differences in social roles and expectations, in the kind and amount of authority and credibility granted to men and women, and in public honor and reward for men's and women's work. Popular films were assumed to be at least partly accountable for reproducing and reinforcing the inequitable treatment of women in society.

More recently, however, feminist film critics like Constance Penley, Laura Mulvey, bell hooks, Mary Ann Doane, Michele Wallace, and E. Ann Kaplan—to name only some of the best known—are more interested in identifying and acknowledging differences among women than in differences between women and men. It is, they say, incomplete, misleading, and irresponsible to attend to issues of gender without simultaneously taking into account differences in race and class. Gender, race, class, and often other variables as well—like sexual orientation and age—need to be understood together if any of these is to be understood adequately.[8] Moreover, identifying differences among women starts with the recognition that even within one person, a unified self is a fiction. Feminist authors like Judith Butler, Iris Marion Young, and Linda Williams have exposed the inadequacy of the search for an original, presocialization true self. This quest, they say, has obscured both the existence of a "mass of contradictions" within the person herself, and—by extension—the existences of others with different perspectives and sensitivities.[9]

Women also differ from one another, of course, in their economic, educational, and social situations. They do not have equal access to the books and universities where most feminist discourse occurs. If feminists are to take differences among women seriously, the many verbal and nonverbal ways in which women express their experiences and ideas must be recognized. Ultimately, to create equal opportunity and access to public discourse, nothing less than the revision of society as a whole is necessary. But recognition of the problem is a necessary first step.

The films I will discuss in this chapter do not highlight issues of race and class, but concentrate on gender. This is not because race and class are not embedded in the narrative structures of the films; it is, rather, that by Hollywood convention, the stories of White people are normative and of universal interest and appeal.[10] Although a film about Blacks is billed as a film about race, films about Whites are advertised simply as films about Americans.

Thelma and Louise and *The Piano*, two films with female protagonists, illustrate the interdependence of Hollywood versions of romantic love and the genre of the cautionary tale. Hollywood movies reiterate the ideal of romantic love that attracts women and men to the gender ideals of their society. The cautionary tale warns us that we will be punished for violating gender norms. Romantic love and the cautionary tale require one another. To be maximally effective, the ideal of romantic love must be supported by an antithetical vision of the painful consequences that occur when gender relations go awry.

In both *The Piano* and *Thelma and Louise*, strong female protagonists enjoy brief moments of exhilarating power and control of their own lives, only to be punished for them. Perhaps the fact that the female protagonists' moments of power are on the screen longer than the moments in which their punishment is shown reflects women's progress in America. Indeed, one's interpretation of both of these films depends largely on whether one attends more to the body of each film, or to its conclusion. There is, of course, no reason to insist that the conclusion of the film is decisive for its interpretation. Nevertheless, the presumed death of Thelma and Louise and the chastened domesticity of Ada place both films in the genre of cautionary tale.

Thelma and Louise (1991)

In *Thelma and Louise*, the title characters abandon husband and boy-friend, respectively, for a weekend fishing trip.[11] On the way, in an Arkansas honky-tonk, a man takes a drunk Thelma (Geena Davis) out to the parking lot where he beats and tries to rape her. Louise (Susan Sarandon), who has suffered sexual abuse in the past, shoots and kills him. The two women take off on a frantic flight from the law toward the Mexican border. They encounter other rude or threatening men along the way, among them a trucker who gestures obscenely and shouts sexual taunts at them, a hitchhiker who steals all their money, and a patrolman they pull a gun on and lock in the trunk of his car. In the end, the law catches up with them, and, surrounded by a fleet of police cars, Thelma and Louise kiss, hold hands, and drive at top speed over a cliff and into the Grand Canyon.

Thelma and Louise combines several film genres. It is a buddy movie, but the buddies are women. It is a road movie, in which the protagonists are desperate, but they are also having fun. It is also an outlaw movie in which the outlaws being pursued are glamorized, but female this time. Critics repeatedly claimed that "this is the first feminist buddy-movie, or at least the first one that matters." If not the first feminist movie—a claim I will contest shortly—it is at least the first buddy movie in which women play characters traditionally assigned to men.

Screenwriter Callie Khouri said she wanted to "write something that had never been seen on the screen before."[12] She was "fed up with the passive role of women" and she wanted to create a film in which women would "drive the story because they were . . . driving the car."[13] Indeed, such moments occurred in *Thelma and Louise*. For example, the buddy genre revised the cautionary tale in that Thelma and Louise are not the traditional solitary heroines. They have each other. Women's friendship is a strong theme, and would have been a stronger one if Ridley Scott, the director, had not "cut scenes that portrayed the close friendship between the two title characters."[14]

Friendship provides the energy that transforms Thelma and Louise from passive reactors into fearless agents. Because the film has no voice-over in which an omniscient narrator interprets dialogue and action, viewers must rely on the relationship as pictured and spoken. Because it has no flashbacks or flashforwards, the moment of interaction is highlighted; the women's relationship is never explained, it is shown. Moments that feature their negotiations, their decisions, and their exchanges of leadership may be unique in film history. These moments made some viewers consider the film a feminist resource.

Virginia Woolf once remarked that although male friendships are frequently celebrated in Western literature, friendship between women has been largely missing. The same is true of Hollywood film. Female friendships have usually been shown as expedient, trivial, temporary, and secondary to women's relationships to men. In the movies, women's friendships frequently collapse into fierce competition over a man. Recently, however, friendships between women have become topics for literature as well as for films like *Thelma and Louise, Fried Green Tomatoes, Desperately Seeking Susan,* and *Entre Nous.*

Traditional Hollywood film conventions contradict the conclusions of social scientists who have researched women's friendships. Robert R. Bell, author of *Worlds of Friendship,* reports on his extensive research, "The evidence clearly indicates that the friendships of women are more frequent, more significant and more interpersonally involving than those commonly found among men."[15] Lillian B. Rubin agrees: "Women between 23 and 55 [the ages on which her research focused] have more friendships, as distinct from collegial relationships of workmates, than men, and the differences in the content and quality of their friendships are marked and unmistakable."[16]

I suspect that the strength of Thelma's and Louise's friendship, in addition to attracting women viewers, also contributed to male allegations of "guerrilla feminism."[17] For reviews of the film were rather neatly divided according to the sex of the reviewer. Women who liked it identified with the protagonists' liberation, power, and spunk, finding even in Thelma's and Louise's death an admirable choice.[18] Men almost unanimously disliked the film; several male reviewers said the film was too violent, that it featured "toxic feminism, man-bashing, man-hating, [and] male-baiting fascism."[19] Yet, as Janet Maslin pointed out, *Thelma and Louise* was far less violent either than road movies of the 1960s and 1970s, or than films of other genres released in the 1990s, like *Total Recall, Another 48 Hours,* or *Die Hard II.* In *Die Hard II* alone there were 264 violent deaths. The true offense of the film is not its violence, Maslin writes, but that "the men in this story don't really matter": "They are treated as figures in the landscape through which these characters pass, and as such they are essentially powerless. For male characters, perhaps, this is a novelty, but women in road movies have always been treated in precisely the same ways."[20]

The film, however, is not a simple role reversal, for the heroism of the female outlaws is punished by death, a fate not usually assigned to most outlaw males. In fact, many aspects of the film reassured the viewer that gender roles, heterosexism, and legal constraint and punishment are firmly in place. From subtle messages, like Thelma's sudden take-charge energy after having good sex (with a man) for the first time in her life, to the film's ending, protest against gender socialization is compromised and subverted. In this Hollywood version of feminist protest, male physical strength, institutional authorization and support for men, and the male privilege of verbal assault are well in place. Moreover, according to scriptwriter Callie Khouri, the director, Ridley Scott, added phallic imagery—"the huge trucks, the giant cacti and a chemical-spewing plane"—which reinforced viewers' sense of the stability of phallocentrism.[21] Lacking such reassurances, the film would not have passed, as it did even for many men who hated it, as good clean fun—entertainment—with the "pleasantly dreamy quality" noticed by Terrence Rafferty.[22] The final image is one in which at least fifty police cars pursue Thelma and Louise to the brink of the Grand Canyon. Overkill.

The ending—joint suicide—received amazingly varied comment by reviewers. Mary Cantwell writes of Thelma's and Louise's suicides as martyrdom, using traditional religious language: "if their leavetaking is tragic, it is also triumphant. Divested of all their worldly goods, and of all their worldly fears, they're not carrying any baggage as they go."[23] Similarly, Kathleen Murphy writes, "(T)hese splendid creatures choose—rather than accept—their fate, they kiss, mouth to mouth, clasp hands, and head into even higher country."[24] Certainly, Thelma and Louise display the increasing alienation from their (male-dominated) society that Christian martyrs of the early centuries described feeling. Also, like Christian martyrs, Thelma and Louise chose to leave an oppressive society.

Thelma and Louise cannot resign themselves to degrading and constraining social roles. But the comparison with Christian martyrs is superficial. The triumph of Thelma and Louise cannot be equated with that of martyrs who believed they would be instantly reborn in a heaven of glorious reward. Despite the film's "cheery, jokey air," and its "moments," Thelma and Louise die.[25] The fact that increments of intensity are frequently confused with actions that lead to death is perhaps unsurprising in a society in which drug and alcohol addiction are epidemic. Richard Grenier called attention to the confusion of life and death in the advertising for *Thelma and Louise*:

> *Thelma and Louise* has been advertised on a level of deceit rare in the history of promotion departments not known for their finicky delicacy. 'Someone said *get a life* . . . so they did,' run the ads. 'For Thelma and Louise it's Independence Day . . . and though it won't be any picnic . . . there'll be plenty of fireworks . . . because they're celebrating life . . . liberty . . . and a clean getaway.' A clean getaway to death, that is.[26]

The cautionary tale is alive and well in *Thelma and Louise*: "the cost of [female] freedom is self-destruction."[27]

But the film must be examined not only as text, but in the context of the society in which it was produced. What is wrong with *Thelma and Louise* is not that it implies that "all men are worthless beasts ruled by degenerate sexual urges, violent impulses and rampant cowardice," as one male reviewer put it,[28] it is, rather, that, as Diane White said, "reality is not, by and large women bashing men, but men bashing women."[29] *Thelma and Louise* inverted social reality at a historical moment when the scale of domestic violence and rape was coming to public attention. Not only are 89 percent of all violent crimes committed by men, but many of them are committed against women. By 1993, the Commonwealth Fund Survey of Women's Health reported that 3.9 million American women had been physically abused by their spouse or partner during the previous year. The U.S. Surgeon General "ranked abuse by husbands and partners as the leading cause of injury to women ages 15–44."[30]

Although many women enjoyed *Thelma and Louise*'s depiction of powerful women holding the gun, the film also carried another, more dangerous, cultural message. Popular films such as *Misery*, *Thelma and Louise*, *Fatal Attraction*, and *Disclosure*, in which women characters harass or violently attack men, reinforce violent men's sense that women are out to get them and suggest that nothing but preemptory male violence will keep women in their place. I am not suggesting that only films that mirror social reality should be made, but that we need to be aware of the social issues and topics of current public interest that provide a context for a film's issues. These social realities included a homicide rate that had increased by 100 percent from 1950 to 1990, public debate about acceptable gender language and behavior as highlighted by the 1991 Hill-Thomas hearings, and epidemic violence against women.[31]

Consider, however, another perspective on screen violence by women on men. Recently Judith Halberstam has argued that filmic representations of "unsanctioned violences committed by subordinate groups upon powerful white men" provides a "place of rage" and volatile power for subordinate groups while at the same time challenging "the hegemonic insistence upon the linking of might and right under the sign of masculinity."[32] In political activism, Halberstam points out, slogans represent a violence that need never be acted out. They produce productive fear in the perpetrators of violence, challenging "white powerful heterosexual masculinity and creating a cultural coalition" among the terrorized.[33]

The argument is interesting, but ultimately, I believe, dangerous. It proposes that a social effect (fear, leading to restraint, in heterosexual men) will result when a filmmaker, whether intentionally or not, questions a form of social violence (men's violence against women) that is taken for granted. Halberstam acknowledges that the social effects of such representations are unpredictable, but she finds that their possible power to effect change makes it worth the risk that the imagined violence may be imitated. But films that glorify violence must be considered in the context of a society in which violence is epidemic, and is largely a male prerogative.

In such a society, the actual effect of producing fear of retaliation in heterosexual men could well be preemptive violence. Indeed, several years ago, the television film *The Burning Bed* did trigger such a reaction. *The Burning Bed* depicted a woman who had suffered years of abuse. One night she doused her husband with kerosene and lit the kerosene with a match as he lay sleeping. According to media reports, the film prompted reactions from both women and men. Battered women found authorization for their anger; they flooded hotlines and shelters, and one woman shot her boyfriend after seeing the movie.[34] But it also made men angry; one man set fire to his wife, burning her over 95 percent of her body after seeing the film; another man beat his wife senseless, telling her that he would "get her before she got him."[35] Halberstam's proposal, in the context of 1990s American society, is dangerously short-sighted.

Under different circumstances, *Thelma and Louise* might be good clean fun, but the film seemed to be the last straw for men already fed up with feminism.[36] Some of them acted out their anger, many others articulated it. As one male reviewer put it, as long as feminist "attacks" were "confined to academic papers, women's magazines, cleverly disguised movies, and novels read only by the elite," men could "suffer in manly silence." But *Thelma and Louise*, he said, "takes aim at the center of mass culture, grievously escalating the war between the sexes."[37] Whatever the filmmakers' intentions—and, as I have described, screenwriter Callie Khouri insisted on her feminist intentions—the film's effects, as revised by the director, may have outweighed them.

Is *Thelma and Louise* a women's film? A distinction needs to be made between women's film (Hollywood films about women aimed at a heterosexual female audience) and feminist film (aimed at a wide range of women, including women-identified, women-loving, lesbian, and heterosexual women). Feminist film is not a Hollywood category, even though several nationally distributed recent films such as *Desert Hearts* and *Go Fish* treat the topic of lesbianism. For example, the women's film *Fried Green Tomatoes*, 1992's most profitable film, eliminated the novel's explicit lesbianism. Similarly, in *Thelma and Louise*, only after each woman's sexual relationship to a particular man is established, may they kiss on the mouth as they leap to destruction. Their kiss is sheltered from a lesbian interpretation *and* is simultaneously a final sign of their outlaw status. *Thelma and Louise* is women's film, not feminist film.

Women's film often succeeds at the box office. Films that feature romance and cooking, such as *Fried Green Tomatoes* and *Like Water for Chocolate*, have been commercial successes, while *The Joy Luck Club*, which "broke every rule of commercial filmmaking with its ensemble of eight women, four of them over 50," was a 1993 hit. Yet, as box office analyst Anne Thompson observed, in a film industry that thinks that to succeed financially it must produce films that attract men, "when such movies are hits, the industry is still surprised."[38] Meanwhile, Hollywood continues to "aim at the young heterosexual male moviegoer."[39]

The price of box office success, as directors and producers have construed it, is the exclusion of the varieties of sexual orientation. I will discuss further filmic treatment of gay men and lesbians in chapter 8. Of the movies I have already discussed, *Daughters of the Dust*, a film that received no Hollywood funding, was the only film to depict the complex forms of love between and among women. It showed women as lovers, as family, and as friends, sharing a rich emotional life, weeping, cooking, arguing, and playing together.

Thelma and Louise also betrayed its adherence to Hollywood conventions by representing theft, alcohol, and casual, unsafe sex as exhilarating, fun, and the best revenge on a sexist society. As Janet Maslin wrote in reviewing *When a Man Loves a Woman*, "the Hollywood esthetic, with its intrinsic prettiness, overwhelms the painful, unglamorous realities that this cautionary tale is supposed to be about."[40] Similarly, at a time when AIDS threatens all people, a film that represents unsafe sex as unproblematic reveals its allegiance to film convention in which sex is essential. One need not propose a simplistic "monkey see, monkey do" hypothesis in order to say that if films have any effect on their audiences—or even on some members of those audiences— *Thelma and Louise*, along with scores of other popular films, is irresponsible in its disregard of a devastating reality.[41]

Although until very recently "safe sex" meant sex in which a woman was protected from pregnancy, safe sex is no longer a women's issue. The gender-blind threat of AIDS has escalated the issue of safe sex to intense national, indeed global, attention.[42] On February 1, 1995, the U.S. Centers for Disease Control and Prevention announced that AIDS is now the leading cause of death among Americans aged twenty-five to forty-four; HIV infection is spreading most rapidly among women and minorities.[43] Yet movies remain largely impervious to efforts to educate Americans to their responsibility for prevention.

The portrayal of unsafe sex in *Thelma and Louise* is just one example in popular films of a major, and very disturbing, issue. Low-budget public service agencies are desperate to communicate, especially to young people, the real and present danger of AIDS for people of all sexual orientations. Yet the largest-budget industries in the United States, Hollywood film, pornography, television, and the recording industry, continue to represent casual, unsafe sex as exciting and unproblematic. Hollywood films could go a long way toward glamorizing safe sex. Glamorizing cultural objects—such as clothing, gestures, cigarettes—is, after all, what the movies do best. There are reasons why it has not done so.

Both film conventions and box office aspirations mitigate against an effort by popular films to establish safe sex as the social norm.[42] Given the media's polarization of women's and men's erotic attractions, which I will discuss more fully, a glamorization of safe sex would seem to suggest that safe sex could occur within the context of the on-screen "foreplay" women are believed to enjoy. It is difficult to imagine how safe sex could be explicitly represented in the context of violence and dangerous sex, Hollywood's idea of what men find erotic. A filmmaker could expect to sacrifice at least a part of the largest box office audience—male teenagers—if s/he were to depict explicit safe sex. Thus it is likely that, despite the recent commercial success of several women's movies, Hollywood will continue to target male audiences. We will shortly see, however, that the portrayal of safe sex is also shirked by the primary genre of women's film, romance.

Before leaving *Thelma and Louise*, however, I want to consider the possibility that powerful filmic "moments" have an influence disproportionate to the cumulative messages a film communicates. Powerful images can, after a time, shed their textual context yet remain in personal and collective image repertoires. Richard Schickel described the force of film images:

> Movies acquire . . . [a] historic stature not because they offer a particularly acute portrayal of the way we live now or because they summarize with nuanced accuracy the opposing positions in an often flatulent quasi-political debate. They work because somehow they worm their way into our collective dreamscape, retrieve the anxious images they find there and then splash them across the big screen in dramatically heightened form.[44]

Although images of two women who temporarily liberate themselves from social constraints are, in the context of American society in the 1990s, deeply problematic on several grounds and a caricature of women's liberation, women who do not have a plethora of images of women's friendship may, by reading against the grain, extract support from *Thelma and Louise*. As a whole, however, and in a society characterized by violence and a backlash against feminism, and threatened by AIDS, the film fails to communicate an empowering vision of women's freedom and responsibility. Moreover, Thelma's unsafe (hetero)sex with a hitchhiker is shown as fun and illuminating. "I don't remember ever feeling this awake," Thelma says, voicing one of the stable conventions of romantic film. Safe sex is as rare in romances of the 1990s as it is in adventure movies. The next film I will discuss in this chapter, *The Piano*, shows why.

The Piano (1993)

The Piano was directed by Jane Campion, the first woman in Cannes' forty-six-year history to win the Palme d'Or.[45] Although *The Piano* is a romance, while *Thelma and Louise* combined several adventure genres, *The Piano* also, I will argue, presents a cautionary tale.

In *The Piano*, Ada (Holly Hunter), a young Scottish woman in the mid-nineteenth century, goes with her seven-year-old daughter, Flora, to New Zealand as a mail-order bride. Ada has not spoken, for an unexplained reason, since she was six, but she has a richly expressive language at her fingertips; she communicates by writing; in sign language that only Flora (Anna Pacquin) understands; and by playing her piano. Her inner voice is also heard in voice-overs at the beginning and end of the film. Ada's opening voice-over explains:

> The voice you hear is not my speaking voice but my mind's voice. I have not spoken since I was six years old. No one knows why, not even me. My father says it is a dark talent and the day I take it into my head to stop breathing will be my last. Today he married me to a man I've not yet met. Soon my daughter and I shall join him in his own country. My husband said my muteness does not bother him. He writes and hark this: God loves dumb creatures, so why should

not he! Were good he had God's patience, for silence affects everyone in the end. The strange thing is I don't think myself silent, that is, because of my piano. I shall miss it on the journey.

Ada brings her piano with her to New Zealand, but her husband-to-be, Stewart (Sam Neill), leaves it on the beach, unwilling to haul it through forest and mud to their home. George Baines (Harvey Keitel), an English neighbor who has partially "gone native" accepting Maori religion and face tattoos, buys the piano—and piano lessons from Ada. But it quickly turns out that George is really interested, not in playing the piano himself, but in watching Ada play. He suggests that she allow him to touch and caress her while she is playing and thus win back— key by key—the piano. Her expressive playing and his gentle touch produce a complex eroticism, and Ada falls in love with George. Stewart, who Ada has rejected sexually, learns of their liaisons, informed by Flora. He forbids her to see George, but when she persists, he takes an axe to the piano and, in a scene more shocking than an axe murder, cuts off one of her fingers.

Soon after, admitting defeat, Stewart sends Ada away to live with George. On the rough sea voyage, and because the boat is in danger, Ada insists that the piano must be thrown overboard. But a rope tied to the piano twirls round her foot and she is pulled into the sea with the piano. Succeeding—not a moment too soon—in freeing her foot, she rushes to the surface and is rescued. As the film ends, Ada and Flora are living with George in a New Zealand town. Ada is learning to speak, and, equipped with a metal finger, she gives piano lessons.

The Piano is devoid of religion, an unlikely representation of a mid-nineteenth-century Scotswoman. In the film, as in twentieth-century secularism, a religion of romantic love has replaced religion as the force that creates and attracts commitment. Salvation through romance has replaced Christian salvation and occupies its place in the film's cultural psyche.

The Piano's images of romantic love are not often seen on screen. The long quiet scenes in which George gently touches Ada, slowly arousing her desire without immediately overwhelming her desire with his own, describe a languid and happy eroticism that is unusual, even for women's movies. If the film had been set in contemporary times, one can even imagine that the delicate art of safe sex could have been, not a mundane interruption, but an integral part of such a scene.

These were the filmic moments that prompted reviewers to call the film "a work of passion and beauty."[46] In an interview, director Jane Campion described her interest in exploring what she calls a "gothic romantic impulse" in the more sexual visual vocabulary of today:

> [Brontë's notion of romance] is very harsh and extreme. I wanted to respond to these ideas in my own century. . . . My exploration can be a lot more sexual, a lot more investigative of the power of eroticism. Then you get involved in actual bodyscape as well, because the body has certain effects—like a drug almost—certain desires for erotic satisfaction which are very strong forces. . . . We've grown up with so many expectations that the erotic impulse is almost lost to us, but these characters have nothing to prepare them for its strength and power. . . . The romantic impulse is in all of us, but it's not part of a sensible way of living. It's a heroic path, and generally ends dangerously.[47]

Filmic romances have seldom explored how a woman's mind and body might be aroused to desire. Moreover, *The Piano* attempts to demonstrate that romance need not end dangerously, but can actually be fulfilled and become daily life.

Whether the film is convincing in that representation is another matter. Indeed, most film versions of romantic love fail at this point. Images of how first love becomes the long daily reality of love are usually absent, as are images of the steady thrill, the quiet excitement of conducting one's life in close and daily proximity to another person who is similarly conducting a life that has a past and a future, reaching back through childhood to—and before—birth, and forward to death. To maintain a vision of the person one is with in his *whole* life is a powerful and trustworthy excitement. We need images that create and encourage such vividness in relationship.

The implicit or explicit promise and premise of romantic love in the movies is that it can be maintained "forever" at something close to its original intensity and passion. Film audiences expect to believe it, but we do not want to see it. As Sarah Kerr put it, in *Casablanca*, nobody really wanted to see Ingrid Bergman and Humphrey Bogart five years later, "sitting down to breakfast in a tract home in New Rochelle."[48] In *The Piano*, this is what we see. Although I will argue that it does not work, it was important to have seen it. When—and if—moviegoers see many undisastrous endings to film romances, directors and audiences will accumulate the repertoire of images that make such happy endings believable. As yet, happy endings to great romances in the movies bear little resemblance to happy endings in life. *The Piano* attempts to show that eroticism and sex do not *automatically* converge with love, but that they can actually become the foundation for a long love.

Does *The Piano* have a hopeful ending, as some reviewers thought?[49] Certainly, Ada has emerged, by means of an implied sexual awakening, into a public world.[50] She no longer uses her piano to express and communicate her feelings, but to earn a living. Nor is she limited to the elaborate signing she formerly shared only with Flora; she is learning to speak. She has adjusted. Yet her silence was a chosen act of defiance, profoundly subversive, an act of self-identity. Ada's closing voice-over summarizes:

> What a death! What a chance! What a surprise! My will has chosen life! Still it has had me spooked, and many others besides! I teach piano now in Nelson. George has fashioned me a metal fingertip; I am quite the town freak, which satisfies. I am learning to speak. My sound is still so bad I feel ashamed. I practice only when I am alone and it is dark. At night I think of my piano in its ocean grave, and sometimes of myself floating above it. Down there, everything is so still and silent that it lulls me to sleep. It is a weird lullaby, and so it is; it is mine. There is a silence where there hath been no sound. There is a silence where no sound can be in the cold grave, under the deep deep sea.[51]

Apparently content with her life, Ada nevertheless, at night, returns to the silence, her piano's silence and her own, recognizing the silence as peculiarly "mine" in a way that her public life as the town freak can never be. What about her sexuality, which prompted such drastic changes in her life? She doesn't mention it.[52] Can any sexual awakening ultimately bear the weight of shaping a new, and lasting, identity? And can this happen with the boorish, illiterate George, who thinks that the best way to find love is to purchase it? Unless the viewer is an uncritical romantic, it may be difficult to conclude that, fascinating as many of its scenes are, *The Piano* is anything more than a classic cautionary tale.[53]

The Piano aroused a storm of diverse responses. Reviewers as respected as Anthony Lane and Stanley Kauffmann disagreed dramatically. Summarizing his evaluation of the film, Kauffmann wrote:

> Every moment is upholstered with the suffocating high-mindedness that declines to connect symbols with comprehensible themes. I haven't seen a sillier film about a woman and a piano since John Huston's *The Unforgiven* (1960), a Western in which Lillian Gish had her piano carried out into the front yard so she could play Mozart to pacify attacking Indians."[54]

Anthony Lane wrote in his *New Yorker* review: "So clever and watertight a film may well be forbidding, but it also picks you up and moves you, and the performers breathe it full of life. Jane Campion peels back the past and finds it shockingly alive, in no need of resuscitation."[55]

Most reviewers focused on sex in *The Piano*, some men finding it anti-male, and some women, like myself, disliking the film's conclusion.[56]

Sarah Kerr, reviewing the film for *The New York Review of Books*, says that these contradictory interpretations arise from "a hollowness at the film's core." *The Piano* offers "no message whatsoever. It merely shows," she says:

> how timebound and rhetoric-laden our expectations about sex are: how much we rate it, classify it as 'casual' and 'serious' . . . look for signs of love or lack of love, for an expression, in miniature, of a character's approach to life. We usually subordinate sex to a larger story, but the point of *The Piano* is the sex; there's no larger story to tell.[57]

But the film is more complex than Kerr indicates; it examines a topic of pervasive importance in popular film, the representation of the erotic, sex, and love. Many or most Americans have learned from the movies what sex looks—or should look—like, but movies have done a less competent job of showing us what love is, how it looks, how it feels, in everyday life.

Philosophers trace the concept of romantic love—love that changes the lover's perceptions of self and world, salvific love—to Dante, and theologians detect its origins much earlier in Augustine's passionate description of love for God. But Hollywood film invented the twentieth-century American version of romantic love as the place at which erotic attraction, sex, and love converge.[58] Although in recent years films frequently represent sex as an end in itself, for the most part erotic attraction has been presented in films as the agent by which sex and love are brought together. Sex, explicit or evoked, has signalled life-altering love. In the movies, romantic love is expected to coordinate men's sexuality and women's sexuality. Romantic love is shown by depicting what men think of as foreplay. *The Piano*'s extended touching and gentle caressing both continues and nuances this film convention. It endeavors to tilt Hollywood films' focus on male heterosexual eroticism toward female heterosexual eroticism, correcting the movies' usual polarization of male and female desire.

It is, of course, impossible to comment on romantic love from an ungendered perspective, but I suspect that the Hollywood version of romantic love has done a disservice both to men and to women, reinforcing the gender stereotypes on which it depends.[59] A recent article in *The New York Times* used a new sex survey to describe these stereotypes, arguing that "men and women live in different sexual worlds." In the article, John H. Gagnon, co-author of *Sex in America*, writes, "Women equate desire with the things that 'indicate the man's interest and caring and affection.'" Men, he reports, "tend to respond erotically to a mix of sex and violence. . . . In fact, it is the combination of ready sex and the possibility of danger that many men find especially alluring."[60] Lynda Obst, a powerful producer, is quoted as insisting that movies [merely] *reflect* the prevailing sexuality of the culture.[61]

Whether or not one agrees that this stereotypical picture of (all?) men's and (all?) women's erotic interest is accurate is irrelevant. Indeed, the underlying heterosexist assumption alone is enough to make these definitions questionable. Under the guise of simply reporting a Hollywood trend, newspaper articles such as this one strengthen the claim of realist film to simply reflect social reality. Yet the polarization of men's and women's erotic attraction may relate primarily to Hollywood's interest in clear marketing hooks, that is, a clearly defined target audience.[62] As Savoy executive Marvin Antonowsky put it: "Females with guns in their hands are difficult to sell. The jocks don't dig it and women don't go to see action pictures."[63]

Clearly, the polarization of male and female erotic interest is culturally constructed. Even if further research someday shows that there is some basis in male biology for men's alleged preference for violent images and in women's biology for images of gentle sex, film images also exacerbate that difference. Recently a young woman described to me talking one day with her boyfriend and some of his friends about going to a movie. "Why don't we go see *Like Water for Chocolate*," she said. "Nah," they replied, "that's a woman's movie. We're gonna go see *Hard Target*." "Why do you wanna see *Hard Target?*" she asked. They replied, "Because there's so many *explosions!*"[64] It is ultimately impossible to distinguish between images that simply reflect male or female preferences and those that strengthen and polarize them, but the long history of religious image-use I described in Part I indicates that images can create desire and define its mode of satisfaction. Screen images both reflect and exacerbate erotic differences.

Journalistic revelations of Hollywood stereotypes at best encourage resistance to these generalizations; at worst, they naturalize and perpetuate them. In either case, the media's normalization of erotic desire to what men like and what women like threatens to weaken a range of erotic attractions that do not fall neatly within either category. Lacking the symbolic authorization and support that polarized male and female images of desire enjoy, alternatives, nuances, and embellishments to standardized erotic attraction are less accessible, impoverishing the erotic imagination of individuals who need a range of images on which to plot their particular sexuality. *The Piano*, I believe, contains such images; it effectively recalls and incorporates into adult sexuality the long-forgotten eroticism of childhood when a delicate fingertip touch could elicit powerful erotic excitement.

Propelled by perennial human longings for images that inspire and support us in imaging our lives, Americans look to the movies. Films, in turn, are advertised, in full-page newspaper ads, on the sides of buses, and on radio and television, for their ability to provide such images.[65] Why, then, do we suffer from normalized imaginations and cultural malnutrition? The short answer is that most popular films are genre films, replete with Hollywood conventions and aimed at box office success. Advertised as different, these films depart only slightly from spectators' expectations, confirming and satisfying our expectations in every other way. Both of the films I have discussed in this chapter provide some new filmic images, and moments in which film's conventions are challenged; both ultimately fail to sustain their nonconventional visions of gender relations.

How different is a road/buddy/outlaw film featuring two women when it is still built on casual sex and violence? How different is a romantic film focused on a heroine who, on her own terms, nevertheless falls in love with a man who purchases and controls her body? The cautionary tale and the romance still divide power and helplessness according to gender, delivering images of women's agency and actualization only to collapse those images into happy endings in which the women are either killed or socialized. The ultimate failure of *Thelma and Louise* and *The Piano*, however, does not render them valueless. It was important to see them, to consider their proposals in a society that is presently negotiating gender roles, and to imagine future films that can incorporate their strengths and not repeat their mistakes.

The long answer to the question of why Americans' symbolic resources are impoverished has to do with a confusion of cultural roles. Movies cannot replace religion in its traditional capacity to define and encourage love. The media's secular imagination relies on caricatures of religion while strenuously trying to fill religion's shoes. Yet popular film contributes to identifying and engaging issues of how to live even in its failure to provide richly imagined pictures of human life and relationships. Even in popular films' striking failure to select images of relationships that honor and augment human life, they reveal the inadequacy of gendered notions of desire, the erotic, sex, and love. But, ironically, to understand this message requires that one think of the movies as more than good clean fun, and that one seriously evaluate the influence of their images on individual and collective experience and longing.

8

Bodies, Pleasures, and Pains

Jungle Fever
Paris Is Burning

The two films I will discuss in this chapter examine American society from the perspective of members of that society for whom the social arrangements and cultural provisions have not and are not working well. *Paris Is Burning* focuses on (mostly) Latino or Black gay, transvestite, and transsexual men, using the documentary form to interview them and to show one aspect of their lives. *Jungle Fever* depicts Black families under the intersecting pressures of city life, racism, drugs, and sexual mythology. Both films also examine concepts of the American family, depicting traditional as well as reconstituted families.

In representing people with whom filmmakers identify, and those with whom they do not, issues inevitably arise. *Paris Is Burning* was directed by a White lesbian woman looking through the camera's eye at Black and Hispanic gay men; in *Jungle Fever*, an African American director examined a middle-class Black man whose social and racial experience are presumably close to his own.

Hollywood films have usually adopted the perspective of those for whom the society generally works. These are the people who can afford to buy tickets at the movie theater. The young White men who constitute film's largest audience are not the wealthiest members of society, but their values and attitudes are likely to dominate in the next generation of leaders in political, social, and legal institutions.

The perspectives and insights of White women and men and women of color have been, until recently, scarce in films. Their lives and stories have not often been featured on the big screen. Obviously, this is a lack that must be corrected, for the victims of ostracism, marginalization, and oppression can reveal the human costs of a society's successes. As in *Daughters of the Dust*, films can also propose alternative values, styles of relating, and cultural resources of women and minority communities. The exclusionary practices of Hollywood film, often taken for granted by moviegoers, are exposed only when we see alternatives. Yet, as we will see in this chapter, neither taking a minority community as the topic of a documentary, nor filming a community with which one identifies guarantees representation of minority perspectives.

Both *Jungle Fever* and *Paris Is Burning* were produced and distributed in 1991, as were several other films I have discussed. On January 17, 1991, the United States launched Operation Desert Storm against Iraq. 1991 was a year of mild recession and unemployment that "hit the upper classes more than most."[1] Since the recession affected those with access to the nation's media soapboxes, the recession was publicized by middle-class out-of-work journalists and other educated people who had assumed they would be cushioned by those more vulnerable than they.[2] The recession may have contributed to Americans' interest, documented by box office receipts, in African Americans and Latinos. White Americans who no longer felt as protected from economic vulnerability as they once had were now interested in the experience of perennially economically marginalized Americans.

Jungle Fever (1991)

In the late 1980s a new phenomenon occurred in the Hollywood film industry. Funded by major studios, young Black male directors began to make films about Black experience in American society, bringing to many moviegoers for the first time the opportunity to learn about American society from their perspective.[3] To understand the importance of these Black filmmakers, one must recall a hundred-year history, discussed in chapter 6, in which African Americans were depicted only in a narrow range of stereotypical roles, such as the Mammy, the brute, the Sambo, and the Tom. By the early 1970s, however, a different kind of representation of Black Americans had become popular.

Catherine Silk and John Silk have described the "blaxploitation" films made by independent Black directors in the early 1970s. Blaxploitation films presented Black men as powerful; they sought "positive self-images" for the Black male, rejecting "traditional racial stereotypes . . . [and] white culture and mores."[4] Blaxploitation films consistently represented "brutal black heroes . . . [and] boorish white villains—the black buck in a new guise . . . as violent criminal or sexy savage."[5] Films like Melvin Van Peebles's *Sweet Sweetback's Baadasssss Song* (1971), and Gordon Parks's *Shaft* (1971) are characteristic of the genre. These films played to a new urban market that was mostly Black, as Whites increasingly moved to the suburbs.[6]

By the mid-1970s, Black film virtually disappeared as White Hollywood directors began to create crossover films like *Rocky* (1976), designed to attract both White and Black audiences. In these films, a tough, often violent, Black man and a tough, often violent, White man team up as protagonists. By the late 1970s and 1980s, Blacks often starred in Black stories, but they were directed and written by White men and appealed to a predominantly White audience. *The Color Purple* (1985) is perhaps the most popular example, a film with virtually an all-Black cast and a White director.[7] Until the end of the 1980s, movies in which African American experience in America was treated seriously and realistically were rare.

Jungle Fever was written, produced, and directed by Spike Lee, who was thirty-four years old at the time.[8] The film revolves around a romance between the protagonist, a young African American architect, Flipper Purify (Wesley Snipes), and his working-class White secretary, Angie (Anabella Sciorra). Flipper's estrangement from his wife and daughter, and his conflict with his gospel zealot father and drug addict brother bring into the film many of the problems of family and inner-city life in the early 1990s.

At the beginning of the 1990s, a number of circumstances brought pressure to bear on the urban life so vividly represented in the film. Among these conditions was a continuing rise in joblessness, public outcry over the beating of a Black man, Rodney King, by Los Angeles police, and the Clarence Thomas / Anita Hill conflict over Thomas's alleged sexual harassment of Hill. In 1992, a Washington, D.C. study showed that 42 percent of young Black men (between the ages of eighteen and thirty-five) in that city had been arrested for crimes and misdemeanors. Moreover,

> the leading cause of death among black males between the ages of 15 and 24 is homicide. The unemployment rate in America for black males is more than twice that of white males. . . . Among recent college graduates with one to five years on the job, white men earned an average of $12.85 an hour in 1991, black women earned $11.41, white women earned $11.38 and black men $11.26.[9]

The breakdown of the inner-city Black community and the marginalization of Black men has accelerated since 1980.[10] In 1974, 48 percent of all employed Black males were in well-paid, blue-collar, semiskilled crafts positions; in 1986, only 25 percent were in similar positions.[11] Moreover, Robert Staples and Leanor Johnson report that "Black and Hispanic males have the highest rate of functional illiteracy among the twenty-three million Americans so classified." They estimate that, in 1995, 44 percent of Black males are functionally illiterate, which may contribute to the similarly high unemployment rate. Staples and Johnson say that "46% of Black males between the ages of sixteen and sixty-two are not active participants in the American labor force."[12] While "Black women who are college graduates have achieved income parity with their white counterparts," Black men have not, as the above figures show. In a symposium called to discuss the situation in which Black men find themselves, Dr. Alvin Poussaint of Harvard University said, "There's a high level of anger among black men, be they low-income or professional, that black women . . . are given preference over them."[13]

The direct relevance of these events and problems of American society to *Jungle Fever* is immediately apparent. *Jungle Fever* is dedicated to Yusef K. Hawkins, who was killed in 1989 at the age of sixteen in a racial confrontation in the Bensonhurst section of Brooklyn. Hawkins was shot in a case of mistaken identity; he was thought to be a companion of a local girl who was ostracized by her White community for dating Blacks and Hispanics.

Jungle Fever treats an urban society *in extremis*. Racism is the primary problem highlighted by the film, reflecting director Spike Lee's statement in an interview with *Rolling Stone* that he considers racism "the number one problem in America." Racism is depicted in many incidents in the film, such as Flipper's White bosses' denying him a promotion, White policemen's assumption that he is molesting Angie when they playfully tussle on the street, and the myriad antagonisms surrounding race, especially Blacks and Italians, in other characters.

Lee talked about the difference between racism and prejudice: "Black people can be prejudiced, but to me racism is the institution. Black people have never enacted laws saying that white folks can't own property, white folks can't intermarry, white folks can't vote. You've got to have power to do that. That's what racism is—an institution."[14] Lee depicts the institution of racism at work in blatant and subtle ways in American urban society. *Jungle Fever* proposes no answer to the problem of racism, except, perhaps, to imply, as bell hooks put it, that "everybody is safest in their own neighborhood."[15]

But, Lee said, "my films don't deal with one theme. They interweave many different things."[16] *Jungle Fever*, Lee said, is "mainly about race, and [when] you add sex and class, you get a much more combustible combination."[17] For example, *Jungle Fever* examines what Lee has called the "racial politics of sex." Angie and Flipper are attracted to each other because of "sexual mythology"—Angie, because of the myth of the sexual capacities of black men, Flipper, because "all his life he's been bombarded with images of white women being the epitome of beauty and the standard that everything else must be judged against." Lee said that the goal of his film was

> to inspect and thereby demolish the sexual stereotypes of the black man as stud and the white woman as beauty incarnate. . . . I'm not saying interracial relationships are impossible. Flipper and Angie are not meant to represent every interracial couple in the world. They are meant to represent two people who got together because of sexual mythology instead of love. Then they stay together because they're pushed together. They're outcasts. And since their relationship isn't based on love, when things get tough, they can't weather the storm.[18]

Near the end of the film, Flipper says to Angie, "I give up. It's not worth it. I don't love you and I doubt seriously you ever loved me . . . Love-can-overcome-everything is only in Walt Disney movies, and I always hated Disney movies."

Interracial heterosexual relationships have a long and burdened history in American society. The first American law banning marriage between White women and Black men—the more prevalent form of interracial marriage—was enacted in 1864; the last laws prohibiting intermarriage were struck from the books in the 1960s. But law is only the most explicit form of social control. Despite more subtle forms of disapproval, interracial marriages have become increasingly common in the United States. In 1975 only 1.5 of every 1000 marriages were black and white interracial; in 1990, 4 out of every 1000 married couples were black and white interracial. Because attitudes toward interracial couples differ a great deal according to class, *Jungle Fever* is also about class, predominantly lower middle-class Bensonhurst Italians and middle-class Harlem Blacks. With the notable exception of Flipper's father, who disapproves of Angie on other grounds, Lee's Blacks are considerably less antagonistic to Angie and Flipper's relationship than the lower-class Italians he portrays as macho and violent, their minds stocked with stereotypes of Blacks.

Lee examined race, class, and sex in *Jungle Fever*, but if one considers, in addition, gender, an even more complex picture appears. One reviewer wrote: "Women occupy the periphery of the worlds Spike Lee brings to life; we never know how Angie feels about the affair, herself, her life . . . she is a reactor, not an actor."[19] Lee is not the first filmmaker to omit a White woman's subjectivity. There is, however, a remarkable scene in *Jungle Fever* that we should consider carefully. In the scene, Black women friends talk about race and sex. Since Black women's subjectivity has been in even shorter supply in Hollywood films than White women's, this scene is all the more striking—and courageous. The scene was rehearsed for three days; it took a whole day to shoot. Spike Lee said: "We just rolled the cameras and kept shooting and shooting, and the women, man, they forgot about that script. They were just vomiting that stuff up! I think it was all from their personal experience and that's why that scene works."[20]

Although African American women speak their minds, however, the scene "works" at their expense, for in *Jungle Fever*, Black men are victimized not only by White culture and society, but also by Black women. The film exaggerates Black women's real achievements and their power in public and private American society in order to blame Black women for their anger against Black men. Within the male director's narrative, Black women express the anger that Lee seeks to highlight.

Considered in relation to blaxploitation films, *Jungle Fever*'s depiction of Black men largely as victims can be seen as a rebuttal to images of Black men as powerful and lustful: "violent criminals and sexy savages." On the other hand, *Jungle Fever*'s depiction of conflict and hostility between Black men and women is apparently an accurate representation of many Black men's antagonism toward Black women, who, they feel, have had greater social and economic opportunity in White society.

Jungle Fever is not the only recent film by a Black director that depicts antagonism between Black men and women. John Singleton, director of *Boyz N the Hood* and *Poetic Justice*, said: "From age 1, black women are taught that black men are nothing. Black men are taught to take their frustrations out on black women. Black men and black women are at war with everything around them."[21] Singleton describes the sad mutual hostility of people "framed" by the larger society, people for whom that society does not work, who experience the tensions first of all in their most intimate relationships.

Despite some Black women's success in demanding and getting income parity in equivalent positions with White women, Black women have not, until very recently, directed Hollywood films. In 1991–92 nearly thirty films by Black male directors were nationally released. Yet Euzhan Palcy, a native of Martinique, was still, in 1993, the only black woman who had directed a Hollywood-financed film, *A Dry White Season* (1989). Patricia Smith writes:

> Brilliant new films by young black directors have set the entertainment world on its ear . . . But look closely. The black women in these films are still mammies, seductresses, whores, mulattoes, matriarchs, victims, servants, and ornaments snapped onto the end of male arms. Only this time the male arms are black.[22]

The point, Smith said, is not to criticize Black male directors, but to urge that "female eyes [be put] behind the camera" as well. Although Black women directors exist, their films are not funded, advertised, and distributed to become box office hits on the scale of *Jungle Fever*, *Boyz N the Hood*,[23] *Straight Out of Brooklyn*, *Poetic Justice*, or a number of other films done by Black male directors.[24]

Julie Dash, with *Daughters of the Dust*, was the first Black woman to direct a nationally released film, though her film received no Hollywood funding. Yet even though *Daughters of the Dust* grossed a very respectable $1.8 million and ran for eight months to sellout crowds in New York City, by 1993 Dash still did not have a Hollywood contract. In 1992, a year in which the average cost of a Hollywood film was more than $27 million, Darnell Martin received just $5.5 million from Columbia Pictures for making *I Like It Like That*; Leslie Harris received only $500,000 from Miramax Films to complete *Just Another Girl on the IRT*. It was not until 1993 that Ruby Oliver (*Love Your Mama*) and Leslie Harris (*Just Another Girl on the IRT*) became the second and third African American women directors to have a nationally released film.

To compound the problems Black women filmmakers have getting Hollywood funding, it seems that funding depends on what White Americans want to see. "The studios can't seem to see beyond the ghetto," says Helaine Head, the director of *Simple Justice*, a television docudrama. "The lack of violence, drug use, and unmarried pregnancies in my scripts were definite drawbacks. . . . A black project without those elements wasn't bankable."[25] One must wonder about largely White popular audience's preference for films that feature Black life and community as troubled and troubling.[26]

Spike Lee was criticized for excluding drugs from his depiction of interracial conflict in *Do The Right Thing*; he takes the topic on in *Jungle Fever*.[27] The film begins on a comic note, but the theme of drugs and violence soon begins to be laced through Flipper and Angie's story. In the character of Gator (Samuel L. Jackson), Flipper's older brother, Lee exposes the desperation, deceit, crime, and hopelessness of drug addiction, not only to the user, but also to families and society.

The families depicted in *Jungle Fever* are suffering from a variety of social ills. The family is perhaps the one institution of North American society that has experienced great changes in the last decade. These changes differ both in magnitude and particularity according to race, class, economic power, and ethnicity. The nuclear family has become weightier in public discourse as it has diminished as a reality.[28] Beginning in the 1970s, the number of people living in a traditional household dropped to less than 30 percent, a statistic that is still accurate.[29] Furthermore, in the Reagan era, the number of American households headed by single mothers increased by 21 percent. In 1988, 54 percent of mothers with children under three were in the work force.

If the White family cannot accurately be seen as the bastion of traditional American values, perhaps the Black family still holds this role. In their book, *Black Families at the Crossroads*, Robert Staples and Leanor Johnson found a vast "dissonance between Black family ideology and actual family arrangements." Although traditional family life remains the ideal among African Americans, American society denies Black men the resources to act as responsible husbands and fathers. They cite some startling statistics, for example: "College-educated Black males earn less than White male high school dropouts."[30] They conclude that "the direction of change is the same for all families in the United States," but since Black families suffer from the racism of American society as well as from class, economics, and gender struggles, the pressures they experience are greater. Measured by out-of-wedlock births and female-headed households, "where Black families were in 1960, White families are in 1990."[31] The UCLA Black filmmakers' commitment to representing the Black family as a site of liberation is not necessarily true to life.

In *Jungle Fever*, the traditional Black marriage of Flipper's parents is contrasted with that of Flipper and his wife Drew (Lonette McKee), a young, upwardly mobile couple caught in changing social conditions. The self-righteous Reverend Dr. Purify and his subservient wife are troubled by their elder son's addiction and by what they see as their younger son's lack of sexual morality in leaving his marriage for Angie. Flipper's own marriage is broken by his affair, and his upward mobility as an architect is brought to a halt when he both loses his marriage and angrily resigns his position in a White-owned firm. Pressures differ according to generation, but both Black families are severely stressed. In both families, it is the men's problems that cause the most stress.

Race, family, inner-city violence, drugs, and sex: surely Hollywood film has come a long way from "pure entertainment" in *Jungle Fever*.

But even this array of issues does not exhaust the film's agenda. Traditional Black religion also comes under scrutiny. A *Newsweek* reviewer wrote of Lee's treatment of religion in *Jungle Fever*: "Lee doesn't spare the church, long considered the moral bedrock of black culture."[32] The film depicts a generation gap in African-American culture and the importance to it of religion. Flipper's father, a gospel preacher, is portrayed as an intolerant, irascible man, who ultimately murders his drug-addict son.

Lee believes that religion is a cause, not a solution, to racism in America. He says of his childhood experience with African American religion: "That's all we did: get on our hands and knees and pray, and sing to the high heavens. [Religion] kept us praying to Jesus and worrying about the hereafter instead of what was happening now. . . . Religion has been used to oppress people."[33] In the character of Flipper's father, *Jungle Fever* presents a Black Christianity that has lost its leadership and is struggling merely to cope and, having done that, to escape into nostalgic Bible reading and listening to the beautiful music of Mahalia Jackson. This picture does not, of course, accurately represent all African American Christianity or theology in the 1990s. Yet as a tremendously popular film, *Jungle Fever* will maintain and reinforce this view of black Christianity.

In an interview with *Rolling Stone*, Spike Lee said that Black self-hatred is key to understanding a lack of solidarity among African Americans: "When you're persecuted, it's natural for people to come together; but when you're also taught at the same time that you're the lowest form of slime on earth, that you're subhuman, then why would you want to get together with people like that? Who do you hate? Yourself."[34] However, self-hatred is not, as Lee's statement shows, a final explanation of a failure to achieve as a people. African Americans live with a legacy of oppression and discrimination in this country, in a society that marginalizes them. *Jungle Fever* may let White America off too easily by its failure to pinpoint the cause of Black self-hatred. In *Boyz N the Hood*, a powerful scene identified Blacks' primary problem in White society very directly as the accessibility, on every street corner in the Black ghetto, of alcohol and guns. Lee also referred to the consequences of Black self-hatred in the *Rolling Stone* interview; but he did not do so explicitly in *Jungle Fever*: "We kill, we kill each other—

shit, White people don't even have to do anything. I mean Black males are killing each other at an alarming rate now. White people can just sit back and watch."[35] But *Jungle Fever* blurs its implicit charge against White society by suggesting that a large part of Black men's problems are due to Black women. Although it may have been no part of Lee's intention to absolve White America of responsibility, the effect of *Jungle Fever* is to make Whites comfortable. In fact, *Jungle Fever* offers precisely the image of a Black community replete with drugs, violence, and broken families that Helaine Head described as the only Black scenario Hollywood will buy.[36]

Another movie about a different minority, *Paris Is Burning*, takes up some of the themes that *Jungle Fever* has highlighted, but its documentary format means that these themes appear obliquely in interviews with its characters.

Paris Is Burning (1991)

Paris Is Burning explores a cultural phenomenon, the Harlem costume balls at which poor, mostly African American and Latino, gay men compete for prizes in different categories, from classic drag queens' formal evening gowns ("Femme Queen Realness"), "Executive Realness" (complete with suit and briefcase), schoolboy or schoolgirl, bangee punkness, to "Military Realness." Realness, or perfection of imitation, is the criterion for judging the competition within each category. One Black gay man said in the film that "realness" is a necessary life skill. It is defined by the ability to get home on the subway in drag without getting beaten up.

The balls begin at 4:00 or 5:00 A.M., and go on for as long as eighteen hours. The men who participate in the balls may work on details of their costumes and their walks for weeks or months before daring to model in the spotlight. Seen from the perspective *Paris Is Burning* illuminates, couture fashion symbolizes and epitomizes the values of a capitalist society. Mimicking the Paris fashion shows, ballwalkers strut their "opulence" while onlookers and rivals criticize or verbally abuse them—"throwing shade"—pointing out features of their costume or gestures that lack "realness." Toward the beginning of the film, as ballwalkers parade, the master of ceremonies says:

This is White America. When it comes to minorities, especially Blacks, we, as a people, for the past four hundred years are the greatest example of behavior modification in the history of civilization. We have had everything taken away from us, and yet we have all learned how to survive. That is why in the ballroom circuit it is so obvious that if you have captured the great White way of living, or looking, or dressing, or speaking, you is a marvel.

In the film, ballgoers tell of their longing for the wealth, privilege, and equality of the great American myth. Desire is one of the major themes of *Paris Is Burning*; I will return to it.

A complex vocabulary and social organization underlies the balls. Ballwalkers—"children"—belong to "houses," each presided over by a "mother" who trains them in the art of voguing, providing support and discipline. Respecting the survivor in each other becomes the basis for noncoercive family and community. Some, however, do not survive. At the end of the film viewers learn that Venus Xtravaganza, a featured character, was found strangled to death under a bed in a sleazy hotel; her body went undiscovered for four days. S/he had repeatedly been cautioned by the mother of her house not to be so reckless as a prostitute—not to enter strangers' cars and not to work the West Side piers.

In fact, *Paris Is Burning* was intended to be read as a post-modern "family values" film. Gay men, rejected not only by affluent American society but also by their birth families, form intentional families for mutual care. Teenagers whose mothers have simply "gone" find a new family, a caring group of human beings in a mutual bond. The film's producer and director, Jennie Livingston, wrote: "*Paris Is Burning* is, above all, about how a group of people under siege—from poverty, from racial prejudice, from homophobic violence—triumph with wit, style and love. [It] is not just about dancing or verbal insults: it's about old-fashioned family values like kindness and tolerance and loving your mother, even if your mother is a drag queen who is taking the place of your biological mother who refuses to speak to you because you're a homosexual."[37]

Livingston, a twenty-nine-year old, White, lesbian woman produced and directed *Paris Is Burning*.[38] After a struggle to fund the film—Livingston sold her car to finance the five-minute trailer she made in order to appeal for funding—the project was funded by the National Endowment for the Arts and by the British Broadcasting Company.[39] The Chicago Resource Center, one of the main gay foundations, turned down Livingston's applications for funding twice on grounds that the film did not "fit our agenda."[40]

Reviewers differed greatly in their interpretations and evaluations of *Paris Is Burning*.[41] Mainstream reviewers generally found the film "touching," "poignant," "funny," and, apparently, infinitely reassuring. Vincent Canby said, "There is a lot of common sense and natural wit behind the role-playing. Yet there is also a terrible sadness in the testimony. The queens knock themselves out to imitate the members of a society that will not have them."[42] These reviews, however, illustrate the limitations of interpreting minority cultures from White, heterosexual, middle-class perspectives. Bell hooks wrote of these positive mainstream reviews:

> What could be more reassuring to a white public fearful that marginalized disenfranchised black folks might rise any day now and make revolutionary black liberation struggle a reality than a documentary affirming that colonized, victimized, exploited black folks are all too willing to be complicit in perpetuating the fantasy that ruling class white culture is the quintessential site of unrestricted joy, freedom, power, and pleasure.[43]

Livingston inadvertently acknowledged that the film permitted predominantly white audiences to relax and enjoy. She said, "At first the audiences were really laughing at the people. Then as the film went along, you could hear the audience click and sympathize. By the end you could sort of tell that they felt this was about life and about them."[44]

Thus, as I will explore later in this chapter, *Paris Is Burning* is not a radical film on the subject of race. What about its perspective on sexual orientation? *Paris Is Burning* is part of a long history of filmic representations of gay and lesbian people. A summary of that history will divert us briefly from *Paris Is Burning*, but it will also reveal that this film is, if not unique, at least a rare effort to let gay men speak for themselves on film.

Vito Russo's *The Celluloid Closet: Homosexuality in the Movies* describes stages in film's treatment of gays and lesbians. Homosexuality first "emerged onscreen as an unseen danger, a reflection of [Americans'] fears about the perils of tampering with male and female roles."[45] "Homosexual" and "homosexuality" were mentioned for the first time on the Hollywood screen in 1962.[46] For at least a decade after, gay characters played "predatory, twilight creatures," monsters, sissies, and aliens, regularly committing suicide, conquered by love, truth, and beauty.[47] In the 1970s, the "perception of homosexual feelings as brutal, furtive, and dangerous" meant that homosexuality "flourished in films of violence and male bonding."[48] Serious treatment of homosexual stories in popular films began only in 1982 with the critical and commercial flop, *Making Love*. A mere twelve years later, the enormous success of *Philadelphia* ($77 million in theater revenues alone), in which the protagonist is a gay man in a committed homosexual relationship, may mean that films about gay men are finally "getting beyond the gay ghetto."[49] Neil Meron, producer of the Broadway musical, *Falsettos*, remarked that the homophobia that has prohibited gay-themed movies "tends to disappear commensurate with box office gross."[50] Yet the success of *Philadelphia* had a great deal to do with its star, Tom Hanks, a straight man; its conventional setting; and the film's treatment of AIDS, a cause of profound anxiety for the middle-class Americans who dominate film audiences.

To achieve box office success, studios will often mount two separate advertising campaigns, one of which targets heterosexuals and minimizes the film's homosexual content, and one that alerts homosexual audiences to that content. Moreover, the heterogeneity of homosexual audiences makes it difficult to devise a marketing campaign that will not alienate large parts of that audience. The gay market cannot be treated homogeneously. "One gay film isn't going to satisfy everybody."[51] Gay men and lesbian women are diverse in class, race, and gender so that, for example, "gay men and lesbians show little interest in each other's films."[52] As late as 1991, Percy Adlon—director of *Salmonberries*—says, "studio distribution executives were 'scared to death' of a lesbian love story."[53] Lesbian films are much rarer than gay films. Just as lesbian-themed fiction is usually published by small presses, while gay-themed fiction is published by large publishers, male homosexual experience on film is considered more universal than women's.

Russo notes that gay men and lesbians have been ambivalent about their moviegoing experience. On the one hand, the movies are where they learned to act straight, and "where [homosexuals] learned the boundaries of what Americans would accept as normal." On the other hand, Hollywood movies taught gays and lesbians that "there were no homosexuals in polite society,"[54] that "homosexuality has only to do with sex, while heterosexuality is multifaceted and embraces love and romance,"[55] and that "a good lay cured homosexuality."[56] Gay and lesbian teenagers learned that there are no gay teenagers in America, a myth that today's films for young people continue to perpetuate.[57]

When Hollywood does focus on homosexuality, gay characters' sexuality tends to be seen as defining their identity rather than being a part of it. The institutional and social discrimination that shapes gays' and lesbians' experience and presumes heterosexuality also tends to be invisible. A vast improvement over almost all filmic treatments of gay men, *Paris Is Burning* nevertheless shares some of the problems of the distorting scrutiny of the big screen.

The commercial success of *Paris Is Burning* occurred in a society and cultural moment in which gay men were thought to be the population most at risk of becoming infected with HIV (although it was no longer true). Although gay and bisexual men presently comprise 77.5 percent of those infected, women are the fastest growing population of AIDS victims in the United States. Gay men have apparently been successful in modifying the sexual practices that made them AIDS' most common victim in the 1980s. Cases among women rose 9.8 percent in 1992, while cases among men rose 2.5 percent.[58]

AIDS statistics are only now, in the 1990s, beginning to convince most heterosexual Americans that they are potential victims of the disease. It is difficult for anyone to ignore the rapidity with which HIV and AIDS are spreading. The first hundred thousand cases of AIDS in the United States were diagnosed in the first nine years of the epidemic; the next hundred thousand were diagnosed in the next eighteen months.[59] Given this reality, moviegoers are interested in and aware of gay life as they had not been formerly.

For most viewers, *Paris Is Burning* appeals largely to their curiosity about the world of balls and voguing. Yet its documentary format, which implicitly claims an impartial or objective representation, masks the standpoint from which the film is made—and for whom.[60] The heterosexual White spectators who dominate film audiences would feel uncomfortable and unsafe if they were to attend a ball in person, but they can look through the camera's eye without discomfort and without risk. Ballwalkers' poverty, race, and sexual orientation combine to position the great majority of viewers as voyeurs, "visiting" a culture they would not otherwise know.

Class, defined on the basis of relative affluence, is central to *Paris Is Burning*. Ballwalkers are poor in a media society that constructs poverty as failure, if not criminality. Culture critic bell hooks writes: "Contemporary popular culture in the United States rarely represents the poor in ways that display integrity and dignity. Instead, the poor are portrayed . . . as seeing themselves as always and only worthless. Worth is gained only by means of material success."[61] This representation of poverty in the media is constantly reiterated; it functions to keep the poor "in their place," blaming themselves for their inability to get rich in America. It also presents the horrifying alternative to the middle-class work ethic in order to reinforce its values and behavior, to produce people who are willing to get up and get to work most mornings of their lives. By briefly posing as opulent at the balls, the ballgoers in *Paris Is Burning* resist both their experience of poverty and media interpretations of the meaning of poverty.

Another aim of the film is to challenge heterosexual privilege. As if it is a dress, heterosexuality is "mopped" or stolen, tried on, and appropriated by the ballwalkers as part of the American dream. By housing White heterosexuality in the bodies of gay men of color, the presumption that heterosexuality is natural—"the original and the norm"—is resisted.[62] Because the characters have studied the stereotype of heterosexual femininity in great detail, they are more skilled at its gestures than many women. One character even teaches femininity in a women's charm school.

For most ballwalkers, realness is achieved through appropriating and wearing femininity. The figure of woman functions to transform them from outsider to the fantasized object of acceptance and approval from White heterosexual men. As not quite "the real thing" in patriarchal society, the image of the woman is "the figure for this theatricality because she is the currency with which men strive to out-purchase one another."[63]

Appropriating the appearance of the White heterosexual woman does not necessarily mean, however, that ballwalkers want to *be* White women or that they identify with women.[64] There is no agreement on this in the ball community as shown in the film. Whether to get a sex-change operation or not is decided largely along generational lines. The fifteen-year-old Venus Xtravaganza was quite clear about what *she* wanted: "I would like to be a spoiled rich White girl. They get what they want whenever they want it, and they don't have to really struggle with finances. . . . I want my sex changed. . . . I want to be a complete woman. . . . This is what I want and I'm gonna go for it."

On the other hand, Pepper LeBeija, who has "ruled" as mother of a house for several decades, thinks that the sex-change operation is going too far. Maintaining male identity is essential to posing as a woman, he feels. Poses are theater; they alone can *appear* real; the actual real, for women, may well be harsh abuse:

I've been a man, and I've been a man who emulated a woman. I've never been a woman. I've never had that service once a month. I've never been pregnant. I can never say how a woman feels. I can only say how a man who acts like a woman or dresses like a woman feels. I never wanted to have a sex change, that's just taking it a little too far. . . . A lot of the kids I know, they got the sex change because they felt, "Oh, I've been treated so bad as a drag queen. If I get a pussy, I'll be treated fabulous." But women get treated bad. They get beat. They get robbed. They get dogged. So, having the vagina, that doesn't mean that you're going to have a fabulous life, it might in fact be worse.

In addition to highlighting class and sexuality, *Paris Is Burning* also thematizes race. Many audiences assume that the film is "inherently oppositional [to mainstream society] because of its subject matter." Yet, bell hooks writes, "the film in no way interrogates whiteness . . . [It] negates that there is beauty to be found in any form of blackness that is not imitation whiteness. [It is] a graphic documentary portrait of the way in which colonized black people . . . worship at the throne of whiteness."[65] As stated earlier, *Paris Is Burning* is utterly reassuring to White heterosexist audiences, reiterating for their consumption the presumption that they have—that they are—the real thing.

As I have noted, gaps of poverty, race, and sexuality separate the subjects of *Paris Is Burning* from the great majority of filmgoers who are heterosexual, white, and middle-class, positioning these spectators as voyeurs. Why are these gaps problematic? For one example, consider voyeurism in relation to the ritual of ballwalking. For the participants, ritual creates a community and marks that community's significant or memorable moments. Yet ritual becomes spectacle when it is watched from a safe distance rather than participated in, and there is a profound difference between ritual and spectacle. Bell hooks wrote of *Paris Is Burning*:

> The film's focus on ritual takes the ritual of the black drag ball and makes it spectacle. Ritual is that ceremonial act that carries with it meaning and significance beyond what appears, while spectacle functions primarily as entertaining dramatic display.[66]

Participants in most rituals dislike being observed by nonparticipants. They find it at best distracting, and at worst, they fear being ridiculed. The characters in *Paris Is Burning*, however, agreed to be filmed because being watched is a necessary part of their ritual. The critical appraisal of onlookers is essential, but they did not predict the effects, within the ballwalkers' community, of being watched by outsiders.

Nevertheless the damages of voyeurism may ultimately be more profound for the viewer than for the viewed. Oddly, the distancing effects of film spectatorship encourage the viewer to identify easily with characters from whom she is, in actuality, very different. In *Paris Is Burning*, the format of interviewing the men and filming the balls—show and tell—gives the impression that one has insight into, or understands, ballwalkers. The film implies that differences of class, race, and sexual orientation are trivial and need not be taken seriously since they are easily overcome by simply listening to others' self-revelations and feeling a facile and temporary empathy with the characters.

Did the production and distribution of *Paris Is Burning* affect the ball community? Since the release of *Paris Is Burning*, there has been anger in the ball world about the film. Many people resent Livingston for making poor Black and Latino people into a commodity for White consumption. But their anger is mostly over money. At the beginning of the filming, seduced by the opportunity of seeing themselves on the screen, attaining visibility, and perhaps even achieving some of the fame they desire, the men agreed to participate without being paid. Now that the film has unexpectedly earned approximately $4 million, they say of the director and crew: "They all got rich, and we got nothing."[67] Most drag queens make a living by prostitution—"it's that or starve"—so resentment about someone from outside the community making money on them is high.[68] Three of the participants sued, but the suits were dropped because they had signed releases. Livingston volunteered to pay $55,000 divided among thirteen performers according to how long they were on camera in the edited version, but this was considered too little and too late.[69] Livingston insists that, for her, the primary reward for making the film was not financial: "The truth is, though I didn't get rich, I am now a filmmaker. And that's something I wasn't before."[70] Although the film's success could not have been predicted, and she was not legally bound to pay performers who had signed the customary releases, I believe that Livingston might have volunteered to share more of the financial benefits with the performers who made it successful.

The more subtle ways that the film may have affected the ball community are more difficult to document. *Paris Is Burning* documents a fragile moment in a community that is disintegrating. In April 1993, at Angie Xtravaganza's (age 27) memorial service, one of her "children" remarked that, although drag balls have been happening in Harlem since the 1920s, the whole world of the gay balls is coming to an end.[71] Partly this is because AIDS is decimating the ball world.[72] Of the nine men featured in the film, five are dead or dying.[73] Did the film also hasten the end of ball culture? Several reviewers thought so. In an article entitled "Paris Has Burned," Jesse Green writes, "Once mainstream America began to copy a subculture that was copying it, the subculture itself was no longer of interest to a wider audience, and whatever new opportunities existed for the principals dried up."[74] Jackie Goldsby concurs that, far from advancing the careers of its subjects, the film has exposed their skillful disguises, reducing society's interest in them:

As much as the film opens the ball world to our view, it also betrays its subjects. The film's form as documentary . . . is inimical to the participants' desire for glamour and mass fame. . . . Simply by representing Octavia St. Laurent, the film exposes the fiction informing her "realness." She'll never become the supermodel she hopes to be. Not surprisingly, it is only Willi Ninja, with his butch looks, who crosses over into *Village Voice* feature stories and Malcolm McLaren music videos.[75]

The issue of representing people and communities with whom the filmmaker is not identified, and representing people with whom the filmmaker does identify should also be considered. One way to begin is to compare *Paris Is Burning* to another film about Black gay men, this one made by and with Black, gay, and HIV-positive men—Marlon Riggs's *Tongues Untied*.[76] Riggs's film treats some of the same material—the balls and voguing—but in an interestingly different way.

Tongues Untied presents the life of a Black, gay, HIV positive man— Marlon Riggs himself—as containing much more than the balls. Riggs treats a broad range of topics, from the ridicule he received as a youth, to the Black gay pride marches of the 1980s, to discovering that he was HIV-positive. He conveys to his audience that life is not all voguing and balls. Riggs's camerawork is quite different from Livingston's accelerated motions and fast cutting. He lets a hand-held camera stay with a slow-moving character or scene so that its full sensuality—as opposed to specularity—can emerge. *Tongues Untied* is the self-representation of Riggs, his lovers, and his community, and it documents a richer range of experience and feeling than does *Paris Is Burning*. Characters are not interviewed; they are not asked to tell their secrets. Rather, they show their anguish, their sexuality, and their moments of solidarity and pride in the context of the Black gay community. Self-representation does not always guarantee an honest and accurate portrait, but it is more likely to achieve it than an outsider's representation. A comparison of *Tongues Untied* to *Paris Is Burning* reveals the difference between inviting a viewer to witness a self-revelation and providing a spectacle for moviegoers. But Riggs's film was not a box office success.

Let us return to the role of desire in *Paris Is Burning*. Although the film does not include any traditional religion, it has a religious subtext in its strong representation of desire. Many historical Christian authors considered the creation and direction of desire to be the primary function of religion. Religion designates what object shapes most fruitfully the psyche that desires it. Desire, delight, beauty: these are key concepts in Western Christianity from Augustine on. And *Paris Is Burning* is centrally and explicitly about desire. Curiously, sexual desire is neither shown nor evoked; it is seldom even referred to. Other people's sexual desires are a way of earning money for many ballwalkers, but their own desires, as far as the film goes, are predominantly if not exclusively social. The perennial desire for self-creation is vivid in the film. The film's remarkable poignancy, commented on by several reviewers, is that the subjects' fantasies of wealth, whiteness, and privilege are probably more satisfying than actually possessing them.

Ballgoers' "playful" mimicry of White America is deadly serious, in the context of a society in which the designer body has never been as fascinating. What messages do poor Black and Latino gay men receive about themselves in a media culture that counsels perfection of body at every turn of a remote control, dial, or page, but the body to be perfected is almost always White, rich, and heterosexual? How playful can ballwalking be in such a context?

As a society, North Americans are "committed"—the rhetoric is recognizably religious—to myriad forms of physical exercise and eating regimes. Many of us also volunteer to undergo painful and expensive surgery to redesign our bodies. In 1989, 681,000 cosmetic procedures were done in the United States. This figure represents an 80 percent increase over cosmetic surgery in 1981.[77] Advertisements for cosmetic "procedures"—the word "surgery" is assiduously avoided—speak of the "transportation of fat from one part of the body to another." These procedures are often compared to hair care and make-up and characterized as play. Yet the motivation to undergo expensive and painful cosmetic surgery is generated by the ubiquitous images in media and advertising that make all women (and, increasingly, men) dissatisfied with their bodies and thus vulnerable to suggestions that their features can be dramatically altered for the better.

In Saul Bellow's novel, *Henderson the Rain King*, the protagonist is tormented by a voice within that says, "I want; I want," but never tells *what* "it" wants. One of the fascinations of *Paris Is Burning* is that characters can and do designate exactly what it is they want. They want the rewards, including the "right" body, of a consumer society. But there is also a subtle subtext of other longings, longings for pleasure, love, and beauty.

Ballgoers represent their yearnings for, and commitment to, the rewards of a materialistic society as ultimate, non-negotiable, absolute—in a word, religious. "I'm gonna go for it," Venus Xtravaganza said. Some would see the quest for material success and fame as misguided compared to a search for God. But while this is no doubt true on some level, I am reluctant to propose it. If a fuller story were told in *Paris Is Burning*, it might well include the betrayal of gay men of color by most organized religions, and by the affiliation of the dominant American religion, Christianity, with white heterosexuality, an association that can certainly be overgeneralized but is not inaccurate for much of mainstream Christianity.[78] It is unlikely that poor gay men of color would find a welcome in most churches, mosques, or synagogues.

No ballwalkers appeared as bishops, priests, rabbis, or imans, though it can certainly be argued that liturgical garments, worn by a largely male clergy, are a perennial and sanctioned form of drag.[79] The subjects of *Paris Is Burning* have found their religion where they could: in the explicit and implicit messages about religion and values circulated in media culture. They have read these messages accurately and appropriated them creatively. In doing so, they call attention to the American values of whiteness, wealth, and heterosexuality. Perhaps ballgoers find traditional religions so peripheral that they do not bother to emulate them as bastions of the values and allegiances of White America.

Most reviewers observed that the men of the ball world revere and imitate a world that rejects them, finding that at best ironic, and at worst deluded. Even director Jennie Livingston remarked in an interview: "There's an intense irony in people imitating people who exclude them."[80] But if the film demonstrates anything, it demonstrates that desire is socially constructed. Power, privilege, and pleasure are clearly defined in a media culture. And the objects of desire offered by a capitalist consumer society are attractive not only to the people who can purchase them, but also to people who can never realistically expect to be a "spoiled rich White girl," and who choose to fantasize rather than to rebel or revolt against society's mores. In fact, people who have the designated objects of wealth, success, and power know that they do not bring happiness, while those who do not may never discover this. Yet the image and possibility—however remote—of conspicuous wealth keeps the have-nots from rebellion. As one character in *Paris Is Burning* put it, "This is not a take-off or a satire, but actually being able to be this. It's really a case of going back into the closet."

In short, just as *Paris Is Burning* allows mainstream Americans one-sided access to a minority culture, the balls themselves both assume and inadvertently support White America. The film publicized ballgoers' admiration for dominant American values. The events that could be interpreted as spoofs of heterosexuality, wealth, and whiteness do not come across as such on the movie screen. Rather, *Paris Is Burning* reveals a spectacular conformity at the core of a counterculture. Judith Butler comments:

> The dreams of economic success, fame, and security articulated by the performers are exactly the dreams circulated in media representations of the good life in America. As much as there is defiance and affirmation, the creation of kinship and of glory in [*Paris Is Burning*], there is also the kind of reiteration of norms which cannot be called subversive. . . . [The film] calls into question whether parodying the dominant norms is enough to displace them; indeed, whether the denaturalization of gender cannot be the very vehicle for a reconsolidation of hegemonic norms.[81]

When poor Black and Latino gay men are represented as longing for consumer goods, the White spectator, representative and possessor of these goods, is "flattered rather than chastened."[82]

Gary Hentzi has pointed out a symbiosis between "subcultural activity" and the dominant culture: "Ironically, the dominant culture is itself often renewed through the eventual reappropriation, packaging, and sale of those innovations."[83] Indeed, that process was already at work as the film was released. One reviewer noted that the ballgoers "vogue on the floor like Madonna dancers." But, of course, Madonna appropriated voguing from the ball world.[84] Jackie Goldsby writes, "Madonna can convert voguing into excess and into a cultural cash crop, banking on the ball world's invisibility and its inability publicly to claim voguing as its own."[85]

*   *   *

Finally, it is instructive to notice the filmic effects of the director's focus on the balls as the center of the lives of poor gay men of color. Two obvious omissions are immediately evident. First, the social world within which the balls have meaning is not explored. Hooks observes that "at no point in Livingston's film are the men asked to speak about their connections to a world of family and community beyond the drag ball."[86] The balls are shown to compensate for the characters' exclusion from mainstream American society. Yet the effect of Livingston's filmic focus on the balls permits the tension of that exuberant compensation to drain away.

Second, the everyday realities the drag balls seek to transcend—violence, drug and alcohol addiction, hunger, and disease—are excluded from the frame. White America is also excluded, except by reference, innuendo, and a brief moment when the camera rests on White heterosexual Americans on the street. By the time this occurs in the film, viewers have become visually familiar with the ballwalkers and the world of the balls. Juxtaposed to the fake "realness" of the ball world, the heterosexual "drag" that dominates the dress and behavior of White Americans becomes evident. The ballwalkers look more real than the White Americans on the street. This is a fine filmic moment, but it does not effectively show the adversarial relationship of the ball world to the world of White heterosexual Americans.

In *Tongues Untied*, White heterosexual America impinges more directly on the film world. The dismissal, heckling, and abuse gay men of color constantly receive is kept in the frame. It is shown as motivating the creation of the balls, an uncolonized space in which these men are free to act out their fantasies. The viewer is not asked to believe that the balls emerge from the spontaneous creativity of people whose difference from mainstream America is only skin deep.

At the conclusion of his analysis of Hollywood's representation of homosexuality, Vito Russo makes a thoughtful suggestion:

> The few times gay characters have worked well in mainstream film have been when filmmakers have had the courage to make no big deal out of them, when they have been implicitly gay in a film that was not about homosexuality. So no more films about homosexuality. Instead, films that explore people who happen to be gay in America and how their lives intersect with the dominant culture.[87]

In order to attract funding, films must promise box office success. And box office success requires that the interest of White Americans be engaged. I have criticized both of the films considered in this chapter as ultimately packaging for White comfort the images they present of Black and Latino people. By representing poverty, drug abuse, sexual license, intolerance, and the endangered family as dark-skinned they ultimately reinforce rather than challenge racist White America. However, both films also provide images of Americans' individual and collective anxieties in the present historical moment. Like beginning preachers, *Jungle Fever* and *Paris Is Burning* do a much better job of presenting problems than of suggesting possible resolutions. Yet they examine in powerful images the ancient question: How should we live? They especially explore, "on location" and in detail, who the "we" is, expanding film audiences' awareness that "we" includes people not often featured in the movies. Finally, that is all that can be asked of a film.

9

What You See Is What You Get: Religion and Values in the Movies

Three queries have been woven through my discussion of particular films in their social context, and it is time to address them more directly. First, I have considered how visual engagement and its effects in film are related to the long history of the religious use of images within Christianity. Second, I have questioned representations of religious and cultural difference in Hollywood films, which are required to make a profit and therefore strive to please and reassure White Americans. Third, I have suggested that films contain images and characters that enable us to discuss the perennial religious question, "How should we live?"

In this concluding chapter I want to consider an issue that brings my three queries together in a way that may not be immediately obvious: the relationship of screen violence to violence in American society. If a connection can be identified, I believe that something further can be said about the effects of screen culture on American values and, ultimately, on the question, "How should we live?" Since a dramatic increase in violence in homes and on streets has alarmed Americans, violence has received public attention in both news media and academic studies, and various efforts have been made to establish a link between screen violence and actual violence.

Culture theorist Todd Gitlin has written, "American culture as a whole . . . cultivates a taste for violence. . . . Today's movies are far more violent than the streets."[1] What is the social setting in which screen violence is so prominent?

The United States is presently one of the most dangerous countries on earth. "The national homicide rate, corrected for population growth, increased almost exactly 100 percent from 1950 to 1990."[2] In large cities the increase has been much higher: in Los Angeles County, with a population that doubled in the last forty years, homicides have increased over 1,000 percent since 1953.

A recent survey of more than a thousand studies over a thirty-year period has shown decisively that "exposure to violent images is associated with anti-social and aggressive behavior."[3] The findings of this survey have been endorsed by the American Medical Association, the National Institute of Mental Health, the Surgeon General's Office, the American Academy of Pediatrics, the American Academy of Child Psychiatry, the American Pychiatric Association, and the Centers for Disease Control. Yet, according to David Barry, evidence of the effects of screen violence has "for decades been actively ignored, denied, attacked, and even misrepresented to the American public, and popular myths regarding the effects have been perpetuated."[4]

How does screen violence promote actual violence? Screen violence is particularly hard to theorize about because of its very different effects on different people. But we do know that movies teach a statistically tiny segment of the population how to kill. Recently *Child's Play 3* inspired two copycat killings in Great Britain, and Joel Rifkin, a Long Island landscape gardener convicted of killing seventeen women, told a psychiatrist that he had "acted out asphyxiations inspired by a graphic scene in the Hitchcock movie *Frenzy*."[5]

Furthermore, the millions of Americans who enjoy screen violence, but are not motivated to imitate it, are not unaffected by it. According to the survey cited earlier in this chapter, actual and screen violence have similar cumulative effects. Like actual violence, screen violence has been shown to anesthetize against empathy with the victim's pain. Gitlin writes: "Over the years of chain saws, sharks, abdomen-ripping aliens, and the like, movie violence has come to require, and train, numbness."[6] He suggests that screen violence functions to habituate Americans to actual violence.[7] Moreover, those who watch screen violence and those who perform violent acts have something in common: desensitization. Martin Amis has observed that "in real life . . . desensitization is precisely the quality that empowers the violent."[8] It is unlikely that someone who had his attention on the victim's pain could bring himself to commit a violent crime.

Violence seen repeatedly on the screen may also normalize violence enough to make a difference to another small proportion of habitual spectators under certain circumstances—such as when they are aroused to anger.[9] Across a large population, the relatively few people who might, in certain conditions, emulate movie violence, become numerous enough to worry about.[10]

Despite this evidence, both media workers and the general public remain unconvinced that screen and real violence are linked. But the media workers who refused to credit the evidence may be acting in bad faith. For television studios sell advertising spots, without which they could not continue to operate, by the use of market research documenting the increased sales attributable to screen advertising. Do media workers believe that viewers are suggestible only during commercials? There is more than a little cynicism in this double-speak.[11]

Many Americans may be reluctant to criticize screen violence because they enjoy it, and not just because it is entertaining. Just as Americans' concern about changing gender relations, religious and cultural pluralism, and racial issues helps make films with these themes successful, so does Americans' concern about *actual* violence aid the success of violent films. What occurs, or threatens to occur, in people's lives needs to be pictured in order to consider how to cope with it. All screen violence cannot, and probably should not, be eliminated.

I will turn later to another reason why most Americans are reluctant to believe that screen violence can do them harm. With this knowledge in hand, however, what can be done to diminish screen violence? David Barry argues:

> There's no constitutional violation in a studio head rejecting a film project out of concern for its possible harmful effect on society. Without even hinting at anything so odious as a regulatory body, it's not hard to imagine activist groups exercising their First Amendment rights by bringing pressure on corporate heads of studios to examine the possible harm done by extremely violent films.[12]

I agree that a combination of group protests and appeals to the social and moral responsibility of studio executives, directors, and screenwriters will be necessary if the kinds of screen violence that have been shown to influence violent crimes are to be diminished.[13] Individuals and groups must protest violence in media entertainment, not just by walking out of violent movies, but by stopping at the box office and asking for our money back. Directors and studio executives could also do a great deal by reducing the violence and depicting violence in ways that emphasize the victim's pain rather than the violent character's strength and skill. I believe that government regulation, on the other hand, is too problematic a form of control, subject as it inevitably is to personal judgments based on the perspectives of those who decide what Americans should and should not see on the screen. Information rather than regulation is, in my view, government agencies' best contribution. In addition to film ratings, information on the content of films is presently given by advertising (which regularly features the most violent moments in a film in the hope of attracting viewers), by reviewers, by the rating code, and by entertainment guides that describe various features of a film that might concern or offend some people. Unless moviegoers in large numbers boycott violent films, however, information alone will not help to reduce screen violence.

Meanwhile, viewers of screen violence can minimize its effects (at least on themselves) by the thoughtful contextual analysis I have urged throughout the book for other issues. For example, analyzing the strategies by which a film containing many violent incidents attempts to make spectators identify with the inflictor(s) rather than the victim(s) of violence might work against some of the numbing effect of voyeuristic violence. Recovering our sensitivity to suffering would, in turn, urge us to work, as individuals, as groups, and as a society toward rectifying the social conditions that foster actual violence as well as screen violence.

Questions concerning the common good, like the question of screen violence, are essentially moral or religious questions, that is, they are questions about relationships, broadly construed. This definition of religion, as I explained in chapter 1, makes it evident that constructions of and attitudes toward gender, race, class, and sexual orientation are not accidental or incidental to religious perspectives. Rather, as *the way religious perspectives are articulated*, they are central to a concrete understanding of religion. Each religion seeks to specify its own values, and these values will result in a particular quality of relationship.

Presumably, although most religions value nonviolent relationships, the present high levels of violence indicate American religions' failure to challenge Americans to shun violence. In a religiously plural society, contending against screen and actual violence cannot be the task of the numerically dominant religion alone; it must be a cooperative goal. If multiple religions are to work, each in their distinctive ways, to instill relational values that can lessen violence in American homes and streets, mutual respect and an equal voice for all religions are necessary. All Americans, not religious and cultural elites alone, must become informed and understand the values and practices of other religious groups. For if multiple religious and cultural negotiations throughout society are to succeed in diminishing violence, they cannot be based on dominant groups' fear of losing privilege and other groups' anger at their marginalization. I do not advocate that religious differences should be overcome or transcended, but that each religion be respected for its capacity to enhance its members' sense of relatedness within society, the world, and the universe.

In fact, an effective medium for transmitting such information already exists: popular film. Yet at present, popular awareness and understanding of the diverse religions of America is rudimentary. Hollywood films could give accurate and colorful pictures of diverse religious groups, their beliefs, and practices. As we have seen for race, class, and sexuality in several films, however, accurate representation is most likely to be achieved when it is self-representation. The same is true of religious identity. Directors, screenwriters, composers, and cinematographers who can communicate an insider's perspective will be needed. But the issue of the accurate representation of America's religions is even more vexed. On at least two of the films I have discussed, a member of the religious group depicted acted as an advisor (*The Mission*, *Romero*). Even when that is the case, however, the representation of difference is often subverted by the film conventions that seek to ensure box office success.

I now return to the question, why do many Americans continue to believe the myth of "pure entertainment," that is, that screen images are innocent of social effect? The long answer to this question must take into account American culture's origins in iconoclastic branches of

Protestantism for which the word was the bearer of both religious and rational discourse. Even Protestants who permit images in churches pay little attention to them; they are not thought of as a powerful part of most Protestants' religious repertoire. On the other hand, language, from political slogans to sophisticated arguments, has been taken seriously. The Protestantism of America has changed to religious pluralism and uneasy secularism without altering the assumption that while language is serious, images are irrelevant.

Nevertheless, Americans are uneasy about images. Throughout the twentieth century, there has been enough popular ambivalence about the power of films to prompt many freedom-loving Americans to support censorship.[14] In 1930 the Motion Picture Producers and Distributors of America successfully compiled a "voluntary Production Code that would restrain the producers' tendency to create ever more licentious entertainment."[15] Colloquially known as the Hays Office (after its first director), it had the power to levy heavy fines for violations of the Code. Until 1952, "no film rejected by the Code had ever had a commercial release."[16] In that year, the Supreme Court gave the film industry First Amendment protection, the same guarantee of free speech held by publications. The public protested strongly, however, against the ensuing "explicit sex and gory violence" of late 1960s films. In response, the rating system was devised in 1968, another attempt at self-regulation by the newly organized Motion Picture Association of America. Religious agencies had attempted to urge parishioners to boycott movies with scenes considered objectionable, but the Protestant Film Office closed in 1966; the Catholic Legion of Decency closed in 1968.[17] Since that time, another self-monitoring effort has been in effect. The rating system describes a film's content to potential spectators. The history of film censorship reveals that each attempt to regulate the movies has been prompted by public protest.

If, as continuing efforts to censor or categorize films indicate, Americans are aware that films have power, it is important to understand the nature and amount of that power. A closer look at a leitmotiv of this study—similarities and differences between ancient religious uses of images and contemporary film spectatorship—may illuminate films' specific power.

Do moving pictures function iconically, as religious paintings traditionally have, to produce or inspire imitation? After considering *The Last Temptation of Christ* and *Jesus of Montreal* in chapter 2, I concluded that these films did not act religiously for Christians who saw them. Was this because of some lack in the quality or content of these films? I think not, for even bad art has been, and is, devotionally efficacious. Is it, then, because of something in the nature of *moving* pictures?

I suggest that film is a weak religious "visual aid" because it is possible to watch a film with little engagement of the imagination. Many, perhaps most, spectators are irritated with films that, because of a weak plot or poorly developed characters, require the spectator to imaginatively embellish the film. By contrast, looking at a painted narrative scene in the context of devotional practice, viewers must imagine a moving scene. What gives the captured moment its intensity is the spectator's knowledge of what came before, and what will come after. In the case of a scene in which sacred figures are posed for the viewer's gaze, one must imagine the figures' heavenly context and all that it implies about human life.[18]

It is this committed and informed imaginative labor that connects the devout to the religious painting, not the subject or style of the painting itself. Modern theories of vision that emphasize the viewer's distance or separation from the object do not describe adequately the religious use of vision. Icon use presumes an ancient theory of vision in which a quasi-physical visual ray streams from the eye of the viewer to touch its object. The form of the object then moves back along the visual ray to imprint itself in the memory of the viewer.[19] This theory emphasizes the viewer's initiative and active engagement, an intentional appropriation of the object that connects viewer and object permanently (in memory). Lacking the spectator's concentrated attention, a religious painting is simply a painting with a religious topic. The setting or surroundings of an image is also important to the use made of it. Paintings that once aroused religious devotion in churches, now, on museum walls, attract artistic appraisal and admiration that may have nothing to do with religious interest.

Like other artistic media, movies do not function iconically unless viewers deliberately augment the visible with imagination, by imagining how it would feel to be in the protagonist's situation, by imagining the smells, the tastes, the touch the film character experiences. In fact, all spectators some of the time, and some spectators all of the time, do contribute such sensory imagination and reflection to film viewing. It is not, then, impossible for films to act iconically; it is just less likely that they will do so. Moreover, to function as an icon, an image must attract a strongly concentrated energy of desire. Ah, but surely this is what films do best! Or is it? Films' limitations in evoking desire will become evident when we consider a recent analysis of desire and its relationship to vision.

In her book, *The Roots of Power*, Maxine Sheets-Johnstone has distinguished two kinds of desire. The first is voyeuristic; it contents itself with the surface and the look.[20] The second kind of desire also originates with vision, but it moves on from vision to engage other senses, especially touch.[21] It is striking that many mystics, such as Plotinus and Augustine, have described their most intense religious experience as simultaneously one of vision and touch. Plotinus writes: "At the moment of touch there is no power whatsoever to make any affirmation; there is no leisure; reasoning upon the vision is for afterwards. We know we have had the vision when the soul suddenly takes light."[22] Orthodox Christians kiss the icons on which they gaze, thereby establishing and acknowledging an intercorporeal connection between the once-living bodies of the sacred figures and their own living bodies. In religious practice the goal of desire is a ritual touch, either the metaphoric touch of the visual ray or the literal touch of a kiss.

Clearly, film spectatorship involves the nontactile desire. The satisfaction produced by films is encompassed by, and stops with, vision. There is nothing to touch. There are no bodies. Touch and the other senses can be engaged only in imagination. Spectators are conditioned, after years of screen-viewing, to a kind of desire that has learned not to long to "place one's body against the other's body,"[23] but views at a distance "the presence of an absence."[24] Those who are alarmed enough about the effects of Hollywood films to urge some form of censorship do so because they assume that we relate to films as a devotee relates to an icon. This is an exaggeration of the power of films.

On one level, we should rejoice that this is so, for it means that most viewers do not develop the kind of attachment to a film that makes us want to appropriate—to incorporate or embody—screen characters' qualities, characteristics, and behavior. Hollywood films seldom show human lives thoughtfully and responsibly lived, in relationship with others like and unlike themselves. Presumably, few adults go to a movie to acquire role models. On another level, however, spectatorship represents a sad curtailment of desire.

But surely film achieves one iconic desideratum of Western Christianity. Film images are more naturalistic than still pictures; they move. And I claimed in an earlier chapter that every increase of naturalism in Western religious pictures has produced an increment of devotional attachment.[25] Why, then, do movies not function as an icon does? It is in part because the imaginative contribution required of the icon viewer is not required of the film viewer; it is also partly because Christians who use icons absorb the form of the same image again and again in a daily practice of concentrated vision. Most people see a film only once. A few people see "cult" films again and again, but most of us buy the video of a film we have enjoyed, only to let it collect dust.

What, then, is the real power of films? No one film has iconic power, but the recurrence of similar images *across* films weaves those images into the fabric of the common life of American society, influencing everything from clothing styles to accepted and expected behavior. Filmic conventions, of which most spectators are never consciously aware, cumulatively affect Americans' self-esteem, expectations, attitudes, and behavior in relationships. That is why it is important to examine and to question them, to ask of them the ancient question of the Holy Grail: Whom does it serve?

When we do so, we will receive a complex answer, and one in which White middle-class Americans are implicated. For it is not box office aspirations alone that dictate film conventions. Box office returns are high only when a large number of Americans attend—and do not ask for our money back. That can be predicted to happen when the largest racial, class, and sexual-preference group of Americans are reassured that our pleasure is paramount. In most of the films discussed here the many choices made in the production of a film often undercut the radical topic filmmakers intended to present sympathetically. One of the surprises I have had in thinking about Hollywood films has been to recognize their profound conservatism.

The answer to my question concerning the power of film, then, is that, to a greater or lesser extent, "we [as a society] are what we look upon and what we delight in," or, in less elegant language, what you see is what you get.[26] But we "get" (the cultural message, as Roland Barthes said), or *are*, what we see not once but repeatedly. We get, at a subliminal and hence utterly effective level, not the narrative but the conventions of Hollywood film.

Because of this, our public self-representations take on a more than casual importance. Who is the "we" in a pluralistic society? Americans need films that help us picture religious, racial, and cultural diversity as irreducible and delightful, if we are to begin to entertain concretely and generously the question, "How should we live?" Films should help all Americans imagine differences that are not erased or transcended, differences of race, sexual orientation, class, and gender that contribute to each person's particularity, rather than positing as different anyone who diverges from a dominant norm.[27]

Moreover, a society in which people are at risk of fatal infection through sexual exchanges needs to see images in which safe sex is sexy. A society in which people are disastrously inept at maintaining committed love relationships needs a media that does not continually polarize men's and women's erotics, and that pictures diverse erotics. We need varied images of beauty on the big screen, images that would help to make the beauty of those among whom we live pop into the eye, for in seeing one another's beauty we augment it. This list of desiderata could be lengthened indefinitely. If any of these desiderata are actually to be met, however, funding for films needs to be diversified so that Hollywood studios no longer control all of the films that are adequately funded, advertised effectively, and distributed nationally.[28]

In a society in which functional illiteracy is high, film images are an important source of information and socialization. The philosopher Suzanne Langer said that the function of a society's art is to educate the emotions, to train the sensibilities to a rich range of feeling, to a perceptual life that misses nothing of importance.[29] To the extent that the arts we live with supply stimulation, articulation, and perceptive delicacy to our relational lives, we are well served. If, however, we find that the arts with which we live are governed by a narrow emotional repertoire, by conventions of representation, and by genre films with minimal elements of surprise, we are not well served. A media diet is not sufficient nourishment for anyone, yet millions of Americans live on it. Ultimately, stocking one's imagination with the rich and varied images that are capable of criticizing and enhancing relationship, community, and society will require more than the movies. But it is the movies, for better or for worse, that have such tremendous potential for informing our individual and collective imaginations. Martha Nussbaum describes the novel's capacity in a way that applies also to movies:

> There may be some views of the world and how one should live in it—views, especially, that emphasize the world's surprising variety, its complexity and mysteriousness, its flawed and imperfect beauty—that cannot be fully and adequately stated in the language of conventional philosophical prose, a style remarkably flat and lacking in wonder—but only in a language and in forms themselves more complex, more allusive, more attentive to particulars . . . in a form that itself implies that life contains significant surprises, that our task, as agents, is to live as good characters in a good story do.[30]

To the question, Are Hollywood films presently so compromised by box office aspirations that thoughtful people would do best to spurn them? I answer, No. When we acknowledge their limitations, then what they can do—and indeed do well—becomes evident. First, they identify social problems and issues and present them in concrete situations in particular lives. Second, Hollywood films often represent conflicts of values, inviting and enabling discussion of how we should live. Films are a resource for viewers who want to entertain questions concerning the value commitments that best inform a responsible, enjoyable, and productive life in our historical moment. Usually, the issues films present are embedded in their narrative; occasionally, a film raises such an issue pointedly and vividly. One example will suffice.

In the 1981 film, *My Dinner With André*, Wally (Wallace Shawn) remarks to André (André Gregory) that when he thinks of his immediate relationships and responsibilities, he feels like "a pretty good guy." He pays his rent; he takes out the garbage; he is nice to his friends; he does his job. But if, for a moment he places himself in the context of a suffering world, a world full of physical hunger, violence, and war, he no longer feels quite so good about himself. He is then forced to recognize that his lifestyle uses more than his fair share of the resources and wealth of the world. He realizes, moreover, that he is oblivious to most of the suffering of the world, and that he has built his own happiness and sense of self-worth on that obliviousness. This was an unsettling and challenging filmic moment.

Films are neither icons to be emulated, nor are they distillations of evil. They are cultural products, deeply informed by the perspectives, values, and aspirations of their makers. They beg for creative discussion, for it is finally the uses to which Hollywood films are put that determines their function in American society. Moreover, films need to be talked about, not merely the emotions they stimulate in diverse viewers, nor whether the images they present of various characters are positive or negative, but what particular anxieties and interests of their social moment they address, whether obliquely or directly.

What films do best, then, is to articulate the anxieties of a changing society. In films, the competing issues of society intersect and can be formulated for consideration, for understanding, and for negotiation of meaning. Films do not provide readymade solutions. But they can vividly articulate specific problems and longings and reveal their complexity and causes. Sometimes, at their best, films can help to identify resources and to imagine alternatives to the social arrangements, the images, and the religious institutions that have contributed to the problems of public and private life. They can contribute to the images with which we work out how we, as a pluralistic society, might live as "good characters in a good story."

Appendix

Using a cultural studies method of film analysis, I asked the following questions about the representation of religion and values in each of the films I discussed:

I. The film as cultural product

    Was the film a commercial success? What was its circuit (funding, production, distribution, and reception)?

II. The film as text

    A. Is religion treated explicitly in the film? Is it central to the narrative?

        Is religion pictured as institutional? As individual spirituality? As communal?

        Are characters religiously motivated? If so, how is this shown?

        How are attitudes toward religion communicated to the viewer?

B. What values are explicit or implicit in the film? This
    question has two distinct but related parts: What did the
    producer and director intend to communicate? What
    effects did her/his filmic decisions have in the film's
    communication?

    How does the film relate to, or differ from, the history
    or novel on which it is based?

    Does the film advocate certain values by glamorizing
    actions that incorporate them? Does it question certain
    values, attitudes, or behavior? Does it denigrate certain
    values?

    Are situations or problems that have traditionally been
    considered religious treated as secular?

    How do gender roles structure the film? Which
    characters have subjectivity in the film? By what filmic
    devices is subjectivity shown?

    Does the film comment on race? Does it imply that only
    people of color have race? What assumptions are made
    about race?

    What social class is depicted? What assumptions are
    made about class? With what class are viewers
    encouraged to identify? By what filmic strategies?

    What objects of sexual desire does the film assume or
    identify? Is heterosexuality assumed? Are there
    references to homosexuality?

III. The film as cultural voice

A. Did the film explicitly relate religious issues and/or
    values to matters of public discussion at the time of its
    production and distribution? Does it refer to a popular
    interest or anxiety? Does it avoid an urgent
    contemporary social issue?

Are attitudes communicated in the film relevant to any issues currently under national discussion?

What social arrangements and institutions does the film depict?

B. From whose perspective (race, class, gender, sexual orientation) was the film created? Did the director identify with the subjects of the film or represent them as an observer?

C. What viewers (race, class, gender) does the film address? From whose point of view is it most easily interpreted? How could it be "read against the grain"?

D. Are treatments of religion and/or values similar across several or many contemporary films? What film conventions (genre, narrative, cinematography) affect the film's representation of religion? Values?

Notes

Preface

1. Although figures for increased church membership in the last forty years can be cited, these figures are often not corrected for population growth. Similarly, figures for financial support of religious institutions are uncorrected for inflation. See, for example, Roger Finke, "An Unsecular America," and Bryan R. Wilson, "Reflections on a Many-Sided Controversy," in *Religion and Modernization: Sociologists and Historians Debate the Secularization Thesis*, ed. Steve Bruce (Oxford: Clarendon Press, 1992). Wilson has argued persuasively that the "social significance" of religion has declined. Religion once "provided legitimacy for secular authority; endorsed, at times even sanctioned public policy; sustained with a battery of threats and blandishments the agencies of social control; was seen as the font of all 'true learning'" (200).
2. Tom O'Brien is an exception; his *The Screening of America: Movies and Values from 'Rocky' to 'Rainman'* (New York: Continuum, 1990) is a thoughtful examination of movie attitudes toward such issues as cultural literacy, work, home, justice, and religion.

3. These phrases appeared in a single film review quoted by Tim Bywater and Thomas Sobchack, *Introduction to Film Criticism* (New York: Longman, 1989), 15.

4. James Carey, "Symbolic Anthropology and the Study of Popular Culture," unpublished essay quoted by Jackie Byars, *All That Hollywood Allows: Rereading Gender in 1950s Melodrama* (Chapel Hill: University of North Carolina Press, 1991), 41.

Chapter 1. Moving Shadows

1. See David Freedberg, *The Power of Images* (Chicago: University of Chicago Press, 1989), and Margaret R. Miles, *Image as Insight* (Boston: Beacon, 1985).

2. For a description of continuities from painting to film, see Anne Hollander, *Moving Pictures* (Cambridge, Mass.: Harvard University Press, 1991).

3. Miriam Hansen, *Babel and Babylon: Spectatorship in American Silent Film* (Cambridge, Mass.: Harvard University Press, 1991), 8–9.

4. Plato, *Republic* VII, 514aff.

5. Ronald Holloway, *Beyond the Image* (Geneva: World Council of Churches in Cooperation with Interfilm, 1977), 48.

6. Ibid., 75.

7. I enclose the word "entertainment" in quotation marks here because throughout the book I will question the assumption that it engages the spectator without effects.

8. Martha Nussbaum, *Love's Knowledge* (New York: Oxford University Press, 1990), 15.

9. Ibid.

10. Ibid., 16.

11. Ibid.

12. Ibid., 15–16.

13. Laura Mulvey, "Visual Pleasure and Narrative Cinema," *Screen* 16, 3 (1975), 6–18; see also Mulvey's "Afterthoughts on 'Visual Pleasure and Narrative Cinema' Inspired by King Vidor's *Duel in the Sun* (1946)," *Framework* (1989), 29–38.

14. Karl Marx, *Critique of Hegel's "Philosophy of Right,"* trans. Annette Jolin and Joseph O'Malley (Cambridge: Cambridge University Press, 1977), 131.

15. Amy Newman, "Feminist Social Criticism and Marx's Theory of Religion," *Hypatia* 9 (Fall 1994), 15.

16. Martha Nussbaum, in *The Therapy of Desire: Theory and Practice in Hellenistic Ethics* (Princeton: Princeton University Press, 1994), repeatedly contrasts the patient careful work of reason and philosophical argument with religion, which "turns the good life over to prayer, making outcomes neither controlled nor fully scrutinized by human reason" (50). See also pp. 217, 233, 261, 489. Yet her concern in *Love's Knowledge*, with "saving our lives," by which she means "giving human beings a life that will be free of certain intolerable pains and confusions" (84), sounds remarkably similar to many of religion's this-worldly salvific aims.

17. David F. Prindle, in *Risky Business: The Political Economy of Hollywood* (San Francisco: Westview Press, 1993), discusses the liberal bias that characterizes Hollywood activism, concluding that "there is no organizational counterweight to balance the leftward hegemony of Hollywood's political groups" (108).

18. Iris Marion Young, "Impartiality and the Civic Public: Some Implications of Feminist Critiques of Moral and Political Theory," *Praxis International* 5, 4 (1986).

19. Nussbaum, *Therapy*, 92. Pity requires that (1) "the person pitied must be thought undeserving (*anaxios*) of the misfortune"; (2) "the person who pities must believe that he or she is vulnerable in similar ways" (87).

20. In "Impartiality," Iris Marion Young identifies impartiality as an ideal of public discourse: "Impartiality means something different from the pragmatic attitude of being fair, considering other people's needs and desires as well as one's own. Impartiality names a point of view of reason that stands apart from any interests and desires. Not to be partial means to be able to see the whole. . . . The impartial reasoner thus stands outside of and above the situation about which she reasons, with no stake in it" (383). Young questions the ideal of impartiality as both illusory and oppressive.

21. Ronald Schiller, "How Religious Are We?" *Reader's Digest* (May 1986), 102. Jeffery L. Sheler, in "Spiritual America," *U.S. News and World Report* (April 4, 1994), quotes a 1992 study by sociologists Roger Finke and Rodney Stark, *The Churching of America: 1776–1990.* Finke and Stark found that America is presently more religious

than it was in 1776, when only 17 percent of America's population claimed a religious affiliation. They estimate that 68 percent now "are members of a church or synagogue."

22. Schiller, 128. Other studies report more ambiguous findings. A 1988 *American Demographics* article cited both a dramatic increase in religious bookstores and a decrease in the percentage of people who say that they read the Bible nearly every day. Also in 1988, a Gallup study, "The Unchurched American," found an increase (from 41% to 44% over a ten-year period), in the number of respondents who identified themselves as outside the church. "Church Membership Down," *The Christian Century* 105 (August 3, 1988), 696. In a 1987 article in *Public Opinion Quarterly*, Noval D. Glenn concludes his examination of a "Trend in 'No Religion' Respondents to U.S. National Surveys, Late 1950's to early 1980's": "It seems . . . that the only honest conclusion to be reached about recent secularization in the U.S. is that no simple and dogmatic conclusion can be reached. . . . a careful and objective assessment of much additional evidence will be required to attain a truly good understanding of what has happened to religion in the U.S. and to the religiosity of the American people during the past several decades." *Public Opinion Quarterly* 51 (Fall 1987), 293–314.

23. It is important, however, to notice the limitations of domestic box office statistics. "Domestic rentals are the actual share of the North American box office grosses returned to distributors." In fact, "domestic theatrical box office seems more and more insignificant—it now represents about 30 percent of an average movie's final revenues." Domestic theatrical rental figures, nevertheless, are influential in determining which films are made into videos and/or become foreign box office hits. It "takes from five to seven years for a movie to run through all its markets in every territory." In 1993, videocassette rentals far surpassed theatrical rentals, climbing to $11.2 billion, and foreign grosses in the same year "accounted for 52 percent of all '93 worldwide grosses." Anne Thompson, "Scent of Green," *Film Comment* (March–April 1994), 79.

24. With the exception of *Go Fish*, which was a modest hit, earning $2.4 million since its 1994 release.

25. Fred Inglis, *Media Theory* (Oxford: Basil Blackwell, 1990), 113.

26. For a discussion of film as "the riskiest art," see Prindle, *Risky Business*, esp. chapter 2.

27. I will not consider films made for television primarily because they require a different analysis, one that takes into account "flow," that is, the whole spectacle, including advertising segments.

28. Tom O'Brien, *The Screening of America: Movies and Values from 'Rocky' to 'Rainman'* (New York: Continuum, 1990), 198.

29. Ibid., 187.

30. *Witness* was on the box office charts for about five months, reaching the rank of number 1 for a month, and grossing $22,657,029.

31. *Tender Mercies* was a critical success, winning Robert Duvall an Academy Award, but it was a box office failure.

32. Inglis, *Media Theory*, 144.

33. "Values may be conceived as global beliefs (about desirable modes of behavior and end-states) that underlie attitudinal and behavioral processes." Boris Becker, Barbara Brewer, Bodie Dickerson, and Rosemary Magee, "The Influence of Personal Values on Movie Preferences," *Current Research in Film: Audiences, Economics, and Law*, 1 (1985), 38.

34. I will focus throughout on values associated with race, gender, and class in films of the 1980s and early '90s. I hope that others will examine these and other values in two film genres that I do not address in this book, war films and science fiction.

35. See Jacqueline Bobo's "Reading Through the Text: The Black Woman as Audience," an exploration of "Black women's seemingly overwhelming favorable response" to Steven Spielberg's *The Color Purple*, in spite of its "neutralization" of the strong Black women of Alice Walker's novel, in *Black American Cinema*, ed. Manthia Diawara (New York: Routledge, 1993), 272.

36. J. Hillis Miller, *Illustration* (Cambridge, Mass.: Harvard University Press, 1992), 10.

37. I accept throughout Clifford Geertz's definition of culture in *Interpretation of Cultures* (New York: Basic Books, 1973), as "a historically transmitted pattern of meanings embodied in symbols, a system of inherited conceptions expressed in symbolic form by means of which men [sic] communicate, [and] perpetuate and develop their knowledge about and attitudes toward life" (89). In Robert A.

LeVine and Richard A. Shweder, eds., *Culture Theory: Essays on Mind, Self, and Emotion* (Chicago: Aldine, 1984), a briefer definition is given: "Culture [is] shared meaning systems."

38. Richard Johnson, "What is Cultural Studies Anyway?" *Social Text* 16 (1987).

39. Miller, *Illustration*, 56.

40. The term 'popular' does not designate anything until defined more precisely and concretely; moreover, "the popular" is not a monolithic entity. I mean by the term cultural products that circulate in the public sphere, i.e., products to which a broad audience has access. Similarly, Raymond Williams cautions that "there is nothing to be gained and indeed much is to be lost, if we go on supposing that within the rhetoric of the 'popular' there is real common ground." "Cinema and Socialism," *The Politics of Modernism* (London: Verso, 1989), 109.

41. Barbara Klinger, "Digressions at the Cinema: Reception and Mass Culture," *Cinema Journal* 28, 4 (Summer 1989), 5.

Chapter 2. *"Were You There When They Crucified My Lord?"*

1. Michel Foucault, *Discipline and Punish* (New York: Vintage, 1979), 27.

2. David Freedberg, *The Power of Images* (Chicago: University of Chicago Press, 1989), 201.

3. Several directors have used the expectation that there is no connection between the world of the viewer and the world of the film to create a startling moment when a film character turns from his world to address the audience "directly." Examples occur in *Love and Death* and *Tom Jones*.

4. Dudley Andrew, *Concepts in Film Theory* (New York: Oxford University Press, 1984), 41.

5. Suzanne Kappeler, *The Pornography of Representation* (Minneapolis: University of Minnesota Press, 1986), 2.

6. Tim Bywater and Thomas Sobchack, *Introduction to Film Criticism* (New York: Longman, 1989), 168.

7. Andrew, *Film Theory*, 44.

8. Ibid., 43.

9. Kappeler writes in *Pornography*, "Representations are not just a matter of mirrors, reflections, key-holes. Somebody is making them, and somebody is looking at them through a complex array of means and conventions. Nor do representations simply exist on canvas, in books, on photographic paper or on screens; they have a continued existence in reality as objects of exchange; they have a genesis in material production" (34).

10. Georgia Frank writes of a visual culture surrounding fourth century Christian pilgrimages: "We are dealing with a highly symbolic language, dictated by its own conventions, values, and clues," a description which is equally applicable to Hollywood film conventions. *The Memory of the Eyes: Pilgrimage to Desert Ascetics in the Christian East during the Fourth and Fifth Centuries* (unpublished Ph.D. dissertation, Harvard University, March 1994), 47.

11. Bywater and Sobchack define "convention" as "a recurrent unit of activity, dialogue, or cinematic technique . . . used in films and familiar to audiences—for example, the shootout in a Western, the line "There are some things that man was not meant to know" in a horror film, the editing of a chase scene," *Introduction*, 124.

12. Ibid., 81.

13. Mary Ann Doane, "Technology's Body: Cinematic Vision in Modernity," *Differences* 5, 2 (Summer 1993), 1.

14. Michael Chanan, *The Dream That Kicks: The Prehistory and Early Years of Cinema in Britain* (London: Routledge, 1980), 15, cited by Doane, "Technology's Body," 1.

15. Ibid., 5.

16. William Hood, *Fra Angelico at San Marco* (New Haven: Yale University Press, 1993).

17. Doane, "Technology's Body," 6.

18. Douglas Gomery says, "The movie industry elevated popcorn to the status of an important farm crop in the United States. The popcorn harvest grew from five million pounds in 1934 to more than a hundred million pounds by 1940." "If You've Seen One, You've Seen the Mall," in *Seeing Through the Movies*, ed. Mark Crispin Miller (New York: Pantheon, 1990), 63. On spectatorship of violent deaths, see Wendy Lesser, *Pictures at an Execution: An Inquiry into the Subject of Murder* (Cambridge, Mass.: Harvard University Press, 1993).

19. Early filmmakers were quick to recognize the spectator's interest in death: *Execution of a Spy* (1902); *Reading the Death Sentence* (1903); *An Execution by Hanging* (1905); and *Beheading the Chinese Prisoner* (1900) are cited by Doane, "Technology's Body," 6–7.

20. *The Last Temptation of Christ* (1988), from the Kazantzakis novel of the same name, was on the box office charts for four months. For writing the book, Kazantzakis was denied burial by the Greek Orthodox Church, and the book was placed on the Roman Catholic Index of Forbidden Books. George L. Scheper, "Jesus Wrestles with God," *Commonweal* (September 9, 1988), 471. The film's highest rank was thirteenth. (*A Fish Called Wanda* was number 1 at the time.) It cost $6.5 million to make, but its total box office gross was only $3,837,639. This box office gross does not tell the whole story, however, as *The Last Temptation of Christ* was an unexpected success in video. In fact, only about twenty films from major studios earn most of their profits from theatrical box office. Anne Thompson, "Industry: The 14th Annual Grosses Gloss," *Film Comment* 25, 2 (March–April 1989), 74. *The Last Temptation of Christ* was made over the objections of marketing advisors who said that religion "just does not sell." In *Risky Business*, Prindle remarks that the film was "kicked around among several studios for three decades" before it was made (151). However, the proven bankability of its director, Martin Scorsese, eventually persuaded Universal Studios to let him make the film. The financial advisors were right: *Film Comment* lists it as a "disappointment in relation to cost."

21. Aljean Harmetz, "Scorsese's 'Temptation' Gets Early Release," *The New York Times*, August 5, 1988.

22. Peter Bien, "Scorsese's Spiritual Jesus," *The New York Times*, August 11, 1988, 25.

23. Terrence Rafferty, *The New Yorker* (September 5, 1988), 78.

24. Stanley Kauffmann, "On Films," *The New Republic* (September 12 and 19, 1988).

25. "Zeffirelli Protests 'Temptation of Christ,'" *The New York Times*, August 3, 1988.

26. Tom O'Brien, *The Screening of America* (New York: Crossroad, 1990), 190.

27. *Last Temptation* was based on a novel by a Greek Orthodox and di-

rected by a Roman Catholic; its screenplay was written by Paul Shrader, a former member of the Dutch Reformed Church and presently an Episcopalian.

28. "'Temptation' and Anti-Semitism," *Harper's* (November 1988), 22–26.

29. Ibid., 26.

30. Prindle notes in *Risky Business* that the cultural moment in which *Last Temptation* was produced is crucial: it "could never have been produced in 1915. Then the film industry could put out a film intensely offensive to blacks but not to Christians. Now, it is the other way around" (162). Prindle does not say what it was about the cultural "moment" that permitted the (contested) release of *Last Temptation*. I do not agree with his judgment that film studios cannot presently offend African Americans. They, in fact, do so regularly, and even intensely, according to my African American students and friends.

31. Quoted by Prindle, *Risky Business*, 151.

32. Most reviewers did not notice or protest the blatant sexism of *Last Temptation*. Andrew Greeley was an exception; in his review in *The New York Times*, August 14, 1988, he said that the film's sexism misrepresents the Jesus of the gospels more egregiously than any other aspect of the film. He wrote: "Jesus related to women as human equals and treated them with respect and affection, with gentleness and wit, with honesty and concern for their dignity. Jesus genuinely liked women, and they liked him. His erotic relations with them differed from those of other men only in that there was no hint of exploitation, manipulation, or violation." As a description of relationships of equality and mutuality, Greeley's description of the "Jesus of the Gospels" leaves a great deal to be desired, but he did notice an aspect of the film that other reviewers ignored.

33. This was first suggested to me in a discussion section of my film course at Harvard Divinity School by Tristan Reader.

34. Scorsese said in an interview that his idea about the Judas character, played by Harvey Keitel, was to "create a . . . stereotypical villain and then make him a hero." *The New York Times*, August 8, 1988.

35. I owe this analysis of the female roles in *Last Temptation* to a student in my film course, David McFarland.

36. A. W. Richard Sipe, *A Secret World: Sexuality and the Search for Celibacy* (New York: Brunner/Mazel, 1990), and *Sex Priests, and Power: Anatomy of a Crisis* (New York: Brunner/Mazel, 1995).

37. Nicholas Dawidoff, "No Sex. No Drugs. But Rock 'n' Roll (Kind of)," *The New York Times Magazine* (February 5, 1995), 66.

38. Ibid.

39. If the film represented Christ's humanity at the expense of his divinity, as some viewers claimed, the fact that, at the end of a lifetime of pleasures, he had the opportunity to revise his earlier decision as to how to live would alone effectively remove him from humanity and imply his divinity! There is, however, something distinctly antiheroic in his choice of death on the cross when he was close to a natural death anyway.

40. It is not clear whether such afflictions as eating disorders should be classified as voluntary or involuntary suffering. Clearly, many people suffer from disorders and other illnesses that they did not choose but that can be overcome or cured with effective help.

41. *Jesus of Montreal* was written and directed by a Canadian filmmaker, Denys Arcand, and produced in association with the National Film Board of Canada. Critics repeatedly called it Canada's best movie of the decade. It was a prizewinner at Cannes and a nominee for best foreign film in the 1990 Oscar awards. Yet *Jesus* had difficulty finding a distributor in the United States, largely because of the furor over *The Last Temptation of Christ* only a year before. (Arcand said that he did not see *Last Temptation* because he did not want to be either influenced or upset by it.) *Jesus* was not as large a box office success as anticipated on the basis of critical acclaim. On the charts for five months, in the week of its highest rank, *Jesus* ranked twenty-eighth (while *Days of Thunder* was number 1), grossing in the period it was on the charts $1,601,612. (By contrast, Arcand's *The Decline of the American Empire* cost less than a million to make and grossed more than twenty times that amount.)

42. John Curtin, "Denys Arcand Offers a 'Jesus for the 1990's,'" *The New York Times*, May 20, 1990, 23.

43. Tom O'Brien, "Jesus of Montreal," *Film Quarterly* 44, 1 (Fall 1990), 49.

44. Suzanne Moore, "Playing Jesus by Night," *New Statesman and Society* (January 26, 1990).

45. Film critic Michael Medved comments on this point: "If someone turns up in a film today wearing a Roman collar or bearing the title Reverend, you can be fairly sure that he will be crazy or corrupt or both," "Does Hollywood Hate Religion?" *TV Guide* (July 1990), 101. The 1984 film *Mass Appeal* is a notable exception.

46. Carrie Rickey, "Saying Good-bye to the Eighties: Twilight of the Reaganauts," *Tikkun* 4, 6 (November–December 1989), 51. Rickey cites the following 1980s Hollywood films as characteristic of this interest: *Risky Business*, *Goonies*, *Gremlins*, *License to Drive*, *Wall Street*, and *Back to the Future*.

47. Caryn James, "A Modern Passion Play in Montreal," *The New York Times*, May 25, 1990.

48. Tom O'Brien, in "Jesus of Montreal," writing about Catherine Wilkening as Magdalen, put this point rather curiously: "[Mereille] is sensuous, spirited, vulnerable—and Arcand's central image for matter yearning for more" (47).

49. Suzanne Moore, "Playing Jesus." Wendy Lesser describes similar requests for executed murderer Gary Gilmore's organs in *Pictures at an Execution*, 112–13.

50. Scorsese commented in an interview on his intention to make a film about "how we should live": "I don't think this will ever be out of my system. I just think I'm too obsessed by it, too fascinated by faith, by this concept of loving, and how we should live our lives." *The New York Times*, August 8, 1988.

Chapter 3. Seeing (as if) With Our Own Eyes

1. However, the top film of 1986 had little to do with religion; it was *Top Gun*.

2. Joseph Berger, "Films Find Spiritual Themes Compelling," *The New York Times*, January 4, 1987.

3. Harvey Cox, *The Silencing of Leonardo Boff: The Vatican and the Future of World Christianity* (Oak Park, Ill.: Meyer-Stone, 1988), 12.

4. Ibid., 11.

5. According to the *Catholic Almanac*, Brazil has the largest Roman Catholic population of any country in the world.

6. Cox writes in *The Silencing* that liberation theology has forced two primary questions: the first is how an ancient church accustomed to

obedience within its ranks will respond to the present "grassroots religious energy." The second issue is the de-Europeanization of the Roman Catholic Church, which is rapidly being transformed from a primarily European and North American church to a church primarily based in Latin America, Asia, and Africa.

7. Roland Joffé, director of *The Mission*, said, "My film is about the individuals who struggle to save other individuals against the broader interests of the Church, which is trying to defend its bureaucratic structures, in this case, the Jesuit order." Quoted by Judith Miller, "The Mission," *The New York Times*, October 26, 1986, 23. However, one reviewer worried in print about whether the "parallels between the eighteenth century and the late twentieth century, when many priests in Latin America have also found themselves at odds with Rome" would be recognized by the "average" viewer. Vincent Canby, *The New York Times*, October 31, 1986.

8. Sharon Welch, *Communities of Resistance and Solidarity* (Maryknoll: Orbis, 1985).

9. Mary Douglas, *How Institutions Think* (Syracuse, N.Y.: Syracuse University Press, 1986), 1.

10. In my view, the film that best achieves the circulating identifications that represent a *community* rather than individuals is *Daughters of the Dust*, a film I discuss in chapter 6.

11. I am indebted to Professor John O'Malley of the Weston School of Theology in Cambridge, Massachusetts, for bibliographical information on the history of the Jesuit missions in Latin America, especially *The Church in Latin America 1492–1992*, ed. Enrique Dussel (London: Burns and Oates, 1992). The best introduction to the Paraguay Reductions in English is Philip Caraman, *The Lost Paradise* (London: Sidgwick and Jackson, 1976); see also C. J. McNaspy, S.J., *Lost Cities of Paraguay: Art and Architecture of the Jesuit Reductions, 1607–1767* (Chicago: Loyola University Press, 1982).

12. Daniel Berrigan, a radical activist Jesuit priest, advised and acted in the film. His book, *The Mission: A Film Journal* (San Francisco: Harper and Row, 1986), describes the making of the film.

13. After a decade-long struggle to raise the production costs of $22 million, *The Mission* was filmed in Colombia. It was on the box office charts for five months—between November 1986 and April 1987. In the week of its highest rank, it was eleventh; its total gross was

$5,236,043. Directed by Roland Joffé, the British director who also directed *The Killing Fields*, *The Mission* won the top prize, the Palme d'Or, at Cannes in 1986. The script was written by Robert Bolt, who also wrote the screenplay for *A Man For All Seasons*.

14. Berrigan, *The Mission*, 26.

15. John Mosier, "Tramps Abroad: The Anglo-Americans at Cannes," *New Orleans Review* 13, 4 (1986), 8.

16. Tim Bywater and Thomas Sobchack, *Introduction to Film Criticism* (New York: Longman, 1989), 142.

17. In *The Mission*, Daniel Berrigan describes asking the director whether there was not some less clichéd way to account for brother turning against brother. He was told that of course there was but that the other ways this might be done "are not so easy to show quickly on the screen" (51).

18. Ibid., 5.

19. Ibid., 11.

20. Keith Tribe, "History and the Production of Memories," *Screen* 18, 4 (Winter 1977–78), 16.

21. Peter Steinfels remarks in his review of *Black Robe* that "even the well-educated moviegoer" finds it difficult to believe that "an apparently sane young French aristocrat [would] impose himself on a people who didn't want him, risking in the bargain a horrid death in a merciless terrain." *The New York Times*, October 26, 1991, 25.

22. Howard A. Rodman, "The Millimeter Review: Director Roland Joffé," *Millimeter* (April 1987), 133.

23. Harlan Kennedy, "Amazing Grace," *Film Comment* (October 1986), 10.

24. Gavin Millar, "The Honorable Dead: The Mission," *Sight and Sound* 55, 4 (October 26, 1986), 285.

25. David Tetzlaff, "Divide and Conquer: Popular Culture and Social Control in Late Capitalism," *Media, Culture, and Society* 13, 1 (January 1991), 28.

26. Profit, however, was not forthcoming. *Film Comment*'s "Twelfth Annual Grosses Gloss" lists *The Mission* as a "big budget disaster": it cost an estimated $24.5 million and grossed in domestic rentals only $8 million. *Film Comment* 23, 2 (March–April 1987), 68.

27. "Jesuits," *New Catholic Encyclopedia* (New York: McGraw-Hill, 1967–79), 902.

28. The most historically knowledgeable of *The Mission*'s reviewers, Richard A. Blake, wrote, without citing the source of his historical information: "As a matter of historical fact, once the Jesuits perceived Pombal's determination to crush the Reductions by military force whether or not they cooperated, they obeyed the orders of their superiors in the vain hope of minimizing the bloodshed." *America*, November 15, 1986, 302.

29. "Jesuits," *New Catholic Encyclopedia*, 907.

30. Mosier observes in "Tramps Abroad" that curiously, although *The Mission* is "technically and ostensibly a British film, [it embodies] all the attributes of the classical Hollywood production" (20).

31. The native population in *The Mission* was portrayed by three hundred and fifty Wanana Indians from the Choco region of Colombia who were transported three hundred miles for the filming. Rodman, "Roland Joffé," 133.

32. In *The Mission*, the Guarani have "no inner life . . . no animating human complexity . . . they are a collective human compass needle. They register the conflicts of beliefs and temperaments between Irons and DeNiro, and they record our own swiveling sympathies between the two. . . . [The Indians] are functions rather than characters, emblems rather than human beings." Kennedy, "Amazing Grace," 10–12.

33. Dave Kehr called the film's treatment of the native population "a positive colonialism"; but he also observed that the native population was depicted as a "brown mass," never differentiated or given character. "Call of the Wild," *American Film* (November 1986), 59. Richard Combs said *The Mission* is "only slightly less demeaning to the exterminated Indians than the cartoon-ecology of *The Emerald Forest*." *British Film Institute Bulletin*, October 1986, 311.

34. Mosier writes in "Tramps Abroad," "It's difficult to believe that a director who has the production of small Central American bananas the chief crop of the oldest Jesuit mission in Paraguay has much of an understanding of that region and its history" (10).

35. The "native" music in *The Mission* was played by the London Philharmonic Orchestra, with the London Voices choir. Second, the quasi-liturgical music which accompanied the slaughter at the Mission San Carlos is itself a film convention. Kenneth Chanko points out that beautiful music is frequently used in scenes of torture and

murder to "blow the audience's boundaries away . . . it heightens and twists the scene." "It's Got a Nice Beat, You Can Torture to It," *The New York Times*, February 20, 1994.

36. Berrigan, *The Mission*, 80–81; 108.

37. Quoted by Raymond Williams, "Cinema and Socialism," *The Politics of Modernism* (London: Verso, 1989), 108.

38. Ibid., 113.

39. Larry Rohter, " 'Romero' Finds a Producer: The Church," *The New York Times*, November 13, 1988.

40. Ibid.

41. Ari Goldman, "A Catholic Film on a Salvadoran Murder," *The New York Times*, August 24, 1989.

42. Stanley Kauffmann, "Truth and Inconsequences," *The New Republic* (September 11, 1989), 26.

43. Archbishop Romero was not the only religious leader killed in the civil war in El Salvador; twenty-two priests and nuns were murdered during the war, including several from the United States.

44. Stephan Ulstein, "Celluloid Evangelism," *Christianity Today* 33 (November 3, 1989), 77–78.

45. Quoted from a *Playboy* review on the jacket of the videocassette.

46. Kauffmann, "Truth," 26.

47. Vincent Canby, "Romero," *The New York Times*, August 25, 1989, 15.

48. For example, the box office success of *Witness* (number 1 for a solid month in 1985, with a total domestic rental gross of over $22 million), has been credited to its star, Harrison Ford. A film that juxtaposed an Amish woman and her community with a tough city detective, with most of the story taking place on an Amish farm, might well have failed to attract viewers without a tried-and-true box office star. I suspect that this lesson was well noted by the producers of *The Mission* and *Romero*.

49. *Salvador* also incorporates the story of the murder of Archbishop Romero, but while *Romero* was a modest success at the box office, *Salvador* was a critical and commercial failure. Part of the explanation for this may be that *Salvador* did not have a hero, but a hard-drinking American journalist for a protagonist. Another explanation for *Romero*'s comparative success was perhaps the Roman Catholic Church's support.

Chapter 4. Not Without My Other

1. Maxine Sheets-Johnstone has recently argued that intercorporeality (a shared condition of vulnerable physicality) is a more accurate and heuristic basis for appeals to a common humanity. *The Roots of Power, Animate Form and Gendered Bodies* (Chicago: Open Court, 1994), 57–59, 110.

2. Iris Marion Young, "The Ideal of Community and the Politics of Difference," *Social Theory and Practice* 12, 1 (Spring 1986), 3.

3. See J. Gordon Melton, ed., *Encyclopedia of American Religion*, 4th ed. (Washington, D.C.: Gale Research, Inc., 1993); J. Gordon Melton, *Religious Bodies in the United States: A Directory*, and *Encyclopedic Handbook of Cults in America*; and Charles H. Lippy and Peter W. Williams, eds., *Encyclopedia of the American Religious Experience: Studies of Traditions and Movements* (New York: Charles Scribner's Sons, 1988). The Pluralism Project at Harvard University, under the direction of Professor Diana L. Eck, will soon publish more accurate figures than are presently available, based on a systematic count of religious populations other than Christians and Jews in the United States.

4. I am grateful to my research assistant, Julia Baird Miller, for compiling these statistics, based on the sources listed in note 3.

5. *Not Without My Daughter* was filmed in Israel; it was directed by Brian Gilbert. It was a critical flop in this country, but its total gross was a very respectable $14,047,556. In the week of its highest gross, *Home Alone* grossed $9,813,012, while *Daughter* grossed $4,962,104. Internationally, *Daughter* was a big hit in Germany, and the book—by the same name—written by William Hoffer with Betty Mahmoody, was a colossal best-seller in Sweden. It has been estimated on the basis of sales that a copy could be in one out of every two Swedish homes. William Hoffer also wrote the script for the anti-Turkish film *Midnight Express*, which, according to Dr. Nayereh Tohidi, is a cult film for Armenians in Los Angeles.

6. *Rolling Stone*, February 7, 1991.

7. Caryn James, "Embrace the Stereotype: Kiss the Movie Goodbye," *The New York Times*, January 27, 1991.

8. The book did somewhat better on this point. It described Moody's incremental disintegration, already fully evident before the family

left the United States, the increasing psychological collapse of a troubled—and troubling—personality. Even the book, however, trivializes the racism Moody confronted in his profession as a significant factor in his increasing depression and hostility.

9. Nayereh Tohidi, "Stop Stereotyping Arabs and Iranians," *Los Angeles Times*, January 21, 1991, F3. Interestingly, Dr. Tohidi told me that when she reviewed the film in the American press, she emphasized its stereotypical treatment of Iranian culture; when she reviewed it in Iran, however, she urged that the picture it presented of Iranian women's constraints in family and society be taken as incentive for social change (Personal communication, March 1994).

10. Dan Nimmo and James Combs, *Mediated Political Realities* (New York: Longman, 1991), 9.

11. *Film Comment* listed *Daughter* as a "recouper," a film that did not recover its production costs in U.S. domestic rentals (first run theaters), but recouped $6.5 million in overseas sales. Anne Thompson, "Scenes from a Mall," *Film Comment* 28, 2 (March–April 1992), 70.

12. Nancy Armstrong, "Fatal Abstraction: The Death and Sinister Afterlife of the American Family," in *Body Politics, Disease, Desire, and the Family*, ed. Michael Ryan and Avery Gordon (San Francisco: Westview Press, 1994), 27.

13. Editorial, "The Rising Storm: Week Two," *Newsweek* (February 4, 1991), 20.

14. George Bush, "News Conference of January 25," *U.S. Department of State Dispatch* (February 4, 1991), 67–68.

15. Noel Carroll, *Mystifying Movies: Fads and Fallacies in Contemporary Film Theory* (New York: Columbia University Press, 1988), 208.

16. Ibid., 172.

17. Ibid., 180.

18. There was also an insistent scorn for a religion whose practices permeate what Westerners recognize as "secular" life; again and again the burdens of Islamic daily life were featured: "Moody taught me Islamic cooking . . ."

19. Betty Mahmoody, *Not Without My Daughter* (New York: St. Martin's Press, 1987).

20. *Chariots*, directed by Hugh Hudson, was on the box office charts for

ten months in 1981–82. It cost $6 million to produce, but reached a rank of number 3, and grossed $18,879,341 in the United States alone. *Chariot's* soundtrack album was among the top five in Great Britain. It won Academy Awards for Best Picture, Best Screenplay, Best Costume Design, and Best Score.

21.   Stanley Kauffmann, "On Films," *The New Republic*, October 7, 1981, 27. The poem itself, however, references a Hebrew Bible passage in which Elijah is carried to heavenly glory in a chariot of fire (II Kings 2.11).

22.   Vincent Canby, "Screen: Olympic Glory in 'Chariots of Fire,'" *The New York Times*, September 25, 1981.

23.   Kaja Silverman, "Dis-embodying the Female Voice," in *Issues in Feminist Film Criticism*, ed. Patricia Erens (Bloomington: Indiana University Press, 1990), 311–12.

24.   Canby, "Olympic Glory."

25.   Kauffmann, "On Films," 26.

26.   Pauline Kael, *The New Yorker* (October 26, 1981), 178.

27.   Michael H. Seitz, "Thatcher in the Theater," *Newsweek* (December 1981), 54.

28.   Steve Neale, "'Chariots of Fire': Images of Men," *Screen* (1982), 50.

29.   Malcolm Moran, "1924 Olympics Recreated in English Work," *The New York Times*, September 20, 1981.

30.   Colin McCabe, "Theory and Film: Principles of Realism and Pleasure," *Screen* 17, 3 (Autumn 1976), 21–22.

31.   Students in my film course found it especially painful to recognize these filmic devices for marginalizing Jewishness in a film that they initially "loved."

32.   The term "anti-Semitism" is misleading if it is taken to mean a monolithic prejudice and/or persecution. In fact, anti-Jewish attitudes and actions take many different forms in different times and places.

33.   Patricia Erens, *The Jew in American Cinema* (Bloomington: Indiana University Press, 1984), 10.

34.   Ibid.

35.   Ibid., 5.

36.   Ibid., 2.

37.   Miriam Hansen, *Babel and Babylon: Spectatorship in American*

Silent Film (Cambridge, Mass.: Harvard University Press, 1991), 15–16.

38. *The Chosen* cost a little more than $3 million. It was a modest box office success in the same year—1982—in which the most popular films were *E.T.*, *Tootsie*, and *Gandhi*. The director, Jeremy Kagan, is the son of a Reformed rabbi in Westchester, New York.

39. Erens, *The Jew*, 378. Subsequently, *Yentl* (1983) also focused completely on Jewish life.

40. Erens, *The Jew*, 378. Even Woody Allen, when he puts a Hasidic character in one of his films, does so strictly as a sight gag.

41. Quoted by Erens, *The Jew*, 6.

42. Despite this scrupulosity, critical responses to the film were disappointing: *The Chosen* was treated by many reviewers as a period piece, so evaluations of the film tended to be in terms of its visual accuracy to the time it portrayed.

43. Point-of-view refers to "a shot made from a camera position close to the line of sight of a performer who is watching the action in the shot." Tim Bywater and Thomas Sobchack, *Introduction to Film Criticism* (New York: Longman, 1989), 230.

44. Lucy Fischer discusses the political implications of film's extensive use of shot/countershot in *Shot/Countershot: Film Tradition and Women's Cinema* (Princeton: Princeton University Press, 1989).

45. Quoted by Richard F. Shephard, "Bringing Brooklyn of the 1940's Back to Life for 'The Chosen,'" *The New York Times*, May 16, 1982.

46. Robert Hatch, "The Chosen," *The Nation* (May 8, 1982), 37.

47. Martin Buber, *Hasidism and Modern Man*, ed. and trans. Maurice Friedman (New York: Harper Torchbooks, 1958), 49.

48. Ibid., 143.

49. Ibid., 163.

50. Ibid., 32.

51. Martin Buber, *Tales of the Hasidim* (London: Thames and Hudson, 1956), 313.

52. Buber, *Hasidism*, 74. Compare similar filmic moments of great intensity and interiority in *Children of a Lesser God* (a deaf woman's solo dance) and *Thirty-Two Short Films about Glenn Gould* (the protagonist listening/dancing/conducting a recording of his own piano performance).

53. Colin McCabe, "Theory and Film: Principles of Realism and Pleasure," *Screen* 17, 3 (1976), 27.

Chapter 5. There Is a Bomb in Gilead

1. *Yearbook of American and Canadian Churches*, ed. Kenneth Bedell (Nashville: Abingdon Press, 1993).
2. Ibid., 12.
3. Richard N. Ostling, "In So Many Gods We Trust," *Time* (January 30, 1995), 73.
4. Introduction to *Yearbook of American and Canadian Churches*.
5. *Handmaid* cost $13 million to make but recovered only $2.3 million in domestic rentals. "Flatliners: The 16th Annual 'Grosses Gloss,'" *Film Comment* (March–April 1991), 32.
6. Ed Doerr called *Handmaid* "shocking . . . but realistic and not at all overdone." "A Chilling Look at a Fundamentalist Dystopia," *The Humanist* (May–June 1990), 25.
7. Robert Duvall, who played the Colonel, commented on the novel in an interview: "I only read a few pages and then gave up on it. I usually do read the book. My girlfriend read it and hated it. But a lot of women love this book: it's like their bible, a feminist bible." Myra Forsberg, "Stars of 'The Handmaid's Tale' Analyze a Grim Fantasy," *The New York Times*, April 2, 1989.
8. Margaret Atwood, *The Handmaid's Tale* (Toronto: McClelland and Stewart, 1985), 389.
9. Doerr, "Chilling Look," 25.
10. Michael Calleri, "Another Example of How Great Novels Make Bad Films," *The Humanist* (May–June 1990), 27.
11. Ibid., 26.
12. Andrew H. Malcolm, "Margaret Atwood Reflects on a Hit," *The New York Times*, April 14, 1990.
13. Michael Calleri, in "Another Example," called the beginning of the film a "colossal misrepresentation" of the novel: "'Once upon a time . . .' places the movie safely in the realm of fantasy" (26).
14. Ibid., 28.
15. For example, Laura Mulvey, "Visual Pleasure and Narrative Cinema," *Screen* 16, 3 (1975). Mulvey has herself reconsidered her early position in "Afterthoughts on Visual Pleasure and Narrative Cinema," *Framework* (Bloomington: Indiana University Press, 1989).

16. Christine Gledhill, "Pleasurable Negotiations," in *Female Spectators*, ed. E. Diedre Pribram (London: Verso, 1988), 67–68.

17. Ibid., 71.

18. Ibid., 68.

19. In chapter 7 I consider popular film's representation of female friendship more generally.

20. Gledhill, "Pleasurable Negotiations," 73.

21. Tolkin is a novelist; *The Rapture* was his first film. Subsequently he also wrote *The Player*. *The Rapture* was on the box office charts for three and a half months. During the week of its highest rank it was number 29, with *The Fisher King* at number 1. It grossed $1,277,404.

22. Quoted in J. Hoberman, "The End," *The Village Voice*, October 8, 1991, 59.

23. Marilynne S. Mason, "Refusing the Rapture," *The Christian Century* (October 23, 1991), 956.

24. The content of her belief is never specified.

25. Quoted in Hoberman, "The End," 59.

26. From the vantage point of the believer, however, even her work acquires meaning: "There's a reason God made me a telephone operator," she says, in response to her supervisor's complaint that she is taking the opportunity to "witness" on the telephone.

27. I am grateful to Adrienne Nock and Kristyn Saunders for pointing this article out to me: Charles Krauthammer, "Why Is America in a Blue Funk?" *Time* (December 30, 1991), 83.

28. J. L. Simmons, *The Emerging New Age* (Santa Fe, New Mexico: Bear and Company, 1990), 18.

29. Ibid., *passim*. See also James R. Lewis and Gordon Melton, *Perspectives on the New Age* (Albany: State University of New York Press, 1992), and Brian R. Wilson, *The Social Dimensions of Sectarianism: Sects and New Religious Movements in Contemporary Society* (Oxford: Oxford University Press, 1990).

30. Lisa Kennedy, *The Village Voice*, October 8, 1991.

31. "The Rapture," *Variety*, June 17, 1991.

32. Hoberman, "The End," 59.

33. Janet Maslin, "Religion Taken to the Breaking Point," *The New York Times*, September 30, 1991; Caryn James, "Zeitgeist Isn't a Snap to Capture," *The New York Times*, October 13, 1991.

34. Mason, "Refusing," 956.
35. Robert Denerstein, in *Rocky Mountain News*, quoted in Mason, "Refusing," 956.
36. *Rolling Stone*, October 17, 1991.
37. Hoberman, "The End," 59.
38. Maslin, "Religion Taken to the Breaking Point."
39. Ibid.
40. David Ansen, "Dark Nights of the Soul," *Newsweek* (October 14, 1991), 70.
41. "The Envelope, Please," *The New York Times*, March 12, 1994. The Religious News Service reports that 72 percent of the top twenty-five box office movies were "acceptable" to the Christian Film and Television Commission headed by Ted Baehr.

Chapter 6. *"Older, Wiser, Stronger"*

1. For example, African Americans were brought to this country by force, while other racial groups have been excluded by law. Beginning in 1882, Exclusion Acts excluded or severely limited immigration of Chinese, Japanese, Koreans, Asian Indians, and Filipinos. Citizenship through naturalization was denied to all Asians from 1924 to 1943. A quota system restricting immigration of Asians to "professionals with postsecondary education, technical training and specialized experience" was in effect until the mid-1960s. Chandra Mohanty, Ann Russo, and Lourdes Torres, eds., *Third World Women and the Politics of Feminism* (Bloomington: Indiana University Press, 1991), 25.
2. Michael R. Winston, "Racial Consciousness and the Evolution of Mass Communications in the United States," *Daedalus: Journal of the Academy of Arts and Sciences* 3, 4 (Fall 1982), 171–82.
3. Jacqueline Bobo, "'The Subject is Money': Reconsidering the Black Film Audience as a Theoretical Paradigm," *Black American Literature Forum* 25, 2 (Summer 1991), 424.
4. Michele Wallace makes the insightful suggestion that "there was a way in which these films [starring Joan Crawford or Lana Turner] were possessed by Black female viewers. The process may have been about problematizing and expanding one's racial identity instead of

abandoning it. It seems crucial . . . to view spectatorship not only as potentially bisexual but also multiracial and multiethnic." "Race, Gender and Psychoanalysis in Forties Film: Lost Boundaries, Home of the Brave and The Quiet One," in *Black American Cinema*, ed. Manthia Diawara (New York: Routledge, 1993), 264.

5. Marlon Riggs, producer/director, *Ethnic Notions: Black People in White Minds* (57 minutes), 1987. Available from California Newsreel, 149 9th Street #420, San Francisco, CA 94103 (415/621-6196).

6. Ibid.

7. James Monaco, *How to Read a Film*, revised ed. (New York: Oxford University Press, 1981), 223.

8. bell hooks, "Representations: Feminism and Black Masculinity," *Yearning: Race, Gender, and Cultural Politics* (Boston: South End Press, 1989), 68.

9. Miriam Hansen, *Babel and Babylon, Spectatorship in American Silent Film* (Cambridge, Mass.: Harvard University Press, 1991), 59.

10. Tom O'Brien, *The Screening of America* (New York: Continuum, 1990), 160.

11. Ibid., 161.

12. Yet *Mississippi Burning* heroized FBI agents and underrepresented civil rights workers, failed to characterize in depth a single black figure, and omitted any mention of the fact that the KKK villains "were never convicted in state courts, and got brief sentences in the federal court." O'Brien, *Screening*, 163.

13. bell hooks writes: "I am fascinated by the appearance of transgression in an art form that in fact is no transgression at all. A lot of films *appear* to be creating a change, but the narrative is always so "sewn up" by an ending that returns us to the status quo—so there's no change at all. The underlying message ends up being completely conservative." *Outlaw Culture: Resisting Representations* (New York: Routledge, 1994), 237.

14. The top films of 1990 were *Home Alone* (grossing $120 million) and *Ghost* ($95 million). *The Long Walk Home*, by contrast, grossed only $1.7 in domestic rentals; it has recovered somewhat in foreign box office and video rentals.

15. In an interview, Whoopi Goldberg related: "During the filming of some of the rougher scenes, where people are screaming 'Nigger,

Nigger, Nigger,' for several hours, Dick [director Richard Pearce] would yell, 'Cut,' and people would instantly just go and grab onto somebody and say, 'I'm sorry. It's not us. We don't do that anymore.' Paul Chutkow, "Remaking Whoopi," *Vogue* (January 1991), 180.

16. Ibid., 181.
17. Taylor Branch, *Parting the Waters, America in the King Years, 1954–1963* (New York: Simon and Schuster, 1988).
18. Elizabeth Clark-Lewis, "'This Work Had a End': African American Domestic Workers in Washington, D.C., 1910–1940," in *To Toil the Livelong Day*, ed. Mary Beth Norton and Carol Groneman (Ithaca, N.Y.: Cornell University Press, 1987), 197.
19. Ibid., 207.
20. Writing about Black women's development of a critical oppositional gaze in relation to Hollywood films, bell hooks says, "We knew that White womanhood was the racialized sexual difference occupying the place of stardom in mainstream narrative film. We assumed White women knew it too." "The Oppositional Gaze: Black Female Spectators," *Black American Cinema*, 294.
21. Chutkow, "Remaking Whoopi," 180.
22. *A World Apart, Cry Freedom, Mississippi Burning,* and *Glory* also depict important moments in Black history from the perspective of a White protagonist. Similarly, *Schindler's List* depicts Jewish history from a Gentile German's perspective, and *Dances With Wolves,* a narrative about Native Americans, focuses on White protagonists. I am grateful to Susan Worst for these examples of assimilations of the history of minority people to the perspective of White Americans.
23. Palcy is from Martinique.
24. Television interview with Euzhan Palcy by Paula Acker, "Black in America Is Not Commercial," quoted in Glenn Collins, "A Black Director Views Apartheid," *The New York Times*, September 25, 1989.
25. hooks, "Oppositional Gaze," 291.
26. *The Color Purple,* despite its flaws as a film, is an exception, as is *What's Love Got to Do with It,* Tina Turner's story.
27. hooks, "Oppositional Gaze," 295.
28. Evelyn Brooks Higginbotham, "Beyond the Sound of Silence: Afro-American Women in History," *Gender and History* 1, 1 (Spring 1989), 51.

29. Ibid., 52.
30. Quoted by Branch, *Parting the Waters*, 140.
31. James Cone, *A Black Theology of Liberation* (Philadelphia: Lippincott, 1970), 17.
32. Branch, *Parting the Waters*, 145.
33. For example, Jonathan Daniels, a white student at the Episcopal Theological School in Cambridge, Massachusetts, went to Alabama to engage in the struggle for civil rights; he was killed as he pushed a Black girl out of the way of a White racist's bullet.
34. *Daughters* was on the charts for six months (from January to July 1992) and grossed $1,642,436. During the week of its highest gross, *Daughters* earned $13,140, while the number 1 film, *Wayne's World*, grossed $12,326,424.
35. Zeinabu irene Davis, "An Interview with Julie Dash," *Wide Angle* 13, 3 (October 1991), 117.
36. Toni Cade Bambara, "Reading the Signs, Empowering the Eye: *Daughters of the Dust* and the Black Independent Cinema Movement," in *Black American Cinema*, ed. Manthia Diawara (New York: Routledge, 1993), 119.
37. hooks, *Outlaw Culture*, 204.
38. Greg Tate, "Of Homegirl Goddesses and Geechee Women," *The Village Voice*, June 1991.
39. Irene Monroe, paper for Religion, Gender, and Culture colloquium at Harvard Divinity School, September 1993.
40. Donald Bogle, *Toms, Coons, Mulattoes, Mammies, and Bucks: An Interpretive History of Blacks in American Films* (New York: Viking, 1973).
41. Monroe, class paper.
42. Bambara, "Reading the Signs," 123.
43. Ibid.
44. Ibid., 135.
45. Ibid.
46. Camera rate is the speed at which the sprocket-driven gears push film stock through the chamber of a camera. Tim Bywater and Thomas Sobchack, *Introduction to Film Criticism* (New York: Longman, 1989), 223.
47. Bambara's description of the scene is in "Reading the Signs," 135.
48. Ibid., 127.

49. bell hooks, in "Oppositional Gaze," comments on Black women's frequent exclusion from feminist film criticism: "It is difficult to talk when you feel no one is listening, when you feel as though a special jargon or narrative has been created that only the chosen can understand" (297).

50. For example, Barbara-O (Yellow Mary) was in Haillie Gerima's *Child of Resistance* and *Bush Mama*, and Adisa Anderson (Eli) was in Ailie Sharon Larkin's *A Different Image*.

51. Davis, "Interview with Dash," 111.

52. Julie Dash, *Daughters of the Dust* (New York: The New Press, 1992), 16.

53. Bambara, "Reading the Signs," 131.

54. hooks, *Outlaw Culture*, 226–27.

55. Todd Carr, *Variety*, February 11, 1991.

56. *The Village Voice*, November 26, 1991.

57. Dash, *Daughters*, 11.

58. Carr also said in *Variety*: "Dash either doesn't know how, or doesn't care, to develop scenes dramatically. Highly emotional moments are sometimes dropped in with no preparation. Other sequences are allowed to seriously wear out their welcome" (11).

59. Keith Tribe, "History and the Production of Memories," *Screen* 18, 4 (Winter 1977–78), 16.

60. hooks, *Outlaw Culture*, 153; see also hooks' "Representations: Feminism and Black Masculinity," and "Counter-hegemonic Art," in *Yearning: Race, Gender, and Cultural Politics* (Boston: South End Press, 1989).

Chapter 7. Good Clean Fun

1. Norma Broude and Mary G. Garrard, eds., *The Expanding Discourse: Feminism and Art History* (New York: HarperCollins, 1992); Whitney Chadwick, *Women, Art, and Society* (London: Thames and Hudson, 1990).

2. See my *Carnal Knowing* (Boston: Beacon Press, 1989) for further discussion of treatments of female nakedness in the Christian West.

3. Constance Penley, "A Certain Refusal of Difference: Feminism and Film Theory," *The Future of an Illusion: Film, Feminism, and Psychoanalysis* (Minneapolis: University of Minnesota, 1989), 376.

4. Paula Rabinowitz, "Seeing Through the Gendered I: Feminist Film Theory," *Feminist Studies* 16, 1 (Spring 1990), 152.
5. Jackie Stacey, "Desperately Seeking Difference," *Screen* 28, 1 (1987), 145.
6. Judith Butler, *Bodies That Matter: On the Discursive Limits of "Sex"* (New York: Routledge, 1993), 13.
7. Ibid., 99.
8. In Great Britain as well as in North America, feminists recognize the importance of identifying and discussing differences among women. Shelagh Young, in "Feminism and the Politics of Power: Whose Gaze Is It, Anyway?," says that feminists' exclusive attention to resistance to male domination has led too frequently to "the suppression of differences in the name of progress." In *The Female Gaze*, ed. Lorraine Gammon and Margaret Marshment (Seattle: The Real Comet Press, 1989), 183.
9. Judith Butler, *Gender Trouble: Feminism and the Subversion of Identity* (New York: Routledge, 1990); Linda J. Nicholson, ed., *Feminism/Postmodernism* (New York: Routledge, 1990); Iris Marion Young, "The Ideal of Community and the Politics of Difference," *Social Theory and Practice* 12 (1986), 1–26.
10. Race is especially important in *The Piano*, in which native New Zealanders provide a foil for the "civilized" quandaries of the English. For a review that criticizes the film's treatment of race, see Stuart Klawans, "The Piano," *The Nation* (December 6, 1993), 704.
11. Directed by Ridley Scott, with screenwriter Callie Khouri, *Thelma and Louise* earned $43,240,638 in its eighteen weeks on the box office charts (cost to make: $17 million). It peaked at a rank of number 4 the same week that *Backdraft* was number 1.
12. Khouri knows whereof she speaks; she has supported herself as a receptionist, salesclerk, and waitress, enduring "the condescension and many of the same slights that infuriate Thelma and Louise." "The Woman Who Created 'Thelma and Louise,'" *The New York Times*, June 5, 1991, C24.
13. Quoted by Janice C. Simpson, "Moving into the Driver's Seat," *Time* (June 24, 1991), 55.
14. Ibid.
15. Robert R. Bell, *Worlds of Friendship* (Beverly Hills: Sage Publications, 1981), 62.

16. Lillian B. Rubin, *Just Friends: The Role of Friendship in Our Lives* (New York: Harper and Row, 1985), 106.

17. Asa Baber charges *Thelma and Louise* with being "prejudiced and sexist at its core," adding: "It faithfully represents our era, a time when feminists can bask in the glory of their increasingly harsh sexism toward men—and even win Oscar nominations for it." "Guerrilla Feminism," *Playboy* (October 1991), 45.

18. For example, Janet Maslin's comment, "The film's bracing end has a welcome toughness," in "Lay Off Thelma and Louise," *The New York Times*, June 16, 1991, 16.

19. John Robinson and Diane White, "The Great Debate Over 'Thelma and Louise': He Hates It, She Loves It," *The Boston Globe*, June 14, 1991, 29.

20. Maslin, "Lay Off," 16. In identifying the film as a road or outlaw film, however, Maslin made an unfortunate comparison. "Traditional reasons for which characters in outlaw movies are disposed of," she wrote, include "because he didn't smile when he said it. Because he stole, cheated, or lied. Because he wasn't lucky. Because it was a good day to die." Placing Louise's killing of Thelma's rapist alongside these conventions of outlaw film, she called screen rape a "new pretext for killing," thus trivializing attempted rape in a moment of "backlash" against feminism in American society.

21. Simpson, "Driver's Seat," 55.

22. Terrence Rafferty, "Outlaw Princesses," *The New Yorker* (June 3, 1991), 92.

23. Mary Cantwell, "What Were the Women 'Asking' For?" *The New York Times*, June 13, 1991.

24. Kathleen Murphy, "Only Angels Have Wings," *Film Comment* 27, 4 (July–August 1991), 29.

25. Richard Schickel, "A Postcard from the Edge," *Time* (May 27, 1991), 64.

26. Richard Grenier, "Killer Bimbos," *Commentary* 92, 3 (September 1991), 51.

27. Richard A. Blake, "The Deadlier of the Species," *America* (June 29, 1991), 683.

28. Robinson, "Great Debate: He Hates It," 36.

29. White, "Great Debate: She Loves It," 36.

30. See Myriam Miedzian, *Boys Will Be Boys: Breaking the Link Between Masculinity and Violence* (New York: Anchor Books, 1991), 7, and Aimee Lee Ball, "The Faces of Abuse," *Vogue* (November 1994), 192.

31. Carol J. Clover calls *Thelma and Louise* a "yuppified" version of a classic horror scenario: "in its focus on rape, its construction of males as corporately liable, its overt mistrust of the legal system to prosecute rape, and its interest in self-help (equals direct revenge) and sisterhood, *Thelma and Louise* is at dead center of a tradition that emerged and throve in the lowest sectors of filmmaking for years before it trickled into major studio respectability." *Men, Women, and Chain Saws: Gender in the Modern Horror Film* (Princeton: Princeton University Press, 1992), 234.

32. Judith Halberstam, "Imagined Violence/Queer Violence: Representation, Rage, and Resistance," *Social Text* 37 (Winter 1993), 187–201. I am grateful to Dr. Ann Pellegrini for pointing out this article to me.

33. Ibid., 199.

34. "TV show spurs calls from battered women," Springfield, Massachusetts, *Morning Union*, October 11, 1984.

35. Andrea Estes, "TV special on family violence 'hits home,'" *The Boston Herald*, October 10, 1984.

36. Robinson, "Great Debate: He Hates It," 29, 36.

37. Ibid.

38. Anne Thompson, "Mo' Money," *Film Comment* (March–April 1993), 85.

39. *Wayne's World* made Penelope Spheeris the highest grossing woman director in the world. Ibid., 86.

40. Janet Maslin, "A Woman Under the Influence," *The New York Times*, April 29, 1994.

41. The 1994 HIV/AIDS Surveillance Report 5 (4), published by the Center for Disease Control and Prevention, reported 47,572 diagnosed cases of HIV/AIDS in 1992; in 1993, the number was 106,949. Gay men accounted for 52.4 percent of the total number of cases in 1993, down from the 58 percent reported in 1992. Women with HIV/AIDS, however, were 5.4 percent in 1993, up from 4.8 percent in 1992.

42. Perhaps it should be acknowledged, however, that movie audiences have what Judith Halberstam called "the safest sex of all," namely, fantasy. Halberstam, "Imagined Violence," 194.
43. "AIDS is Top Cause of Death for Young Adults in U.S.," *San Francisco Chronicle*, February 1, 1995.
44. Richard Schickel, "Gender Bender," *Time* (June 24, 1991), 53.
45. *The Piano* was the tenth largest grossing film of 1993. In the seven months it was on the box office charts, it grossed $40,132,527. It reached the rank of number 7 the same week that *Mrs. Doubtfire* was number 1.
46. Brian D. Johnson, "Rain Forest Rhapsody," *MacLean's* (November 22, 1993), 72.
47. Mary Colbert, "Jane Campion on Her Gothic Film 'The Piano,'" *Sight and Sound* (October 1993), 34.
48. Sarah Kerr, "Shoot the Piano Player," *New York Review of Books* (February 3, 1994), 30.
49. Edward Rothstein, "A Piano as Salvation, Temptation, and Star," *The New York Times*, January 4, 1994.
50. But *is* it her sexual awakening? Ada's relationship with Flora's father was of such physical and mental attunement that, for a time at least, he could hear what she thought.
51. Jane Campion, *The Piano* (New York: Miramax Books, 1993), 9.
52. The ambiguous power of "sexual awakening" has had a notoriously volatile range of interpretation throughout Western literature. For example, in one of the earliest documents of civilization, the *Epic of Gilgamesh*, Enkidu's sexual initiation changes him from a wild man who runs with the gazelles to a socialized member of his society. An opposite interpretation was accorded to the power of sexuality by the twentieth-century author Herbert Marcuse, who thought of sexuality as subversive of socialized behavior, an energy by which the "true self" could be recognized and social conventions overthrown.
53. In "Shoot the Piano Player," Kerr writes that "the scene is a negation of everything that preceded it. The reckless logic of the film has prepared us to reject Baines and Ada as a happy domesticated couple" (30).
54. Stanley Kauffmann, "A New Spielberg; and Others," *The New Republic* (December 13, 1993), 31.

55. Anthony Lane, "Sheet Music," *The New Yorker* (November 29, 1993), 151.

56. The *Off Our Backs* reviewer was by far the most disgusted with *The Piano*: " 'The Piano' is a gorgeously shot, utterly repellent film about a woman trapped between two rapists: a sleazy, blackmailing rapist and a violent possessive rapist." *Off Our Backs* (February 1994), 21.

57. Kerr, "Shoot the Piano Player," 32.

58. Denis de Rougemont, *Love in the Western World* (Princeton: Princeton University Press, 1983); Margaret R. Miles, *Desire and Delight: A New Reading of Augustine's "Confessions"* (New York: Crossroad, 1992).

59. Psychoanalyst Maria Torok, commenting in a 1963 article on the phenomenon of "penis envy," concluded that the social effects of Western societies' gender arrangements are damaging to both women and men. Although it is initially "easy to grasp" why men enjoy heterosexual relationships in which women are passive and dependent, on closer inspection it is not so obvious: "The insincerity, ambivalence, and the refusal to identify with the other that this type of relationship entails should appear to men as so many obstacles thrown in the way of their complete and authentic fulfillment. . . . What benefit does the male derive from subjecting to his mastery the very being through whom he could both understand and be understood himself? Self-to-self-revelation . . . would be the realization of our humanity and this is what eludes nearly all of us." Maria Torok, "The Meaning of 'Penis Envy' in Women," reprinted in *Differences* 4, 1 (Spring 1992), 36.

60. Guy Garcia, "Women = Coy Banter, Men = Nude Blonds," *The New York Times*, October 23, 1994.

61. Ibid.

62. Thompson, "Mo' Money," 87.

63. Quoted by Anne Thompson, "Scent of Green," *Film Comment* (March–April 1994), 82.

64. Personal communication, February 1994.

65. Mark Crispin Miller states that the publicity for a film "takes up more cultural space than the film itself." *Seeing Through the Movies* (New York: Pantheon, 1990), 16.

Chapter 8. Bodies, Pleasures, and Pains

1. Charles Krauthammer, "Why Is America in a Blue Funk?" *Time* (December 30, 1991), 83.
2. Ibid.
3. Spike Lee's highest grossing film to date was *Malcolm X* ($35 million). It was backed by a major studio—Warner Brothers—"to a degree unprecedented for an African American movie." Anne Thompson, "Mo' Money," *Film Comment* (March–April 1993), 85. See also bell hooks's critique of *Malcolm X*, "Spending Culture: Marketing the Black Underclass," in *Outlaw Culture: Resisting Representations* (New York: Routledge, 1994), 145–54.
4. Catherine Silk and John Silk, *Racism and Anti-Racism in American Popular Culture: Portrayals of African Americans in Fiction and Film* (Manchester: University of Manchester, 1990), 164.
5. Ibid.
6. Ibid., 163. Both of these films were produced on extremely low budgets but grossed $11 million and $18 million respectively.
7. Other examples listed by Silk and Silk include *A Gathering of Old Men* (1987), *A Soldier's Story* (1984), and *Freedom Road* (1979). For criticism of *The Color Purple*, see bell hooks, "Stylish Nihilism," in *Yearning: Race, Gender, and Cultural Politics* (Boston: South End Press, 1989), 155.
8. *Jungle Fever* was on the box office charts for three months, during which time it reached the rank of number 3 (while *City Slickers* was number 1), grossing $13,739,045. Expected by many to win the Palme d'Or at the Cannes Festival, it actually won only in the category of "Best Supporting Actor," for Samuel L. Jackson's portrayal of Gator, Flipper's older brother.
9. Bob Herbert, "Who Will Help the Black Man?" *The New York Times Magazine* (December 4, 1994), 74.
10. Ibid.
11. William Julius Wilson, quoted in Herbert, "Who Will Help?" 74.
12. Robert Staples and Leanor Boulin Johnson, *Black Families at the Crossroads* (San Francisco: Jossey-Bass Publishers, 1993), 226, 235.
13. Quoted in Herbert, "Who Will Help?" 74.
14. Ibid.

15. bell hooks, "Counter-hegemonic Art: Do the Right Thing," in *Yearning: Race, Gender, and Cultural Politics* (Boston: South End Press, 1989), 173.

16. David Breskin, "Interview: Spike Lee," *Rolling Stone*, July 11, 1991, 64.

17. Ibid., 71.

18. Jack Kroll, Vern E. Smith, Andrew Murr, "Spiking a Fever," *Newsweek* (June 10, 1991), 44.

19. Julianne Malveaux, "Arts: Spike's Spite," *Ms.* (September–October 1991), 80.

20. Kroll *et al.*, "Spiking a Fever," 47.

21. John Singleton, quoted in Herbert, "Who Will Help?" 110.

22. Patricia Smith, "Black Women's Voices Struggling to Be Heard," *Boston Sunday Globe*, September 1, 1991.

23. For example, *Boyz N the Hood* grossed $57 million.

24. John Singleton received $18 million from Columbia Pictures for the production of *Poetic Justice*.

25. Bronwen Hruska and Graham Rayman, "On the Outside, Looking In," *The New York Times*, February 21, 1993.

26. The following statement by Michael Nathanson, president of worldwide production at Columbia Pictures, expresses the impasse between new perspectives and old conventions: "We are looking for the most interesting and commercial pictures possible. At the same time, we are looking to give opportunities to whatever minority groups can bring them to fruition." Of course Hollywood studios need to make money. Nevertheless, the judgment on "the most interesting and commercial pictures" will be made by studio bosses who are likely to be unaware of their own bias toward the kind of pictures they think will be commercially successful. Quoted by Hruska and Rayman, "On the Outside," 26.

27. Kroll *et al.*, "Spiking a Fever," 47.

28. In 1993 family movies made a dramatic comeback. *Jurassic Park* broke all records, making $339.4 million in domestic rentals alone.

29. Nancy Armstrong, "The Death and Sinister Afterlife of the American Family," in *Body Politics: Disease, Desire, and the Family* (San Francisco: Westview, 1994), 24.

30. Staples and Johnson, *Black Families*, 234.

31. Ibid., 224.
32. Kroll *et al.*, "Spiking a Fever," 47.
33. Ibid.
34. Breskin, "Interview," 64.
35. Ibid., 71.
36. hooks also questions in "Spending Culture" whether Lee's work can be "revolutionary and generate wealth at the same time." In order to achieve commercial success, she says, a film about Blacks must reproduce "conservative and even stereotypical images of blackness" (150).
37. Jennie Livingston, letter to *The New York Times*, April 28, 1991.
38. *Paris Is Burning* grossed slightly more than $4 million. The highest rank it achieved was twenty-sixth (while *Hot Shots* was number 1, grossing over $13 million in the same week that *Paris Is Burning* grossed slightly over $496,000). But *Paris Is Burning* cost only $375,000 to make, including $175,000 for music clearances, so it represents a tremendous hit for an independent filmmaker. It was also a critical success, playing at the New York Film Forum for a record-breaking seventeen weeks. In 1990 it won the Los Angeles Film Critics Award for best documentary; and it shared the Grand Jury Prize with Barbara Kopple's *American Dream* at the 1991 Sundance Film Festival.
39. Paul Minx, "House Frau," *The Village Voice*, March 19, 1991, 56.
40. It is difficult to interpret this rejection. It might be because gay and lesbian people want more "positive" images of homosexuals in film. Middle-class gays and lesbians may not want to be represented by the drag queens that comprise popular caricatures of gay life. Curiously, previews on the videocassette showed the following: *The Lunatic*; *Chameleon Street* (Latino and African American subjects); and *Tour Disaster* (horror).
41. bell hooks says that the title of the film evokes "images of the real Paris on fire, of the death and destruction of a dominating white Western civilization and culture, an end to oppressive Eurocentrism and white supremacy." "Is Paris Burning?" *Z Magazine* (June 1991), 61. Jesse Green suggested another meaning. She writes: "*Brennt Paris?*" ("Is Paris burning?") Hitler demanded after he had ordered the city bombed as his troops retreated in 1944." Paris survived, of

course, but Green contends that the Paris of Ms. Livingston's movie may not. "Paris Has Burned," *The New York Times*, April 18, 1993, 14.

42. Vincent Canby, "Aching to Be a Prima Donna, When You're a Man," *The New York Times*, March 13, 1991.

43. hooks, "Is Paris Burning?," 62.

44. Quoted in Minx, "House Frau."

45. Vito Russo, *The Celluloid Closet: Homosexuality in the Movies*, rev. ed. (New York: Harper and Row, 1987), 6.

46. Ibid., 128.

47. Ibid., 21, 48, and 95ff.

48. Ibid., 72.

49. Howard Feinstein, "Getting Beyond the Gay Ghetto With Gay Films," *The New York Times*, August 21, 1994.

50. Meron is co-authoring an adaptation of the Broadway musical for a film; Feinstein, "Beyond the Gay Ghetto."

51. Chris Pula, president of marketing at New Line Cinema, quoted by Feinstein, "Beyond the Gay Ghetto."

52. Christine Vachon, who produced *Go Fish*, said, "Lesbians go to gay men's films because there aren't enough lesbian films for them. But how many gay men do you know who want to see two women kissing on each other?" Ibid.

53. Ibid.

54. Russo, *The Celluloid Closet*, 176.

55. Ibid., 132.

56. Ibid., 161.

57. Robin Wood, "Images and Women," in *Issues in Feminist Film Criticism*, ed. Patricia Erens (Bloomington: Indiana University Press, 1990), 348.

58. *Gay Men's Health Crisis Facts* (May 1994), 1. Although women comprise 10.9 percent and men 89.1 percent of diagnosed victims of AIDS in the United States, by November 1993 40 percent of AIDS cases worldwide were among women. Three out of four women with AIDS in this country are women of color. The grouping of lesbians with gay men and bisexuals results in the invisibility of lesbians with AIDS. Moreover, because definitions of "lesbian" vary, it has proved difficult to count the number of lesbians with AIDS. I am grateful to

Carol Johnson for suggesting the following source of information: Anne Harris, "Silent Crisis: The Invisibility of Lesbians with AIDS," *Network* (July 1994), 23–26.

59. Ibid.

60. Essex Hemphill writes in *Ceremonies* (New York: Plume, 1992): "What I find commendable about Livingston's *Paris Is Burning* is that she allows the voices of this highly transgressive ball community to emerge without her interference, without excessive questioning. . . . We are not exposed to Livingston's judgments, if she has any, of the subject. The authentic voice of this community emerges unfettered" (115). Peggy Phelan, bell hooks, and others have offered more subtle analyses, criticizing the filmmaker for representing a community of which she is not a part and describing how Livingston's perspective dominates the film, despite her attempt to let the characters speak for themselves. Livingston, hooks wrote in "Is Paris Burning?," "is represented both in interviews and reviews as the tenderhearted, mild-mannered, virtuous white woman daring to venture into a contemporary 'heart of darkness' to bring back knowledge of the 'natives'" (62).

61. hooks, *Outlaw Culture: Resisting Representations* (New York: Routledge, 1994), 168–69.

62. Judith Butler, "Gender Is Burning," *Bodies That Matter: On the Discursive Limits of "Sex"* (New York: Routledge, 1993), 125–26.

63. Ibid., 104.

64. The misogyny of gay imitation of women has often been noted; Marilyn Frye calls this imitation "a casual and cynical mockery of women." Quoted by Phelan, "The Golden Apple: Jennie Livingston's 'Paris Is Burning'," *Unmarked* (New York: Routledge, 1993), 101.

65. hooks, "Is Paris Burning?" 62.

66. Ibid.

67. Green, "Paris Has Burned."

68. Ibid., 13.

69. Ibid.

70. Ibid.

71. For the early twentieth-century history of Harlem gay balls, see Eric Garber, "A Spectacle in Color: The Lesbian and Gay Subculture of Jazz Age Harlem," in *Hidden From History: Reclaiming the Gay*

and Lesbian Past, ed. Martin Dubelman, Martha Vicinus, and George Chauncey, Jr. (New York: New American Library, 1989), 318–31.

72. Nearly 50 percent of Americans with AIDS are people of color, according to the *Gay Men's Health Crisis Newsletter* (May 1994).

73. Green, "Paris Has Burned."

74. Ibid.

75. Jackie Goldsby, "Paris Is Burning," *Afterimage* (May 1991), 11.

76. Marlon Riggs died of AIDS in April 1994.

77. Susan Bordo, *Unbearable Weight: Feminism, Western Culture, and the Body* (Berkeley: University of California Press, 1993), 267.

78. Don Lattin, "Many Religions Revising Their Views on Right and Wrong," *San Francisco Chronicle*, November 29, 1994, summarizes attitudes toward homosexuality in the most populous Christian denominations and churches, in Judaism, and in Islam.

79. Marjorie Garber does, in fact, argue this in *Vested Interests: Cross-Dressing and Cultural Anxiety* (New York: Routledge, 1992).

80. Minx, "House Frau."

81. Butler, "Gender Is Burning," 125.

82. Phelan, "The Golden Apple," 102.

83. Gary Hentzi, "Paris Is Burning," *Film Quarterly* 45, 2 (Winter 1991–92), 36.

84. Richard Corliss, "A Happy Birthday for the Kids of Kane," *Time*, May 13, 1991, 70.

85. Goldsby, "Paris Is Burning," 10.

86. hooks, "Is Paris Burning?" 64.

87. Russo, *Celluloid Closet*, 326.

Chapter 9. What You See Is What You Get

1. Todd Gitlin, "On Thrills and Kills: Sadomasochism in the Movies," *Dissent* (Spring 1991), 246.

2. David Barry, "Screen Violence: It's Killing Us," *Harvard Magazine* (November 1993), 38.

3. The survey of studies examining the relationship of screen violence to actual violence was conducted by Ron Slaby of the Harvard Education Development Center; Ed Donnerstein of the School of Com-

munications, University of California; and Leonard Eron, professor emeritus of the University of Illinois. Cited in Barry, "Screen Violence," 40.

4. Ibid. Bywater and Sobchack discuss a history of studies from 1928 to the 1970 *Presidential Commission's Report on Obscenity and Pornography.* This commission concluded that no relationship between antisocial behavior and violent or sexual behavior on screen could be documented; media reporting of these studies no doubt also influenced many Americans' belief that screen behavior does not affect actual behavior. Tim Bywater and Thomas Sobchack, *Introduction to Film Criticism* (New York: Longman, 1989), 116–19.

5. Joyce Johnson, "Witness for the Prosecution," *The New Yorker* (May 16, 1994), 41.

6. Gitlin, "Thrills and Kills," 247.

7. Gitlin attributes screen violence overload to a current crisis of masculinity: "What is spilling all over the screen is the fury of men who hate and fear women, hate and fear homosexuals, and don't know what kind of masculine performance is expected of them" (246).

8. Martin Amis, "Blown Away," *The New Yorker* (May 30, 1994), 48.

9. David Linz, Edward Donnerstein, and Steven Penrod, "The Effects of Multiple Exposures to Filmed Violence Against Women," *Journal of Communication* 34, 3 (Summer 1984), 130.

10. The numbing effects of ever-greater increments of screen violence may operate, however, primarily on adults. Children are taught to find violence funny. In Barry, "Screen Violence," Deborah Prothrow-Smith, assistant dean of the Harvard School of Public Health, said:

     From their very first cartoon all the way through the latest super-hero movie, we teach our children that violence is funny, is entertaining, is successful, is the hero's first choice, is painless, is guiltless, is rewarded. . . . If you watch little children watch their first cartoon, they literally learn when to laugh. It's not a natural response to violence to laugh. But they learn, because the other children around them laugh. Because there's a laugh track, because there is music that tells them when to laugh (41).

11. Not all media workers dismiss evidence of the effect of screen violence; screenwriter Ben Stein, a participant in the Senate hearings organized by Senator Paul Simon, expressed his conviction that "moviemakers have a responsibility to consider the consequences of their

work. People who make the culture have as much responsibility to think about its effect as people who make cars have to think about the effect of their product." Quoted in Barry, "Screen Violence," 43.

12. Ibid.

13. Dr. Park Dietz, forensic medicine expert, has been hired as a consultant for several Hollywood thrillers and for the television series "Law and Order." Thus far, he says, producers have taken his advice "about avoiding the kind of graphic depictions of violence that promote copy-cat crimes." Johnson, "Witness," 50.

14. Bywater and Sobchack discuss the public's concern about film's moral effects and the organizations that have endeavored to monitor films in *Introduction to Film Criticism*, Chapter 5, "The Social Science Approach: Films as Social Artifacts."

15. The Code was primarily devised to impose moral conventions on films. For example, punishment for sexual or other moral offenses had to occur within the plot; no references to sexual intercourse were permitted; no characters could be prostitutes; there could be no shots of animals' sexual organs or of toilets; and there could not be the sound of a human burp. David F. Brindle, *Risky Business: The Political Economy of Hollywood* (San Francisco: Westview Press, 1993), 155–56.

16. Vito Russo, *The Celluloid Closet: Homosexuality in the Movies*, rev. ed. (New York: Harper and Row, 1987), 145.

17. Joe Maxwell, "The New Hollywood Watchdogs," *Christianity Today* (April 27, 1992), 18.

18. See Anne Hollander, *Moving Pictures* (Cambridge, Mass.: Harvard University Press, 1991), for a distinction between "cinematic art," which "sets the viewer's psyche in motion, reveals arbitrarily rather than describes thoroughly, disturbs more than it satisfies, and strongly suggests the impossibility of seeing everything at once," and "classic art," in which the painter's skill in selecting and posing figures is primary: the "appeal [is] to the viewer's appreciation of the way the painter brought the universe inside the picture to completion" (7, 14).

19. David Chidester, *Word and Light: Seeing, Hearing, and Religious Discourse* (Urbana: University of Illinois, 1992), 2ff.

20. Maxine Sheets-Johnstone, *The Roots of Power* (Chicago: Open Court, 1994), 24.

21. Ibid., 28. A connection between vision and touch is attested to by numerous Western authors, among them Plotinus, *Ennead* 6.5.7, and Augustine, *Confessions* 9.10 and 7.17.

22. Plotinus, *Ennead* 5.3.17, trans. Stephen MacKenna (London: Faber, 1969).

23. Sheets-Johnstone, *Roots*, 26.

24. Dudley Andrew, *Concepts in Film Theory* (New York: Oxford, 1984), 44.

25. Iconic power is culturally determined, however. In Eastern Orthodoxy, a different visual rhetoric exists. Iconic figuration is systematically distorted in order to signal the "presence of a presence," a spiritual world that is fundamentally different from the world of everyday experience and which the viewer must not confuse with her ordinary world, but must endeavor to enter in spirit. In anagogic representation, the sacred and saintly figures are slender and elongated, their eyes—the windows of the soul—enlarged, their mouths tiny.

26. Plotinus, *Ennead* 4.3.8.

27. For an excellent description of reconceptualizing difference, see Henry A. Giroux, "Living Dangerously: Identity Politics and the New Cultural Racism, Towards a Critical Pedagogy of Representation," *Cultural Studies* 7 (Spring 1993).

28. Funding institutions like the National Film Board of Canada have been quite effective in enabling the production of films that would not have been likely to pass the scrutiny of a Hollywood studio, such as *Strangers in Good Company* and *Jesus of Montreal*.

29. Suzanne Langer, "The Cultural Importance of Art," *Philosophical Sketches* (Baltimore: Johns Hopkins, 1962).

30. Martha Nussbaum, *Love's Knowledge* (New York: Oxford, 1990), 4.

Index

Library of Congress Cataloging-in-Publication Data

Miles, Margaret Ruth.
  Seeing and believing : religion and values in the movies /
Margaret R. Miles.
      p.   cm.
  Includes bibliographical references and index.
  ISBN 0-8070-1030-8 (cloth)
  ISBN 0-8070-1031-6 (paper)
    1. Motion pictures—Religious aspects.   2. Religion in motion
pictures.   I. Title.
  PN1995.9.R4M56   1996
  791.43'682—dc20   95-24927